World Anthropology

General Editor

SOL TAX

Patrons

CLAUDE LÉVI-STRAUSS
MARGARET MEAD
LAILA SHUKRY EL HAMAMSY
M. N. SRINIVAS

MOUTON PUBLISHERS · THE HAGUE · PARIS
DISTRIBUTED IN THE USA AND CANADA BY ALDINE, CHICAGO

Development from Below

Development from Below
Anthropologists and Development Situations

Editor

DAVID C. PITT

MOUTON PUBLISHERS · THE HAGUE · PARIS

DISTRIBUTED IN THE USA AND CANADA BY ALDINE, CHICAGO

41426

General Editor's Preface

In the less industrialized continents of the world, villagers, including those who move to cities to make a living, are the major population of the nations in which they live. They are critical factors in economic development. Programs for development are planned by government administrators, economists, and technicians who are characteristically of the elite classes in the nation or abroad. These planners rarely know the particular grass-roots societies and cultures which are being affected or grasp the theory needed to analyze the part they must play in the process. Therefore, the development efforts are often inefficient and destructive. The question asked in this book is why the appropriate knowledge of anthropologists and sociologists is not used much more in such programs, and what anthropologists might do to make what they know more useful. What answers there are owe much to a small international conference associated with the Congress which brought together scholars from all parts of the world, including those from the very regions which are the subject matter of this book.

Like most contemporary sciences, anthropology is a product of the European tradition. Some argue that it is a product of colonialism, with one small and self-interested part of the species dominating the study of the whole. If we are to understand the species, our science needs substantial input from scholars who represent a variety of the world's cultures. It was a deliberate purpose of the IXth International Congress of Anthropological and Ethnological Sciences to provide impetus in this direction. The *World Anthropology* volumes, therefore, offer a first glimpse of a human science in which members from all societies have played an active role. Each of the books is designed to be self-contained;

each is an attempt to update its particular sector of scientific knowledge and is written by specialists from all parts of the world. Each volume should be read and reviewed individually as a separate volume on its own given subject. The set as a whole will indicate what changes are in store for anthropology as scholars from the developing countries join in studying the species of which we are all a part.

The IXth Congress was planned from the beginning not only to include as many of the scholars from every part of the world as possible, but also with a view toward the eventual publication of the papers in high-quality volumes. At previous Congresses scholars were invited to bring papers which were then read out loud. They were necessarily limited in length; many were only summarized; there was little time for discussion; and the sparse discussion could only be in one language. The IXth Congress was an experiment aimed at changing this. Papers were written with the intention of exchanging them before the Congress, particularly in extensive pre-Congress sessions; they were not intended to be read aloud at the Congress, that time being devoted to discussions — discussions which were simultaneously and professionally translated into five languages. The method for eliciting the papers was structured to makes as representative a sample as was allowable when scholarly creativity — hence self-selection — was critically important. Scholars were asked both to propose papers of their own and to suggest topics for sessions of the Congress which they might edit into volumes. All were then informed of the suggestions and encouraged to re-think their own papers and the topics. The process, therefore, was a continuous one of feedback and exchange and it has continued to be so even after the Congress. The some two thousand papers comprising *World Anthropology* certainly then offer a substantial sample of world anthropology. It has been said that anthropology is at a turning point; if this is so, these volumes will be the historical direction-markers.

As might have been foreseen in the first post-colonial generation, the large majority of the Congress papers (82 percent) are the work of scholars identified with the industrialized world which fathered our traditional discipline and the institution of the Congress itself: Eastern Europe (15 percent); Western Europe (16 percent); North America (47 percent); Japan, South Africa, Australia, and New Zealand (4 percent). Only 18 percent of the papers are from developing areas: Africa (4 percent); Asia-Oceania (9 percent); Latin America (5 percent). Aside from the substantial representation from the U.S.S.R. and the nations of Eastern Europe, a significant difference between this corpus of written material and that of other Congresses is the addition of the large proportion of contributions from Africa, Asia, and Latin America. "Only 18 percent" is two to four times as great a proportion as that of other Congresses; moreover, 18 percent of 3,000 papers is 360 papers, 10 times the number of "Third World" papers presented at previous Congresses. In fact, these 360 papers are more than the total of ALL papers published after the last International Congress of Anthropological and Ethnological Sciences which was held in the United States (Philadelphia, 1956).

The significance of the increase is not simply quantitative. The input of scholars from areas which have until recently been no more than subject matter for anthropology represents both feedback and also long-awaited theoretical contributions from the perspectives of very different cultural, social, and historical traditions. Many who attended the IXth Congress were convinced that anthropology would not be the same in the future. The fact that the next Congress (India, 1978) will be our first in the "Third World" may be symbolic of the change. Meanwhile, sober consideration of the present set of books will show how much, and just where and how, our discipline is being revolutionized.

This volume is one of a number in the series which deal with the bearing of anthropological knowledge on the social and economic problems of our rapidly changing world. Others, for example, treat political anthropology; colonialism and war; population growth and the migrations of peoples; competition for resources of ethnic groups and social classes; development of cooperatives; and educational innovations.

Chicago, Illinois
March 10, 1976   SOL TAX

Table of Contents

Introduction

DAVID C. PITT

COMMUNICATING

The papers in this volume emerged from a concern about boundaries between anthropologists and other social scientists working in the development field. There can be little doubt that communication is greatly restricted between those who work in development agencies and those in academia, between disciplines within academia, and across national, cultural, theoretical, and ideological boundaries. The breakdown in communication has contributed to the relatively poor performance in many areas of development programs. The meetings at the IXth International Congress of Anthropological and Ethnological Sciences in Oshkosh and Chicago, where these papers were presented, represented first of all an attempt at communication. These efforts are continuing, for one positive result of the Oshkosh meeting was the formation of an international network of development scholars and practitioners.

Apart from those whose papers appear in this volume, we are grateful to many people for helpful suggestions and ideas given both at the meetings and before and after them. Among these people were: Ajato Amos (Nigeria), David Brokensha (U.S.A.), Mihail Cernea (Romania), Paul Henri Chombart de Lauwe (France), Wayne Dye (New Guinea), Karam Elahi (Pakistan), Mary Lindsay Elmendorf (U.S.A.), André Gundar Frank (W. Germany), Nancie González (U.S.A.), Irving Horowitz (U.S.A.), Tariq Husain (Pakistan), Claude Meillassoux (France), Amnon Orent (Israel), Paola Palmeri (Italy), Jim Riddell (U.S.A.), Roma Stendefer (Canada), H. Sang Lee (U.S.A.), and Rieck Hannifin (IAF). We owe a special debt to James Riddell and the University of Wisconsin for making the Oshkosh meeting possible.

BOUNDARIES

The first boundary between the pure and the applied originated from
the very small number of anthropologists and sociologists working in
development agencies and from the relatively minor utilization of anthropological or sociological knowledge. There were many reasons for
this situation, notably the traditional and mutual suspicion that existed
between government and university and later the stigma that attached
to anthropology because of its connection with colonialism. There were
exceptions certainly. Mathur shows, for example, in his paper on
applied anthropology in India that there the discipline has had a long
and generally respected development role. But India is one of the few
Afro-Asian countries where anthropology is not a dirty word.

In the postwar period if any social scientist has been important in
development agencies it has been the economist. However this situation
seems to be changing. The United Nations Second Development Decade
has of course placed a major emphasis on social factors, on the quality
as opposed to the quantity of life, and development agencies, national
or international, are increasingly employing anthropologists or sociologists as full time staff or consultants. This process of integration is
taking place partly because of a growing interest by anthropologists
themselves. Cochrane's paper, for example, shows how anthropology
has penetrated into one of the economist's most exclusive preserves, the
World Bank. But this could not have happened had there not been
sympathy within the organization. In another paper an official from
the Bank, Tariq Husain (this volume), shows how anthropological expertise was increasingly sought in project appraisal. Widstrand shows
more specifically how the anthropologist's role has developed in evaluating procedures, and other roles that anthropologists have performed
in development agencies are discussed by Bornstein and den Hertog.

How successful has the anthropologist been in the development
agencies? Obviously it is too early to tell but there are some pessimistic
signs. In some agencies the anthropologist or sociologist is something
of a luxury, only added to the establishment in the fat years and the
first to go in times of retrenchment. He may be in some senses a status
symbol for the organization or department which posseses him, a sure
sign of being up with the fashion of building in the social dimension.
Consequently his reports may be politely received but left in a file to
gather dust. There is often, too, a certain uneasiness about the anthropologist's qualitative penchant and his often obviously sympathetic
attachment to real life rural people. The more remote sociologist with

his quantitative questionnaire may be marginally more acceptable.
The utilization of anthropology or sociology in most development organizations is still basically in an economic frame, and overall anthropological influence has not been great. The anthropologist, though in the door, has hardly reached the first floor. He is typically on the periphery of the power in the organization. He is a consultant, on a short-term contract or low down in the hierarchy, too low certainly to significantly influence either policy at the top or even the middle power range of the technocrats where the locus of knowledge often lies.

One reason for the increasing inclusion of the anthropologist or sociologist in development agencies is the realization that interdisciplinary approaches are most useful in solving development problems. This theme is taken up here in the paper by Streeten, an economist with much practical experience, who stresses the readiness of the economists to cooperate. There remain many obstacles to communications, however, notably social distance between the different disciplines in different regions and countries and even within the same university between very closely related departments such as anthropology and sociology. Our colleague Suda showed how close the anthropological interests in development are to the sociological concerns about modernization. In many countries sociology and social anthropology are virtually synonymous, even if basic methodologies (questionnaires as opposed to participant observation) are different. In development agencies, too, the designations are used interchangeably or, rather, lumped together under the anonymous umbrella of terms like social affairs. Once in the field studying a specific problem, a specific region, or a specific village, the disciplinary boundary tends to fade away. For example Ajato Amos (i.p.) in his paper on ethnicity in Nigeria which was presented to the meeting argued that the classical division of Nigerian social structure into a small number of tribes was an armchair assumption and that there were in reality 250 ethnic groups. This involved research that was at the same time geographical, historical, anthropological, sociological, and legal.

Difficulties in crossing interdisciplinary boundaries are compounded when different languages, cultures, or ideologies are involved. But again the increasing mobility of scholars is easing this problem. The great divide, the iron curtain, as the paper by Galeski demonstrates, need not be a fundamental obstacle.

ALTERNATIVE MODELS

Ideological differences in the development field have centered around those arguments between theories which we may broadly call exploitative and those which emphasize more harmonious patterns in the social structure. The first group of theories is dominated by conflict approaches, usually Marxist, in which development is seen as an effort by rich countries or rich classes in one way or another to dominate or exploit, a process in which development agencies are willy-nilly involved. Opposed to these conflict models are the structural-functional, consensual, or altruistic models. The ideology of many development agencies is often of the latter kind, seeing development as an undisputed benefit bestowed on the poor people of the world.

A major task of the Oshkosh group and a major thrust in the arguments centered on this particular debate. The concern was not however to argue that conflict or consensual models were right or wrong, rather the feeling was that they were, if not irrelevant, then less relevant as a model for explaining development and, in particular, for explaining the failure of development programs. The participants were in fact searching for an alternative approach, which came to be called "development from below."

Development in conventional theory or practice characteristically comes from above, externally imposed by governments or bureaucracies, whether conceptualized as altruistic or exploitative. Knowledge of and links with the recipients is often minimal. Development plans reflect ethnocentric tendencies or similar structural features in development agencies or donor subcultures. Apthorpe's paper shows clearly how great the separation can be between planistrator and peasant. Widstrand in his vignette of a Kenyan village shows how social distance usually means that nothing is achieved.

Separation not only means inappropriate images and objectives or the ineffective transmission of development, it also means that there is little recognition or understanding of the processes of internally generated development. The paper by Robineau shows how traditional institutions can survive into the modern economy and are, as Rutz argues in his paper, relatively efficient in agricultural development. Pitt, in his contribution, links tradition and identity and sees this as a crucial part of the development process underlying the basic decision of whether to cooperate with the outside world or to seek other means of self-expression. Most examples of development from below are derived from the grass roots, from rural villages away from the power and influence of the development bureaucracies. Isolation is itself an aid to independence and a stimulus to internal generation, but there are also examples of development from below in urban settings, as de Goede shows using material from Pakistan. Nor is action confined to the economic sphere. Huizer analyzes the stages of peasant mobilization, proceeding from economic grievances to the wider political sphere and eventually to revolutionary activities.

A final but important theme in the Oshkosh discussions concerned the role of the anthropologist or sociologist working in development situations. In general the underlying ethos was evolutionary in character, for although it was recognized that there may be situations calling for more radical change, it was felt that it is important that the possibilities of utilizing and influencing existing institutions be first exhausted. It was also felt that the traditional role of anthropological interest in the welfare of the rural people they study is important and should be continued.

Anthropologists outside the development agencies can exert pressure for, in an age of mass media politics, agencies in many countries are susceptible to publicity. Anthropologists, particularly in the field, may in fact serve a very useful liaison function. Salisbury suggests that the anthropologist might become a kind of ombudsman. Eventually it is to be hoped that the depressed societies of the world will produce their own students and spokesmen. Even when working full time within organizations, anthropologists can use their influence to promote local welfare and freedom of action and trying to strenuously resist the misuse of anthropological or sociological expertise or knowledge.

REFERENCES

AMOS, AJATO
   i.p.   "Nigeria's 250 ethnic groups," in *Perspectives on ethnicity*. Edited by Regina E. Holloman and Serghei Arutiunov. World Anthropology. The Hague: Mouton.

Development from Below

DAVID C. PITT

Until recently, social scientists have been rather reluctant to turn a hard, analytical light on themselves, although, at least from the time of Kant (Moore 1972: 6), it has been realized that the social situation of the human observer greatly affects (some would say determines) the resulting analysis. But now there is a resurgent interest[1] in at least the sociology, if not in the anthropology, of the scholarly world. The time seems appropriate, as Myrdal (1972) has recently suggested, to take a long hard look at the social context of development which scholars and practitioners have used as a background for analysing their theories and practices.

In this paper, we want to contribute by briefly looking at this development subculture. We want to suggest that certain of its features have played a part in making development what one writer (Apthorpe 1971–1972) has called the greatest failure of the century.

At first sight, the world of development thinking seems extremely fragmented. For one thing, there is not much agreement about the definition of development itself; Freyssinet (1966), for example, has over 300 different usages. The social structure itself is diffused and dispersed, reflecting the broader structure of academic and administrative institutions. In universities (which are characteristically atomized) development courses may be found in many different departments and in

---

[1] E.g. Friedrichs 1970; this, however, is mainly concerned with theoretical modes. Much research has been done on the social origins particularly of American scholars (e.g. Glenn and Weiner 1969), but much less has been done on different kinds of academic subcultures, especially those in which anthropologists participate (but see Dumont 1971).

parts of many different kinds of courses. Where there are courses explicitly concerned with development, most are options or are only loosely associated with anthropology or sociology degrees. In a recent survey in Britain (Barnett 1972), for example, of the thirty sociology and/or anthropology development courses in tertiary institutions (mostly universities), only one was an integral part of the undergraduate degree. Cross-disciplinary courses seem to be relatively rare, and where they do exist, they seem to be federal in structure rather than genuinely integrated.

The academic research world appears equally fragmented. Research workers remain within disciplinary national or cultural boundaries, and communication is not well developed. Certainly, there are academic institutions, journals, societies, etc. that are broadly concerned with development studies, but these are restricted networks which often simply reflect other social divisions. Certainly too, there are emerging networks of social scientists interested in cross-disciplinary approaches.[2] But in this and other cases, most of the scholars are located in the American university system and exist under the patronage of small groups or institutions. The crossing of national and especially linguistic boundaries is still difficult despite the great improvements that have been made in abstracting and translating and the more extensive movement of scholars. Difficulties relating especially to relations between East and West remain, but it could be argued now that the reason for the lack of scholarly communication is not critically affected by ideological communication obstacles. We will return to this important point later. It is certainly also true that some kind of communication takes place through the common reading of the literature; but this does not necessarily lead to a wider communication, partly because the literature itself is rarely integrated. The great debate in anthropology in the 1960's about substantivism, for example, hardly caused a ripple in other disciplines (Dalton 1971).[3] Often too, the ideas and arguments, even when communicated, are scaled down and translated into local terms. Arguments about theoretical issues turn into arguments between cliques, groups, etc.

If there is fragmentation within academe, there is a veritable chasm between the academic developers and the practitioners. Very few of the development research workers and teachers are involved in the appli-

---

[2]   E.g. the *Bulletin of Comparative Interdisciplinary Studies*, which is explicitly designed to be a medium through which social scientists can communicate.
[3]   Admittedly the link (despite the title of Dalton's latest book) with development was never very explicit.

cation. This is partly due to prejudices and stereotypes on both sides. The academic, especially when a critic of the development establishment, feels that working for agencies, such as those in the United Nations system, is an immoral act, an aid to the process of imperialism, of which the United Nations is felt by some to be an integral part (Rhodes 1970; Riddell 1972). Within the agencies themselves, there are often very mixed attitudes on the employment of academics, especially anthropologists and sociologists. In many organizations concerned with development the economists have maintained a hegemony and quite often they allow the social context to remain a shadowy and sometimes irrelevant factor. Political factors may also intrude in recruitment procedures.

There are other sources of conflict. Applied development takes place within a bureaucracy, the cadre of which is built up over long years of discipline. The academic, especially on a short-term contract, is seen as a reluctant and potentially unreliable bureaucrat. The Jackson report on the United Nations system (United Nations 1969), for all its criticisms, still firmly supported the principles of early recruitment and undivided loyalty. But behind the prejudices and stereotypes is the simple fact that the academic and the administrator often come from different subcultures, which rarely overlap. They do not intermarry; they have different tastes and styles of life, different conceptions of wealth, status, and power.

The internal structure of the development organization further complicates the patterns of communication. There is very often great rivalry and competition between departments. Sometimes if one department employs a sociologist or anthropologist, it is only because it regards itself as progressive in contrast to other more conservative departments that are staffed by a large number of economists and lawyers.

We might suggest several important consequences for development studies which result from this fragmented and divided structure. In the first place, and most significantly, the experts, whether academic or administrative, are quite often remote, in one way or another, from the object of their studies — the poor people in the countryside or the towns. Apart from anthropology, the tradition of fieldwork is not well developed. The economist and the demographer deal in statistics; the political scientist reads the newspapers, interviews the politicians, does a psephological poll, interprets the election results or the revolutionary casualties; and the sociologist conducts a survey. Certainly, the revolution in air transport and the growth of Afro-Asian universities have meant that the social scientist now usually visits or resides in his country of study, while much less time is spent in the depressed rural villages or slums. Factfinding for the applied agencies is usually an even more restricted affair. Reports may be written without any visit to the country concerned. When a visit is made, the experts may not proceed any further than the charmed circle of the Intercontinental, the government offices, and the elegant cocktail parties.

Other problems, however, remain even if there is a tradition of field-work and close continuous contact, problems very relevant to contemporary anthropology. In some ways, the Malinowskian ideal has been watered down. Anthropologists still spend long ritual periods in the field, but the social distance between them and the people is considerable and perhaps growing. For example, the fieldworkers are now often married, with children and, even if not, are insulated in other ways by such things as cars, appliances, trips to town, etc.

But probably more important still (and this applies to most social scientific study conducted in the Third World) is the fact that the local people are rarely represented among the students of their own social situation. It is the outsider who conducts the research, and despite the supposed usefulness of stranger value this is a very great obstacle to rapport and intimacy. This is especially true when, as often happens, the Euro-American social scientist is seen as some kind of agent for a colonial or neocolonial power. Camelot may have come as a shock to the academic world, but there has always been a widespread belief in the Afro-Asian villages that all anthropologists were spies of some kind or other. Finally, and most significant of all, the outsider cannot interpret the nuances of the situations with the same insight and penetration as the insider.

Problems of perspective and interpretation are related to social distance and difference in other ways as well. First of all, it can be argued that many ideas about development have more to do with the academic or administrative subculture than with the reality of the development situation. This ethnocentrism or culturocentrism has a number of consequences which contribute to a greater or lesser extent toward the failure of development itself. In the first place, development and underdevelopment are seen in terms of known features of the social landscape. In most of the development literature there is an assumption that there is a continuous evolution that proceeds from a traditional state toward a modernization goal and follows steps that are similar to those presumed to have been followed by Western industrialized nations (Lerner 1964). Some (e.g. the development agencies) regard this process as desirable and beneficial; others (e.g. the Marxists) see it as exploitative. And while there certainly are variant definitions and interpretations (e.g. of what constitutes tradition[4] or modernization), the process of social change is regarded as inevitable.

In this process the stimulus for development is seen to come from above and outside, from the developed countries in the form of aid, trade, and the transplanting of European institutions. In fact, a major characteristic of much development thinking, deriving essentially from internal subcultural features, is its simplicity and inflexibility. In many senses it functions as a myth within organizations and institutions. Like all myths, there are positives and negatives and ineluctable processes. It would be interesting to analyze in the Lévi-Straussian manner the "mediation" between development objectives and achievements. In both Marxist and structural-functionalist analyses (including systems approaches) (e.g. Kunkel 1970), the large number of variables breaks down into a small number of oppositions. Certainly, in the development agencies there is a checklist of social conditions, which are considered to be conducive to development, just as there are supposed to be levels that can be precisely monitored by socioeconomic indicators (e.g. Piatier in Lengyel 1972).

The myths are perpetuated partly because their bureaucratic contexts are inflexible and partly because of the weak development of communication with others working in the same field and with the field itself. In addition, the ways in which the ideas and theories resist attack are very significant. In the development agencies there are many examples of what has been called *projectismo* (Fayerweather 1959: 77), a situation in which the plan is the only, sacredly inviolable reality. Some plans (especially the more utopian variety) have their own built-in success inevitability before there is any attempt at implementation. The academic analogy is in the elegant but remote abstractions that grace many serious studies.

It seems obvious that more realistic development thinking and more appropriate avenues for the anthropology of development lie in increasing the lines of communication between disciplines, institutions, and cultures. But, in order to achieve this and ultimately in order to achieve greater development success, it is first necessary to develop much more flexible and more realistic models and methods, capable of multi-

---

[4] There is a growing literature (and argument) on tradition (see Bendix 1967; Shils 1971; Eisenstadt 1969). Scholars working in the Indian field particularly have commented on the modernizing aspects of tradition (e.g. Gusfield 1968; Rudolph and Rudolph 1967). See also Pitt (1970) for another case study.

disciplinary usage. I would now like to outline briefly the form that some of these models might take.

The first requirement would seem to be a redescent, or a return if you like, to the field, to the village, or to the suburb. Some recent arguments have emphasized that by doing this, by being empirically grounded, to use the new fashionable phrase,[5] we will get nearer to a more realistic appreciation of the facts or to a more sensitive understanding of the village life-world. However, one might argue that this is only part, perhaps a small part, of the benefit. I think we should be cautious of becoming obsessed with finding hard facts. I remember a Samoan who once said to me that truth was like a fish — certainly there, but extremely hard to catch and hold in the hand. Indeed, the interpretation of any fact depends very much on the perspective and viewpoint, the situation of the observer. I would rather argue that the real benefit of the descent is theoretical; it would provide us with a useful perspective and a point of departure.

Many commentators have noted that the impetus for development comes from above, from social groups outside the peasantry or the proletariat. The structural theories of development of whatever hue follow this assumption. The active groups, whether donors or exploiters, are outside the village, which is seen as passive or, at best, as reacting to outside stimuli.

I am not trying to deny the activism from outside, but I think it can be argued that development also can come, and often does come, from below. What I am saying is that there are alternative models of development in which the village, rural or urban, is the center. To some extent we need in development studies an analogy of network theory at a structural rather than an individual level (e.g. Mitchell 1969; Boissevain 1973).

The decentralization of theory also necessitates the modification of many existing development frames. Macroconcepts need to be reinterpreted. The national or international development structure can no longer be seen as consisting of classes or sectors, but must be viewed as being composed of different overlapping situations, in which communities are taking a variety of kinds of social action (including no action). Decentralization requires a more radical reconceptualization. Useful categories might be situational ones, which would stress a fluid, dynamic set of relationships, rather than structural ones that imply a relatively static, ordered universe.

[5]   The phrase was coined by Glaser and Strauss (1967) and has been explicitly applied to development studies, e.g. Wells (1972).

One of the first tasks of a multidisciplinary approach to development might well be to make a systematic study of these development situations, their origins, and their consequences. Even a very cursory glance at the literature shows that there are many different types of development situation. In some cases the pessimism of the developers is not warranted. Development, in the usual Western sense of increased consumption or production, often takes place in the most unexpected places and quite unknown to the developers. Elsewhere I have described how some Samoan villages describe themselves as developed, and how they may, in fact, have unrecognized wealth in the forms of unrecorded consumer goods, hoarded money, and undeclared income, etc., despite the fact that their country is classified by the United Nations as one of the twenty-seven least developed countries in the world. In many Pacific Islands a considerable proportion (sometimes all) of a family's income derives not from cash crops, family labor, investment, or entrepreneurship, but from gifts remitted by relatives. In many underdeveloped countries, some villages, some regions, and some subcultures are distinguished by virtue of their much greater wealth or success in the outside world, relative both to other groups and to development indicators. Depressed and developed villages or groups may be found side by side. Good examples in the literature are the Antioqueños in Colombia, the Monteros in Mexico, the Kikuyu in Kenya, the Ibo in Eastern Nigeria, the Parsis or Jains in India, the overseas Chinese or Indians, the Jewish community etc. (Rogers 1969; Horton 1963; Hagen 1962). But these examples are obvious because of their involvement in entrepreneurial activity. Less obvious are those villages, or families, or individuals, who achieve such distinctive characters in an agricultural, rural setting. These cases tend to be overlooked in aggregate statistical compilations or by officials who are only looking for failures.

For the many examples of what we might call absolute development, there are also many more examples which show substantial development when the inputs of production factors are considered. Production figures in many areas in the Third World do not take into account the background difficulties of climate, soil, technology, capital, expertise, or marketing.

Quite often, absolute or relative development is achieved through what are regarded as traditional institutions, which are usually regarded by the developers as synonomous with underdevelopment. Elsewhere I have tried to show how in Samoa traditional institutions can be flexible and adaptive (Pitt 1970). There, as in many societies, it is assumed by both the people themselves and the development agencies that the traditional *fa'aSamoa* [way of life] has existed for a very long time if not from time immemorial. In fact, it can be demonstrated from the historical record that what is now regarded as traditional evolved during the nineteenth century and some elements appeared even later. It is true that the basic elements of the so-called traditional Samoan social structure, the *'āiga* [extended family], the *matai* [chief], and the *nu'u* [village], extend much further back in time. But the form and functions of these institutions were flexible and could accommodate a great deal of change. For example, the *'āiga* [the extended family] quickly adapted to becoming a cooperative, of which the *matai* was the manager. In some villages land was divided up into individual plots. In many cases these informal cooperatives did not bother to go through the formal procedures of registration and so were generally unrecognized by the administrations. The chieftainship itself became somewhat democratized insofar as most adult men became chiefs. New titles were created; old titles were resurrected, split, or shared. In practice, the demands of the community or the chiefs on an individual were not excessive, certainly not excessive enough to effectively decrease the demand for goods or prevent status or monetary rewards for economic activity.

It was not only institutions that were flexible, but capital and technology as well. Traditional agriculture, for example, had many built-in conservation features, and although it was, perhaps, not productive in terms of land or labor input, it was adequate for consumer needs and did not harm the environment. The methods used in traditional agriculture, medicine, and education all adapted to the changing socioeconomic environment.

One of the reasons for much of the blame for Samoan underdevelopment (or, perhaps, for Third World underdevelopment generally) being placed at the door of tradition is that there is an appearance of inflexibility and incompatibility. The developers in Samoa, for example, believe that the status of chief is ascriptive and that chiefs are despotic. There is evidence to support this stereotype in Samoan society. Genealogies, for example, reflect primogeniture and continue to do so even when the facts are quite different. The real point is that the images of this traditional structure are theoretical, even mythical; hard lines are inevitably softer in practice. In Samoa, and perhaps in many Third World societies, the plasticity and complexity of real life situations is not well understood. On the one hand, I think we often assume that the myth is the reality, a deceptively easy misconception when the myths are believed by the developers and the developed alike. On the other hand, when fieldworkers or developers go into the field with hard structures or ideal types in mind (e.g. both Marxist and Weberian development structures), facts to fit these images can be found. I wonder how often what is looked for is what is found. Certainly, this would help us explain some of the contradictory reports that occur in the literature about the same village or situation.[6]

This is not to say that the myths and their functions are not worth studying. In Samoa, for example, *fa'aSamoa* [the traditional way of life] may not have been traditional, but it is very important to Samoan people in emphasizing their identity. Calling upon the past, upon tradition, gives great weight and purpose to activities. It is a way for people to say "we are different" and in Samoa *fa'aSamoa* [the Samoan way of life] is opposed to *fa'apalagi* [the European way of life]. Local pride, ethnocentrism, is a very important stimulus to development.

Identity, in fact, plays a very important and largely unrecognized part in some development situations. Often the kind of behavior adopted in a village or in any group is closely related to the image this group has of itself. If this image stresses an identification with the outside world, an environment suitable for development is created. Good contacts will be formed with the development bureaucracy, with the traders, and with other institutions like the missions. There will be agreement to change local customs, even down to selecting personnel. In the early days of contact, the prestige or power of the colonizers was so great that the emulatory image was paramount. The success stories in the entrepreneurial sector are also related to identity, but in a different way. In these cases, trading relations allowed more room for maneuver and for the retention of identity, which was, in fact, an important social base for economic activity.

Identity is also often very significant in situations where development does not take place. So far, we have looked at examples where development can be achieved through local, traditional organizations. But we tend to overlook the fact that in many cases development itself is not wanted. An official once said that the essential problem of development was to make people want what they need. In Samoa, for example, and perhaps for many Third World people, development is not a neutral process; on the contrary, it involves culture contact and, in many people's minds, the fear of alien domination. To participate in a development program, however indirect it is intended to be, involves in people's minds the concept of subordination at some point. Even goods or money are not neutral. Many people feel that something of the char-

---

[6] E.g. the celebrated case of Tepoztlán.

acter and spirit of a person is absorbed into goods. In Samoa, again for example, people feel that the European style and perhaps the European success are related to eating certain kinds of foods such as bread. Goods of all kinds become imbued with *mana* [good] or *tapu* [bad] characteristics.

To many people the loss of their local identity is more important than becoming wealthier and more developed. In addition, a greater emphasis may be placed on the quality of life (especially spiritual values in Samoa) rather than on the quantity of goods. People will even point to the balance of payment difficulties, inflation, etc. as being caused by excessive consumption.

It is also widely believed that development benefits the superior groups in the local social stratification system rather than those intended to be the ultimate beneficiaries. Increased income flows into the pockets of the merchants, who belong to a different subculture; the administration of development programs becomes yet an additional power in the already overpowerful central government.

Attitudes to population, the other important side of the development coin, are often radically different from accepted development thinking. Most Samoans, for example, want large families. There are many traditional and effective methods of birth control available to them if they do not wish to have large families. But they want large families because fertility is a symbol of prestige, because more hands around house and garden mean the production of more food which can be disbursed at *fiafia* [prestige-giving ceremonials], because they honestly believe the world would be a better place if there were more Samoans, and because they suspect that outside interference in population questions is a disguised form of domination.

In some cases, no development or opposition to development may involve very similar internal structural contexts of development, especially a strong sense of local identity and local pride. The external difference often lies in whether the local people feel they can cope with the situation of culture contact or are not overly subordinate in that situation.

Too often these kinds of feelings about development are either not known or, if known, rejected by developers, both academic and administrative. The effects of internal social stratification are seldom adequately taken into account in development programs. Aid is given to country X and it is assumed that every man and woman in that country will share the aid to some degree. By the time this aid, even when it is in the form of experts or machines rather than money, percolates down to the villages through the channels of corruption, venality, and inefficiency, little is left. And what is left is likely to flow back to the landlords, merchants, or government. In general, it is the local Afro-Asian governments who are the most insistent on centralization; it is the urban subcultures, attempting to emulate a European lifestyle, which raise consumption rates of imported goods to levels where deficits in foreign trade create grave development problems.

Summing up, my argument is simply that there are many roads to development and many different conceptions of development. Far more attention needs to be paid to the differing social contexts of development, especially at the grass-roots level, and to the complexity of the social relations involved in the exchange of goods and services. Multidisciplinary approaches are needed for the study of these situations because the insights of all social scientists can be useful. But although the perspectives need to be broadened and to be made more flexible, a greater concentration on understanding the local cultures is also needed. This not only means a rigorous study of language and culture, more fieldwork, and the encouragement of local social scientists, but also a more significant and much more careful interpretation of the data that does exist because local people will increasingly become involved in studying, reporting, and implementing development. To be realistic, very few Western social scientists will be able to make the transition needed to become part of the world below. Theoretically and methodologically, more flexible alternative models and strategies need to be utilized.

REFERENCES

APTHORPE, R.
   1971–1972   The new generalism: four phases in development studies in the first U.N. development decade. *Development and Change* 1:62–73.
BARNETT, A.
   1972   "The teaching of the sociology of development in Britain." Paper presented to the annual meeting of the British Sociological Association, Rugby.
BENDIX, R.
   1967   Tradition and modernity reconsidered. *Comparative Studies in Society and History* 9:292–351.
BOISSEVAIN, J.
   1973   *Friends of friends: networks, manipulators and coalitions.* Oxford: Blackwells.

COHN, B. S.
1962   An anthropologist among the historians: a field study. *South Atlantic Quarterly* 61 part 1:13–28.
DAHRENDORF, R.
1959   *Class and class conflict in industrial society*. London: Routledge and Kegan Paul.
DALTON, G.
1971   *Economic anthropology and development*. New York: Basic Books.
DUMONT, L.
1971   *Introduction à deux théories d'anthropologie sociale.* Paris: Mouton.
EISENSTADT, S. N.
1969   Some observations on the dynamics of traditions. *Comparative Studies in Society and History* 11:451–475.
FAYERWEATHER, J.
1959   *The executive overseas*. New York: Syracuse University Press.
FREYSSINET, J.
1966   *Le concept de sous-dévéloppement*. Paris: Mouton.
FRIEDRICHS, ROBERT W.
1970   *A sociology of sociology*. New York: Free Press.
GINSBERG, M.
1934   *Sociology*. London: Oxford University Press.
GLASER, B. C., A. L. STRAUSS
1967   *Discovery of grounded theory*. Chicago: Aldine.
GLENN, N. D., D. WEINER
1969   Some trends in the social origins of American sociologists. *The American Sociologist* 4:291–296.
GUSFIELD, J.
1968   Tradition and modernity. *Journal of Social Issues* 24.
HAGEN, E.
1962   *On the theory of social change*. Homewood, Illinois: Dorsey.
HORTON, W. R. G.
1963   The boundaries of explanation in social anthropology. *Man, Journal of the Royal Anthropological Institute* 43:10–11.
KUNKEL, J.
1970   *Society and economic growth*. New York: Oxford University Press.
LENGYEL, P.
1972   *Approaches to the science of socio-economic development*. Paris: UNESCO.
LERNER, D.
1964   *The passing of traditional society*. New York: Free Press.
MITCHELL, J. C., *editor*
1969   *Social networks in urban situations*. Manchester: Manchester University Press.
MOORE, BARRINGTON, JR.
1972   *Reflections on the causes of human misery*. London: Allen Lane Press.

MYRDAL, G.
1972 "The need for a sociology and psychology of social science and scientists." Paper presented to the annual meeting of the British Sociological Association, Rugby.
PITT, D. C.
1970 *Tradition and economic progress in Samoa.* Oxford: Clarendon Press.
RHODES, R., *editor*
1970 *Imperialism and underdevelopment: a reader.* London: Monthly Review Press.
RIDDELL, D.
1972 Towards a structuralist sociology of development. *Sociology* 6: (1):89–96.
ROGERS, E. M.
1969 *Modernization amongst peasants.* New York: Holt, Rinehart and Winston.
RUDOLPH, L. I., S. H. RUDOLPH
1967 *The modernity of tradition — political development in India.* Chicago: University of Chicago Press.
SHILS, E.
1971 Tradition. *Comparative Studies in Society and History* 13:122–159.
UNITED NATIONS
1969 *A report on the development capacity of the United Nations.* New York: United Nations.
WELLS, A.
1972 Towards an empirically grounded theory of development. *British Journal of Sociology* 23:312–329.

Peasants and Planistrators in Eastern Africa 1960-1970

RAYMOND APTHORPE

The rural development planning in Africa in the 1960's that engaged the attention of "development studies" did not stem from decision making by people in and of the rural areas themselves. Development studies laid emphasis on a lopsided interchange (whether cooperative or competitive or both) between what in practice were regarded as two distinct sets of persons. The "diffusion of innovations" studies, that were so characteristic of social science thinking in the decade, called one set of persons "planners," "initiators," or "change agents," depending on the level of reference. The other set was known rather as "receivers" who, potentially or actually, were simply supposed to accede gratefully to the well-intended ministrations of the former.

For the argument to be explored in this paper, which is addressed especially to some problems of secondary studies (Boudon 1969) and their interpretation in the social sciences, it would be useful to agree on a terminology that would catch the spirit of this give-and-take approach. The first set of persons could be called PLANISTRATORS,[1] because at the local level, especially, distinctions between central planning and public administration (the latter including implementation of central planning) are difficult to sustain. They engage in planistration.

This essay reflects on social science experience in middle Africa 1957–1968 and comparative study of certain aspects of African rural development planning in the two years following that period, carried out while Visiting Professorial Fellow in Sociology at the Institute of Development Studies at the University of Sussex and Project Director for Africa at the United Nations Research Institute for Social Development, Geneva. A companion piece is "Peasants and planistrators in northern Africa 1960–1970" (1972c).

[1] A term introduced in my note on the subject (Apthorpe 1969).

"Planistrator" and "planistration" are coined terms. For the second set of persons, the most widely prevalent term used by the planistrators was PEASANTS. Other "types" of humankind known to planning, administration, and the social sciences in the 1960's included "tribesmen." As they appeared to planistrators, "tribal" societies responded even less favorably to development planning than "peasant" societies — the "peasants," in the language of the times, were at least "sedentarized." Perhaps they were "villagized" as well.[2]

For much social science in the 1960's, a principal question for secondary (that is, comparative) development studies was to discover just what, precisely, constituted the mixture that was "peasant" society. This led, for instance, to much play in the interpretation of primary (that is monographic) materials, using such concepts as "dependence mentality" and "limited good." The best of the creative-historical and ideological-social anthropological analyses that resulted distinguished, for instance, between peoples and their societies who were and who were not taxed, or who were and who were not dependent on wage labor, or who were and who were not bound to the land. Insightful descriptive understandings of social forms considered such distinctions to be structurally basic. As the decade advanced, however, and as the varieties of social and other change "inside" and "from within" peasantries were brought more and more to the fore in social analysis, social science could, and, to some extent, did recognize more of the common humanity of man. By the end of the decade even an international committee (consisting mostly of economists) could, in its reflections on "development" and public policy, safely assume that "... the peasant farmer is not hopelessly fettered by custom and tradition ... he is not insensitive to prices" (Pearson 1969). Thus, at the very end of the period under review, it had come to be somewhat generally recognized that earlier suppositions made to the contrary by development planners needed to be revised.

Social survey research, monographic analyses, and particular policy statements, as a general class of pronouncements, often tend to relate or to be relatable to characteristically *post factum* explanations. Secondary analysis, which must transcend individual case studies and be addressed to general theories, has its own problems. What is suitable for the one kind of inquiry is seldom suitable also for the other. Received dichotomies such as sacred-secular, *gemeinschaft-gesellschaft*, etc., however

[2] "Sedentarization" and "villagization" are concepts developed especially in ILO (International Labor Organization) studies of nomadic societies and planned change in Africa and the Middle East.

useful, in limited ways, their contribution might be to social survey work or monographic studies, will usually be useless for secondary analyses. The latter have to recognize above all that any (indeed every) social situation can usually be characterized by each pair of these at one and the same time.

In the reflections that follow, three regions of conceptualization in peasant and planistrator studies will be explored: first, some aspects of analysis that are best illustrated by an inspection of these terms themselves and how they are used; second, the notion in development studies of "social prerequisites"; third, concepts of "traditional-modern" social change and public policy.

PEASANT AND PLANISTRATOR — A PAIR OF FICTIONS

Depending on the point of view from which it is considered, in planistration (i.e. central planning or public administration or both) political components or aspects may be deemed to predominate over functional, professional, or technological aspects. To continue with our word game for a moment, for it is instructive, planistration may at times seem to some to be more like POLIplanistration. That is to say, what may be understood in a central planning office or a university faculty as essentially, or merely, a matter of science, may seem nothing of the sort to cultivators on their farms, for whose benefit the whole planning operation may have been intended by its authors. It is especially in such a one-way process, understood as proceeding from one set of persons to another, that there is likely to be a clash of understandings, resulting in misunderstandings. To the first set of persons, who probably were making recommendations on the basis of what to them were standard textbook principles, there was nothing specially innovative about the innovation (though probably they lacked any practical personal experience of it in their own walks of life). It was considered by them to be novel with reference only to the second set of persons (with whose mode of life the first set of persons probably also had little, if any, personal contact).

Three observations critical of this planistrator-peasant orientation must be made. The first concerns the various kinds of problems that result from attributing categorical identities to individual persons or groups. Any (perhaps every) individual or group of individuals in real life shares some qualities with peasants and some with planistrators, if not always exactly at one and the same time, then more or less intermittently. Categorically, peasants have these attributes or those (depending on the particular theory about peasant societies invoked), in contrast with this or that characteristic of planistrators. To support this, reference is made to a number of monographic studies. There is no question that these generalizations are based inductively on empirical studies. But when one tries to apply the generalizations made in secondary studies to people in real life, one finds that the process cannot be reversed. This is particularly so concerning the generalized terms that are used as terms of reference, terms that would never be used by one of the sets of persons to address the other, except with the deliberate intention of exploiting their specious and derogatory nature. In that case, they would be more like epithets to be hurled at others than ordinary descriptive words such as one might apply to oneself. Our scholarly terms, then, are fictional as well as factual, MORE fictional than factual when they are applied back again to real life. This is because they allude primarily to categories of attributes rather than to groups of people. It is in sliding from one of these universes of discussion into the other that endless problems have been caused in social sciences and in development theories and practice alike.

Second, where planistrator-peasant categories of attributes have indeed been correctly recognized as such and applied in social science accordingly, difficulties for secondary analysis have arisen where they have been understood alogically or illogically. Since the attributes to which these categories refer are considered more often to be continuous rather than discontinuous in their distribution among persons or individuals, their application in sociological theorizing should be as contraries, not as contradictories. A dichotomous pair of terms exhausts its universe of discourse completely. Contraries, on the other hand, are flexible and fallible. In remarking on this analytical principle, however, one should keep in mind that it is the USE of a pair of categories to describe social and other relationships that is under review. It would be simplistic to suppose that relationships HAVE only one categorical character, expressed falsely by contradictory and correctly by contrary categories.[3] Relationships are, in a word, multiplex.[4] In any event, intent alone is seldom categorical.

[3] E. R. Leach (1961) merely moves from the frying pan into the fire when, for example, he rejects dichotomies (contradictory categories) outright in favor of continuum constructs (contrary categories) as conceptualizations of social relations (as, for instance, the sacred and the profane). As construed by and among the population in which they are current and acted upon, these concepts are acted upon sometimes as contraries, sometimes as contradictories. The important thing for secondary studies is that they should recognize a range of possibilities, rather

We have moved from factual to fictional terms, and then from contradictories to contraries. Third, it is to be observed that the ways in which "peasants" themselves analyze and predict their own patterns of social and economic activities perhaps exclude none whatsoever of the characteristics of rationality that planistrators like to attribute to planistration alone. Recently, as we have seen, planistrators also have come to understand this better. But if peasants, when they plan, are no longer peasants, surely it would be best to drop the planistrator-peasant approach and terminology altogether. Because "planistrator" is a coined word, it is easy to argue that it is best used only as a term of abuse where abuse is called for. Because "peasant" is not a coined word, it is more difficult to abandon it — except, again, as an epithet.[5] Least of all would the authors of social anthropological studies of peasants and peasant society wish to be considered as abusing their subject.

The most basic defect of planistrator-peasant development studies is that they have conceptualized planned change as a kind of confrontation, not merely between two sets of persons, but even between two kinds or types of societies — or rather, a confrontation between a type of society at the receiving end (a peasant society, receiving an input) and an output at the giving end thought of as being without any institutionalization at all, in a real sense. Peasant society has been considered, positivistically, to be economically underdeveloped. Planistrators put this down to social rather than economic reasons. Theorists (even in the discipline of economics) who addressed themselves to development studies and did fieldwork (probably as creatively as was possible within the paradigms that prevailed at the time) could distinguish between social factors (such as "a person's class or job") and economic factors (such as "the level of a person's spending on food . . . income . . . price"), and then submit that the connections between economic items were stronger than connections between any one of these and any one of the so-called social factors — all this within the framework of a general theory that denied the relevance of constraints, if

---

than only (any) one case. C. Lévi-Strauss' thinking about oppositional social relations is, similarly, insensitive to the different varieties of opposition actually perceived and acted upon in socal situations.

[4] This term we owe principally to M. Gluckman's studies of Barotse jurisprudence.

[5] Epithets are very commonly metaphors. It is the abusive use of metaphors that is at issue here. In a more extended analysis, "peasant" (and for that matter "planistrator") should, of course, be considered also as praise names, as well as disparaging epithets.

they were perceived only externally and were unknown to the farmers being studied (e.g., Lipton 1968).

In social anthropological analyses it was considered that while social institutions (such as kinship and family structure) were interrelated with economic and ecological circumstances, it was only the social institutions which provided common "basic norms." Economic and ecological circumstances amounted merely to external or limiting factors. It was as if social institutions had been formed prior to the situations to which they referred, so that, in the organicist language that was used, it was merely local adaptation of the institutions that followed or was needed. Social factors being viewed thus as somehow prior to economic ones, it followed, especially in diffusionist studies, that it would be necessary and sufficient for social policy and social science alike to focus on the difficulties (in rare cases, the ease) of economic-ecological adaptation alone.[6] If social anthropologists did not, as economists often did, attribute the economic underdevelopment of peasant society to social factors, they — we — nonetheless intellectually imposed a kind of sequential factor priority in secondary social science — in deed, if not in intention.

Divergences in understandings — misunderstandings — between persons in government who plan or administer and those for whose benefit the exercise is intended may vary locally due to the degree of social distance between the two. Where (still speaking metaphorically) peasants' expectations are rising rapidly so that the target income levels planned for them by planistrators are seen by the peasants to be much lower than those which the planistrators themselves enjoy, the ground is especially fertile for local reactions to planned change that planistration has not anticipated or planned for. This is especially likely to be the case where the planistrators constitute a new social class in the rural area and are perceived as deriving their better position somehow at the expense of the peasants.

In Africa, as elsewhere, such reactions have often taken one of two extreme forms. On the one hand, the theory has taken root among peasants and their intellectual protagonists that development planning is a conspiracy to siphon off or dampen their aspirations. Classically, John Stuart Mill discussed cooperatives as a conspiracy to limit gains in this way. However, the main proposition in Calvert's standard work on the law and principles of cooperation is that cooperatives, more than

---

[6] "Economic" and "social" are distinguished in many other ways as in social anthropology, economics, and the other social sciences. It is only one of the distinctions that is at issue here.

any other kind of instrument, provide the only path to economic (and social) development for poor people. Problems have arisen at the local level when rural cooperatives have been seen as a means of keeping poor people poor, as devices that insulated rural populations from better opportunities. On the other hand, a very different reaction to planned change is possible. Cooperatives, as well as other projects, have triggered new wants for education and other social services. When educational (social) advancement is seen locally to be more immediately critical for progress than, say, the only marginally higher agricultural (economic) output and income levels that planistration has proposed, a conflict has been set up, between what have been identified as social and economic objectives, that only works against the attainment of either. In both situations, social distance and levels of aspiration or expectation are crucial considerations for local populations, but with different effects in the two cases.

In the postcolonial Africa of the 1960's rural cooperatives were commonly the most favored social instruments for structural change at the forefront of public policies.[7] I contend that a major reason why this continued to be the case, despite the fact that the actual performance of these instruments at that time was seldom very successful, was what might be called the intellectual subculture of planistration and the applied social science commissioned by and contributed to it. In this regard, the following observations concerning the concept of social prerequisites which played such a dominant part in social science applied to cooperatives have a particular relevance. Before identifying and then critically reviewing the trends in African applied social science in the 1960's, however, some alternative conceptualizations of "peasants" and "planistrators" to those of the model examined thus far should be illustrated by means of some historical and substantive remarks on cooperatives and public policy in eastern Africa.

Peasants Are Not Always Passive

Any approach to planning or to social science that excludes the possibility of dynamism "from below" is defective, however difficult peasant mobility may be to sustain in reality. As a recent study by Eric Wolf (1969) concluded, especially significant here might be the landowning "middle" peasantry located in a peripheral area outside the

---

[7] A synoptic account of rural cooperatives in action in Africa is to be found in Apthorpe (1972b).

domains of major landlord control who, for example, are relatively most vulnerable to economic change brought (or expressed) by commercialism in a situation in which equilibrium is continuously threatened ". . . by population growth; by the encroachment of rival landlords; by the loss of rights to grazing, forest and water; by falling prices and unfavorable conditions of the market; by interest payments and foreclosures." It is, Wolf suggested,

> . . . precisely this stratum which most depends on traditional social relations of kin and mutual aid between neighbours; middle peasants suffer most when these are abrogated, just as they are least able to withstand the depredations of tax collectors or landlords.

Drawing in part on Germaine Tillion's work on northern Africa (1961: 120–121), he went on to point out how

> . . . the middle peasant . . . stays on the land and sends his children to work in town; he is caught in a situation in which one part of the family retains a footing in agriculture, while the other undergoes "the training of the cities." This makes the middle peasant a transmitter also of urban unrest and political ideas. The point bears elaboration. It is probably not so much the growth of an industrial proletariat as such which produces revolutionary activity, as the development of an industrial work force still closely geared to life in the villages.

The conclusion Wolf presents is that "it is the very attempt of the middle and free peasant to remain traditional which makes him revolutionary." As he puts it:

> The peasant rebellions of the twentieth century are no longer simple responses to local problems, if indeed they ever were. . . . Industrialization and expanded communication have given rise to new social clusters, as yet unsure of their own social positions and interests, but forced by the very imbalance of their lives to seek a new adjustment. Traditional political authority has eroded or collapsed; new contenders for power are seeking new constituencies for entry into the vacant political arena. Thus when the peasant protagonist lights the torch of rebellion, the edifice of society is already smouldering and ready to take fire.

The particular interest of these challenging arguments is that, while they assume a peasant order or type of society, they also recognize how both "anarchism and an apocalyptic vision of the world" can exist within a peasantry and can change society outside of it as well as within.

In Zambia and in Uganda the early beginnings of marketing cooperatives as we know them today date from the second decade of this century. In Uganda for instance, four farmers in Singo County formed The Kinakulya Growers in 1913. In 1933 The Buganda Growers' Association, which initially comprised five groups of farmers attempting to sell their cotton cooperatively, was reconstituted as The Uganda Growers' Cooperative Society. Though little has been recorded of these incipient "movements," they were basically voluntary organizations, devised at the local level. Government legislation on cooperatives in Uganda was not forthcoming until after World War II. The government did go so far as to draft a cooperatives bill in the 1930's, but vigorous opposition by expatriate-controlled processing and marketing interests soon led to its withdrawal in favor of the continuance of welfare and basically nonfinancial improvements in farming that did not include, for example, credit. In the interwar years, government depended on cotton for some 80 percent of its revenue. No doubt it was in connection with this that the administration developed the view that, while government intervention in trade was dangerous, the growing of crops for export by "a population of primitive natives"[8] represented an abnormal situation in which "excessive competition" should be limited and "rationalization" was all important. British and Indian firms joined to act in harmony against any free trade in ginneries.

During his visit to the Uganda Protectorate in 1944, W. K. H. Campbell found well-developed local economic improvement organizations already existing and a well-defined interest in the running of cooperatives, despite the lack of an ordinance for the recognition of such societies (Engholm 1967: 402–420). With the understanding that politics, in no shape or form, would or should be involved in the cooperatives, he recommended a modest degree of official assistance to the movement in the form of legislation. What planistration envisaged here (as elsewhere in Africa soon afterwards) was an apolitical, welfarist form of self-realization and democratization that would not radically change the existing status quo but would make it more tolerable to the farmers now firmly within the cash-economy sector. By then the class of trading middlemen that had been so prominent in the 1920's was almost defunct.

In 1948 a government report found the immigrant-controlled ginning industry to be in a decrepit state and dependent on antiquated

---

[8]   Brett's dissertation (1968) cites the *Report on closer union in eastern Africa* (the Milton-Young report) 1929. I have drawn here especially on Brett (1968: Chapter 7).

machinery. It allowed a five-year period in which to reform. Riots in April 1949 against the Buganda Government, organized by the Bataka Party and the Uganda African Farmers Union (UAFU), brought matters to a new explosion point. The UAFU was registered under the Business Names Ordinance by Ignatius Musazi, Uganda's first nationalist leader, as a commission agent mainly for sales of cotton and coffee. The Buganda government, however, was also exerting pressure on the administration for higher prices for primary produce and for a share in the ginning industry. The UAFU was banned, but continued under another name, the Federation of Uganda Farmers. This organization invited John Stonehouse (with his experience of cooperatives in Britain) and George Shepherd (from the United States) to help with the task of further organization of what was virtually an unofficial movement. The problems of the movement, as these two animators saw them, were twofold. They included: (1) troubles with members of the administration in the Cooperative Department who knew or cared little about cooperative principles and (2) manipulation locally by "black sheep, tricksters and crooks who came into this mushroom organization to make a quick penny for themselves" (Stonehouse cited in Engholm 1967: 413). Government continued to devote its reformist attentions mainly to the ginning interests, but also blocked further expansion of immigrants' interests in favor of eventual participation by the cooperatives' unions. As in Tanzania, the cooperatives had come to be a force to be reckoned with, negotiated with, and finally absorbed or harnessed. In 1952 the results of a new government investigation into the cooperative movement were published. The 1946 Ordinance was greatly amended — in particular the supervisory duties of the Cooperative Department were relaxed. The way was now open for the government-sponsored policy of registering societies, that eventually came to be seen as a force more for social control than for social change.

In their beginnings, cooperatives in Tanzania were also voluntary, grass-roots movements. The beginnings of cooperatives in Tanzania were associated with the considerable expansion of coffee planting after 1921. In the 1930's, government contemplated the possibility of introducing cooperatives legislation, and indeed the registration of cooperative societies was possible from 1932. It was not, however, until twenty years later that government positively fostered cooperatives — apart, that is, from provision for the purely formal functions of legal registration, audit, and financial supervision (*Tanganyika Standard* n.d.). The

Kilimanjaro Native Planters' Association was formed in 1933, and the Kilimanjaro Native Cooperative Union (KNCU), one of the best known of all African cooperatives, in 1933.

The cotton cooperatives in Sukumaland developed only after World War II, as will be discussed below. The Victoria Union Federation of Cooperative Unions was the largest African-owned and African-operated cooperative organization in Africa and the single largest enterprise in the economy of Tanzania (Maguire 1969).[9] As one would indeed expect with an undertaking on so large a scale, an intermixture of political as well as economic factors determined its growth. Although in its early years it represented a protest against the existing regime, from the start it had the support of the administration in Mwanza, which was also concerned with abolishing that system of trade under which the unsalaried Asian buyer depended on a commission for his livelihood. Originally, as the first government cooperatives officer in Mwanza put it, the cooperative movement in Tanzania was defensive rather than aggressive in character. Only later did tensions develop at the local level between chiefs and would-be organizers of cooperatives, when the activities of the cooperatives intertwined with those of the political associations.

In 1955, under multiracial formulas that had been adopted, Paul Bomani, the prime mover of the Muranzo organization, became the first representative of the new politics to find a voice in the higher councils of the Tanganyikan Administration. When, in the mid-1950's, the government moved against the political associations (one of which was to lead to TANU, the Tanganyika African National Union), the cooperatives in Tanzania mobilized some ten times as many members as either the TAA or the Sukuma Union. At the local level, a wide range of participation developed. Bomani worked sometimes with the constituted authorities of local government but more often with traders, ambitious cotton farmers, and occasionally traditional village leaders (such as leaders of the young men's societies and elders). Committee members in the primary societies differed widely in age. The cotton cooperatives in Tanzania

... were never simply collections of discontented and vociferous young men. The new societies responded to a need felt throughout the community and they engaged the efforts, leadership and membership of many segments of any community in which they were active (Maguire 1969).

[9] See especially Chapter 4: "Traders, cotton cooperativs and politics."

The organization of the cooperatives was such as not to permit chiefs and headmen to use it to augment the power that the administration had conferred on them. What the northern movement did achieve in Tanzania was

...to awake.... thousands to a conscious definition of their economic and political plight. They offered concrete machinery for the alleviation of latent grievances and the achievement of new aspirations (Maguire 1969).

The KNCU, for example, devoted much of its wealth (coffee prices were at their height in the mid-1950's) to building a school of commerce and a secondary school. In addition, the tax paid to the Chagga local treasury was the main resource that allowed for the great improvement of social services in that area at that time.

In the mid-1950's in Tanzania the organizing of political protest and mobilization passed essentially to the political parties. Having thus far been mainly concerned to negotiate with a force for change, of which the enormous potential was unmistakable, the government now began to identify with it so completely that henceforth the cooperatives and the cooperative movement ceased to have any independent existence at all. The year 1953, when the government forbade its servants to take any part in the affairs of the political association, marked an important turning point in Tanzania. The division between administration and politics that this signified deepened as Tanzania saw its last years of trusteeship status.

Coming now to the 1960's, and the achievement of independence in the different countries in East Africa, some of the new explosions of energies and aspirations that marked this period at the local level expended itself in the formation of new cooperatives. These were of the high-principled variety, like the earlier ones during the voluntary beginnings of the 1920's or so. Whether these new societies were launched quite spontaneously in the local context (as in Kenya) or in response to a specific call to the nation from the president (as in Zambia) is not particularly important, given the release of energies at all levels that *uhuru* [freedom] (in Swahili) in Africa meant.

Planistration Is Not Always Active

In the 1960's an important continuity with past public policy lay in the fact that the government of the new states, like their precursors, found poverty, ignorance, and disease to be endemic in rural areas, and built crucial ideological implications around this. Above all, these included a distinct separation, not of powers, but of the central from the local levels as regards virtually all decision-making matters that concerned political organization and the distribution of economic resources. As before, the purpose of this was to make it quite clear where authority rested. As regards details and timing, of course, countries and districts differed, and in some respects the organization of the central governments was in constant change throughout the decade. But the most important single socioeconomic structural feature of East Africa — namely an all-powerful system of district commissioners and public servants on which the center relied for the control of the periphery and to which, to facilitate this, certain measures of autonomy were allowed — remained in force. Where, as in Uganda, the earlier years of the decade did see a move away from this, in later years the old system was reinstated so as to give the center even stronger powers than it had possessed before.

Initial policy emphasis on Africanization, combined with more priority on growth aims, in many ways had the effect of reinforcing rather than reforming the structures inherited from the past regime. The Arusha Declaration (Nyerere 1969) was a notable reaction to this on the part of one of the governments (Tanzania) in the region under discussion here. It is to be noted that the continuities with past organizations, within inherited boundaries,[10] are essentially at the level of the state and its servants. For the greater part, the privileged material conditions of the previous administrators were simply passed on to nationals without significant change. At the same time, as goals for rural productivity were raised, generally speaking the emergence of income and wealth differentials in the countryside in effect received a new impetus, rather than the opposite. Of the many observers who have commented on this in East Africa, Brian van Arcadie (1969) went on to show that

... even some explicit attempts to reduce economic inequality have perverse results — minimum wage increases, aimed at improving the miserable lot of the unskilled employed worker had as its effect the restriction of employment, with a closing of the income gap amongst the employed being combined with the emergence of an increased contrast between the economic well-being of the small minority who could gain jobs and the unemployed and self-employed majority.

The same author describes the pattern that has emerged:

---

[10] The re-forming of colonial boundaries having been regarded initially as an insuperable task, this was not undertaken upon the achievement of independence.

... as inherently more stable, at least in the short term, than the previous colonial system because it allows upward economic mobility, it draws support from nationalist rhetoric and, when export conditions are favourable, generates short-term economic success (van Arcadie 1969).

The correctness of this judgment depends, however, on a number of factors, including the force (military and other) with which the tendencies toward opposition within it are suppressed or instated. Much depends also on the nature of the independence movements in the first place.

Planistration in eastern Africa has long supposed that there are two extremes between which public policy must choose. Competition has been identified with *laissez-faire*, and cooperation with a planned economy. It is for the latter that the governments have opted. The view has steadily gained ground that (as in the case of coffee, cotton, and pyrethrum, for example) marketing should be a monopoly of the cooperatives. It was presumably well understood that the centripetal tendencies that would follow from competition would lead to the establishment of points of influence and development independent of the center.

To begin with, one of the arguments for monopoly functions was that the new ventures needed much protection. It was seen that the cooperatives were, as in Tanzania,

... usually not equal to the competition of Indian traders. Obligatory sales are necessary if they are to succeed. In the short run, traders may give better service to the producer than cooperatives. Traders have no monopoly. Competition among them is keen. They have long experience in commerce. However, the cooperatives are ... African institutions. Their members learn through failures, set-backs and difficulties, and gain commercial knowledge and experience in dealing with economic power. In the long run this advantage is certainly more important than any possible losses due to lower efficiency. Obligatory sales may be regarded as an unavoidable protective measure for the emerging cooperative movement (Ruthenberg 1964: 101–102).

In Uganda events took a somewhat different course. In the middle 1920's, government prohibited the building of new ginneries. Ten years later it limited competition between those that were already in existence. By the 1940's, the position of the independent middleman had virtually been eliminated. Competition had been all but eliminated from the structure of the industry when, eventually, government cooperatives were introduced. As E. A. Brett (1970: 118) notes:

... as a result of this monopolistically controlled situation, profits were exceedingly high during the 1950's and the market price for ginneries correspondingly inflated. Since the cooperatives were forced to buy at these very high prices they were thereafter committed to heavy interest rates and capital repayments.

The best evidence from Uganda of inadequate relations between the rewards, the controls, and the work done by the cooperatives [11] came when, in the 1965–1966 season,

> ... the government cut the ginning allowance by about 30%, and then cut it even further in the following year, The earlier generous margins had vanished, and heavy losses were general. Weaker unions have been brought to the verge of the financial collapse, and even the better organized have made losses on their cotton trading. Unless the allowance is increased or radical changes in management introduced the Unions which do not have substantial interests in crops other than cotton cannot expect to develop themselves as viable economic institutions. The reduction in formula took place principally because the government was under extreme pressure to maximise the price which could be paid direct to the grower, but it was also justified on the grounds that it would force the Unions into efficiency. It has probably been at least partially successful in this, since costs have been reduced and management somewhat improved. At the same time it has led to an immense amount of upheaval among the Unions, not all of it of a beneficial nature. The Department and the Banks have had to intervene more directly to ensure that improvements would take place, and the movement as a whole has not been able to accumulate any surpluses which could be used to finance further expansion. Since the Government is no longer giving the cooperatives the unqualified support which it manifested in 1962–65, and since a general shortage has now developed in the availability of long term finance, the movement has been able to initiate relatively few new projects during the last two years. In addition few Unions have been able to pay a bonus to their members and this has been an important factor in contributing to the widespread lack of support for them.

An attempt to introduce a monopoly for maize marketing by the cooperatives in Kenya failed in 1967–1968. At the same time, attempts to give the cooperatives the same powers in the distribution of seeds to smallholders in the Western Province were considered to have such poor results that, as of the end of the 1960's, the Ministry was reported to be highly reluctant to try it again. Planistration in Kenya was less ideologically committed to cooperatives as instruments of public policy (Hyden and Karanja 1970) than it was in Uganda, Tanzania, and Zambia.

[11] " ... in the early years the rewards were certainly excessive and the controls inadequate, in 1965–1967 the rewards have probably been too small and the controls probably too direct. The old system encouraged waste, the new system will lead to stagnation" (Brett 1967: 4).

SOCIAL PREREQUISITES

Rural development policies such as the formation of cooperatives in the 1960's were, in practice, devised and implemented by one social group, but for the benefit chiefly of another. It was not, however, just ANY other category or group, or ALL others, but ONLY THAT PARTICULAR ONE whose qualities planistrators deemed somewhat likely to favor the success of the policies they proposed. Precisely what these qualities were stated to be or assumed to be varied widely. Very commonly, however, two features (one particular, the other general) were given prominence in the lists enunciated. First, literacy, not to mention school education itself, was regarded as a universal solvent. Second, societies with a "traditionally hierarchical social structure" were considered to be more receptive to planistration than others. A critical examination of the concept of social prerequisites is necessary.[12]

Two observations about social prerequisites can be made immediately. First, very often it will be found that the supposed predisposing qualities in effect cancel each other. If there were such close functional interrelations between one aspect of society and another as the prerequisites approach assumes, it would be reasonable to suppose, for example, that the appearance of literacy in a "traditionally hierarchical society" would change either its traditional aspect (however that was defined) or its hierarchical character or both. In any event, the very fact of a higher and external authority being accepted as having the power to impose a cooperative's policy from above and from the outside would mean that any previously-obtaining authoritative ordering no longer existed in the autonomous sense it may have had before. Second, there is the intellectual and practical futility of a tautological approach. What is recommended as facilitating the initial establishment of a cooperative is very often nothing other than the desired qualities of the cooperative itself.

---

[12]   The following is based on Part A of my "The golden eggs of cooperation" (1968a), a conference paper read at the Institute of Development Studies Conference at the University of Sussex in May 1968, which was contributed mainly as a criticism of views represented at that time by L. Joy and R. Dore. This conference paper was not, however, included in the book of the conference, *Two blades of grass,* edited by P. Worsley (1972). Instead, another paper of mine was included, namely, "Some evaluative problems for cooperatives studies with special reference for primary societies in highland Kenya" (1971), which was then in press for another volume, *Cooperatives and rural development in eastern Africa,* edited by C. G. Widstrand (1971). In the papers under the authorship of Joy and Dore in the Worsley volume, some of the views expressed are similar to those which were proposed in "The golden eggs of cooperation."

Of all possible rural development policies, those which put their main emphasis on "cooperation" may lean heaviest on a search for pre-requisites (Apthorpe 1968a). If the fundamental premise of development planning is that it should have some chance of guiding events into directions in which they would otherwise not be expected to go, it is odd, in any case, that so much effort should go into looking for ready-made receptacles for the new central politices. What most need to be critically reviewed here, however, are two ideas mixed together in the notion that it is less difficult to introduce "modern cooperation" into "traditional society," which includes among its characteristics the right "social prerequisites" for cooperation. The prerequisites approach in input-output models in systems analysis, especially when applied to cross-cultural comparison and policy formulation, has, as I have already implied, the disadvantage that it confuses prerequisites (whether functional or causal) with consequences. The 1945 Fabian report on co-operatives made this point most cogently when (in arguing that it was a mistake for policy-recommenders for rural Africa to assume that the cooperative methods and technology of highly-prosperous agricultural countries like Denmark were entirely irrelevant) it observed that "the very high level of mutual trust and widely diffused business ability" that the Danish system demands were "[NOT] SO-CALLED PRE-REQUISITES . . . [BUT] THE PRODUCTS of cooperative Danish agriculture" and the cooperative folk schools (Fabian Bureau 1945: 27, emphasis added). Here all that the prerequisites theory achieves is to put the cart before the horse, rather than the other way about, as its name would suggest.

Another difficulty arises when:

The terms "social pre-requisites," "social factors," and the like . . . envisage a developmental process that is centrally economic but that will run more smoothly if social lubricants are added to the machinery and social grit flushed out of it. Under such an interpretation social specialists complain that they are likely to be called in only at a secondary stage to propose additives or tactical modifications for economic plans constructed without their full participation (Economic Commission for Latin America 1966).

It is the first part of this statement that is most germane to the present line of argument. In focusing too exclusively on "the system" and the various inputs and outputs that are needed to make "it" work, the prerequisites approach in effect neglects, completely contrary to its author's intentions, what it calls "the human factor." Really, there is a paradox here. It is precisely because planistrators have aimed to take "the human factor" into account that, at the practical level, they and others have looked for lines of least resistance.

Next to be discussed here are the neglected questions: whose prerequisites and for what? With respect to WHOSE prerequisites, it must first be noted that while "the system" is an abstraction so, at a different level of discourse, is "the individual." It would not go very far toward solving our problem, then, merely to substitute the latter for the former. When something goes wrong with "the economy" or "the polity" that gives rise to planning concern, project evaluations have shown that in particular districts some of the effects or casualties are very specifically located at the level of particular age/sex/occupation categories. But even if there were agreed prerequisites to assure benefits for the people affected, it would remain to be demonstrated that the prerequisites were equally valid for other population categories or groups. In any event, there are DIFFERENT KINDS OF prerequisites, not all of which relate equally to the same (or different) categories or groups. For example, the procedures [13] required by professional planners for what they see as technical operations may differ considerably from those on the basis of which they might allocate popular participation. Also, as we have seen already, what by some parties in the process is regarded as technical in content, by others is regarded as political. Variations with respect to different kinds of prerequisites and different kinds of policies — e.g. for education, health, welfare — must also be distinguished. Then, of course, conditions on the use of international aid or technical assistance may differ significantly from the strings attached to domestic sources. And so on.

Concerning the problems of social prerequisites FOR WHAT, given terms of reference may make it clear that such and such a particular project is what is to be evaluated. But seldom do they go on to state with the same (or indeed any) precision the objectives or standards against which it is to be evaluated. To ask, simply, what contribution such and such a new cooperative has made or might make "to development" is virtually to ask nothing at all when "development" is undefined or defined only in the vaguest terms.

It is an excessive and simplistic preoccupation with a prerequisites approach that we have aimed to illustrate here and then to review critically. Questions about WHAT KIND and WHOSE bring into relief some of the limitations of such an approach. If any purpose at all is to be served by working with prerequisites in secondary analysis, then, to begin with, several complementary and conflicting classes of pre-

---

[13]   A fuller analysis would need to distinguish, for example, between principles, procedures, and personnel.

requisites would need to be distinguished. Social prerequisites thinking has jumbled together (providing no means for ranking in any causal, functional, or dialectical ordering) at least the following: nonsensical kinds of facilitating conditions — nonsensical because they are advanced by "general theorists" without any general theory to account for their possible efficacy; requirements (e.g. of a procedural kind) for professional planning, popular leadership, moral equity, fiscal success, or scientific analysis, which vary according to the social groups or categories involved; and inducements demanded or expected by the different parties involved in planning and its execution (e.g. high salaries for short-term contract staff, career prospects for long-term clerks or inspectors, changes in modes of livelihood for farmers, etc.). In the short run, different kinds of prerequisites, as well as different instances of the same kind, may conflict. It is in the short run that a new development project has to prove itself worthy of continuing institutional support. For these among other reasons I would agree with Fredrik Barth (1967) that ". . . the anthropological predilection for going from a generalized type construct of a social form to a list of prerequisites for this general type" has thus far proved notably fruitless in development studies. To parallel Barth's remarks on entrepreneurial studies, it is less what makes cooperatives, than what cooperatives make as a contribution to planned social change, that is the more promising line of social science inquiry. The 1960's trends in idealization in social science (Lopreato and Alston 1967) are not helpful in this respect.

Social structures are best seen in development studies not as unitary but as situational and diverse in their characteristics. Up to a point, conflicting tendencies can be contained within the same social structure. Social prerequisites thinking masks this important social fact. Hierarchical, nonhierarchical, or antihierarchical social organization in, say, industrial relations or in agriculture, does not necessarily also mean hierarchical, nonhierarchical, or antihierarchical values in, say, religion or kinship. The appearance of factionalism in a cooperative is not necessarily a mark of its failure. If factionalism has any special relationship at all to the cooperative organization as such, it may be an indication of success rather than failure. Not all groups in a society or parts of a social structure are, or can be, harmoniously linked with one another. Prerequisites thinking in effect always views peasants and planistrators only as contradictory categories, thus leading social analysis to ignore, among other things, the intervening or countervailing power elites. The dogma that if cooperatives — and other rural organizations — are to work satisfactorily they must function as formal organizations quite free from underpinning, undermining, or intersecting informal organization and primary or interpersonal influence, is based on a sociocentric assumption that planistration is — or should be — purely functional, free from informal structures. No existing organization actually works (or could conceivably work) on formal principles alone, without shortcuts, delays, or other adjustments to local circumstances, or without errors or false beginnings.

In the early 1960's, something of a turning point came when new trends of diversification began to appear in monographic studies on administrative organization in change. Lloyd Fallers' important book, *Bantu bureaucracy* (1958), had crystallized a notion that was then widely held, namely that African social structures that were traditionally centralized would "adopt" (or "adapt to") what were called "Western civil-service conceptions" more readily and with less conflict than would African social systems that were not already hierarchical in form. Research and discussion set off by this study opened the way to new thinking.

To some extent, two stages in this work can be discerned. First, a converse hypothesis was entertained, viz. that it was in the noncentralized social structures at the local level that the rapid introduction of a bureaucratic element (such as the administration of cooperatives, for instance, would represent — though this was not a case specifically discussed at that time) stood the best chance (Apthorpe 1960).[14] Second, a few years later, as it became equally clear that even the converse of the old hypothesis had little meaning, the traditionalmodern dichotomy itself in its various forms (here African-Western) came into disrepute. Some of the models of modernization that were invoked, indeed, were nothing other than readings of what in the history or traditions of one society or situation were somehow to be recommended for another. I will turn to this in a moment.

In my inaugural lecture as incumbent of the Makerere Chair of Sociology,[15] I returned to an issue that had first attracted me ten years earlier, recalling that my colleagues and I, then in Zambia, had found Fallers' hypothesis to neglect completely what we considered some of the most significant factors in social and political change. In particular, we had been of the view that certain powers and interests of individuals or groups could not be redistributed, *in vacuo* as it were, without social norms being thereby necessarily affected in the process. However,

---

[14]   See also works on African politics by B. J. Dudley and others.
[15]   Partly published as Apthorpe (1968b), this inaugural was given, in fact, as a valedictory lecture.

looking back in 1968 at my own position ten years earlier, I noted that my argument failed to extend beyond the presence or absence of a hierarchy in dominant social structure. Worse, it had not for the most part gone beyond its term of reference, which were confined to the social values theory of development (Apthorpe 1968a, 1968b) that then prevailed so much in social science in Africa and elsewhere. I realized that, and if I were to rally to that particular debate aagin I would find myself in sympathy with neither Fallers' thesis nor our counter-thesis. Both belonged to typological or classificatory social science, the intellectual ground of planistrator-peasant approaches. When applied to the study of political and administrative change (and for that matter, economic change), unfortunately it posed problems in terms of a one-sided emphasis, a series of intellectually-created gaps that events have to be made to jump, so to speak, just to please the predilection of the theorist. The solution to the problem, proposed by the typological method (as in the Busoga analysis), invoked a double standard for which logical proof is hard to find. Social change within any one type is conceived as evolution, but "the same" social change between any two types is called diffusion.

To return to Fallers' analysis, let us call the Soga State "A" and the bureaucracy that was to be introduced into it "B." The Soga State is described as having been incipiently bureaucratic even before colonial contact — that is, "A" was said to be incipient "B." But, according to the theory put forward, pre-Western "A" can become Western "B" only by the diffusion of "B" into "A." The theory does not explain how "A" could be incipiently "B" BEFORE colonial contact, but proceeds, nonetheless, on the basis that this is a historical fact. Admittedly, however, the classic African political systems approach which that particular Ugandan study exemplified did have the merit that it recorded many varieties of social organization in rural areas, all the way from the cephalous to the acephalous, as it were. Therefore it did not necessarily assume the city to be the source of all diversity in rural organization, nor did it assume that self-evident urban circumstances existed which could dictate necessities of a social-organizational or administrative kind.

The typological approach to the study of change forces analysis to assume that change must always take a collision course, somehow at the same time evolutionary and revolutionary, not to mention diffusionary (between kingships, feudalisms, republics, democracies, and so on). It assesses the authority of a kingship or a presidency, but not the effective power of an individual king or president; it tests the theory of a democracy, but not the actual policies of a particular democratic party. Probably, type theory distorts the study of kingships and presidencies above all because, even according to typological premises, the personal qualities of an individual at the center in a centralized regime can exert a determining influence on events which then may have little if anything to do with any -ism or -ship or -cracy. Historical accounts of political development in Uganda leading up to the crisis of 1966, duly followed by the usurpation of the usurper in 1971, demonstrate this perfectly.

SOCIAL CHANGE — "MODERN" AND "TRADITIONAL" MODELS

The varieties of social change are infinite. Some cooperatives policies — to continue with these as illustrations — are reformist. Others are more revolutionary in intent. Some have a high development content. Others come closer to a care-and-maintenance approach. Some planned social changes relate to models, rather specifically defined. Others rest content with more general terms of reference. Probably the most prevalent of all of the more general approaches in cooperatives studies in the 1960's was epitomized in the question posed by planistration of social research: should "modern" cooperatives be built on "traditional" cooperatives or not? This is a systematically misleading question, which should be sent back to its authors for rephrasing, or should be rephrased for them! It supposes, first, that there are two distinct kinds of social organization; second, that they differ fundamentally; and, third, that one rather than the other necessarily affords or connotes the best strategy for planned change.

In addition to the shortcomings that have been listed already, the simplistic social prerequisites approach to applied social research reinforces a number of suppositions that we must now discuss. First to be examined will be the notion of social change towards "modernity."

Compared with all other development "models," that of "modernization" is vague and ambiguous in the extreme. Often, indeed, it is not a model at all so much as just an affirmation that something — something drastic — must be done, on a total scale. The emphasis is on this enormous and urgent need for action "to modernize," rather than on any details of the action itself. Typically, added to this vagueness is the notion that the introduction of the change deemed necessary will be opposed by those for whose benefit it is supposed to be intended so that compulsion or coercion will be needed to realize it. Frequently the main weaknesses of the concept of "modernization" for development studies as well as for development planning lie in these two aspects. Diffusion studies in social science are, of course, not new. But "modernization" stands not so much for a transfer of this or that item or trait, as for the replacement of an entire way of life by another entire way of life. Inasmuch as the justification for this replacement is usually that the former way of life was "underdeveloped," one must ask: UNDERDEVELOPED IN COMPARISON WITH WHAT? Here is a key question to be explored. More often than not, the standards of comparison are exogenous in the extreme, or otherwise farfetched and fantastic. In the new states, the comparisons have sometimes been with affluence in the colonial past. The sources have varied and the models with which comparisons were made have varied. Often it is not easy to discover exactly what they were, precisely because the objectives of the study were so strongly idealistic or utopian.

Then again, there is the related question of aspirations. High though these may have been on the part of the planistrators, seldom perhaps were they matched by similarly high aspirations on the part of the peasants for whom they were planned. Concerning the "revolution of rising expectations" in Africa, then, in particular instances there is some question as to WHOSE expectations were involved. As has been suggested for Uganda by Anthony Oberschall (1969a, 1969b), perhaps the need for change felt in rural areas in the 1960's was not urgent and wholesale in nature. If that is correct, then the premise of much "nation-building" politics that a great deal of state intervention was necessary to prevent political turmoil was wrong. Of course, inasmuch as this is an empirical question that was seldom asked and hence seldom answered, little specific evidence on the subject has been gathered. But it is my impression, based on various indirect evidence, that the Ugandan and Nigerian studies are illustrative of many situations in Africa in the 1960's (Engholm 1967).

To probe "modernization" as a theory and practice of planned change and cooperatives policies, it would be necessary to discuss at least four aspects: Westernization (including capitalization), industrialization (including urbanization), rationalization, and technological change. As regards cooperatives, at any rate, the entire subject can be conveniently introduced in compact form with three or four extended "theoretical" statements taken from a much wider review of the literature than can be undertaken here.

The "new sociology" found systems analysis to stand not in the neutral or objective dispassionate center, as it typically claimed, but too far to the right. Irving Horowitz, in *Three worlds of development*, is one who criticized from the left that modernization

... is NOT synonymous with economic development [in general] .... [but] related to a special form of economic change which emphasizes bureaucratic innovation and a host of mending processes such as education and legal reform. In contrast to modernization, the structuralist school of development holds that the process of development requires an overhaul in social relations as well as in industrial productivity as such ... [Wilbert] Moore tends to speak of modernization as an autonomous social process. Hence, in the name of pluralism he avoids the political problems of development occasioned by the role of planned processes.... Moore has broadened the equation of development with industrialism to one which asserts that development equals modernization (Horowitz 1966:317–418).

Another criticism from the left raised other issues. Branding modernization as the "theology of a new capitalism," *The May Day manifesto* (Williams 1968: 45), went on to show that:

... modernization opens up a perspective of change but at the same time it mystifies the process, and sets limits to it. Attitudes, habits, techniques, practices must change: the system of economic and social power, however, remains unchanged. Modernization fatally short-circuits the formation of social goals.... All programmes and perspectives are treated instrumentally. As a model of social change, modernization crudely foreshortens the historical development of society. The whole past belongs to "traditional" society, and modernization is a means for breaking with the past without creating a future.... human society [is] diminished to a passing technique. No confrontation of power, values or interests, no choice between competing priorities is envisaged or encouraged. It is a technocratic model of society, conflict-free and politically neutral, dissolving genuine social conflicts and issues in the abstractions of "the scientific revolution", "consensus", "productivity". Modernization presumes that no group in the society will be called upon to bear the costs of the scientific revolution — as if all men have an equal chance in shaping up the consensus, or as if, by some process of natural law, we all benefit equally from a rise in productivity.

Turning, finally, to modernization viewed not critically from the left but with approval from the center, in Tunisia, a country in which the state at that time was to a great extent committed to cooperatives policies, especially as a means of land reform and rural development, one aspect of the rationalization they stood for was

... préparer l'économie, les populations et les mentalités traditionnelles aux mutations exigées par l'industrialisation. La mise en place du système coopératif dans les campagnes tunisiennes est en même temps une mise en place de structures d'accueil favorables à l'urbanisation et à l'industrialisation (Zghal 1967:98).

Specially with regard to the cooperative farm area itself, the aim was to extend

... tous les aspects de la vie sociale. Dans le village coopératif, l'espace sera en quelque sorte désacralisé et réduit à des formes géometriques rationnelles obéissant aux rythmes et aux formes géometriques agricoles. Les paysans d'un village coopératif modèle feraient en quelque sorte abstraction de l'arbre genéalogique des différentes exploitations intégrées dans le village coopératif. Le village coopératif idéal n'a pas "un terroir"; il a des zones: zone A, zone B, etc.

Comme l'espace du village coopératif, le travail des coopérateurs serait un travail désacralisé. Ni l'age, ni la parenté, ni le sexe n'interviennent pour la répartition du travail. La productivité est la seule norme qui guidera la répartition du travail. Poussée à son maximum, la logique de la rationalisation ne désacralise pas seulement la terre, le bétail, mais assimilera le travail humain à celui de la machine. Comme la terre, le bétail et le matériel mécanique, le travail de l'homme sera aussi considéré comme un facteur de production qu'on doit pouvoir partager en unités élémentaires pour mesurer son efficacité par rapport aux autres facteurs de production.

La rationalisation du système coopératif conduit, en plus de la désacralisation de l'espace et du travail humain, à la desacralisation de la famille traditionnelle. Dans le village coopératif, les paysans sont des agents de production et non des membres d'un groupement ethnique. La répartition des logements dans un village coopératif doit se faire au hasard ou selon l'ordre alphabetique des coopérateurs (Zghal 1967:98–99).

Here, pushed, I suppose, just about as far as it will go, modernization as rationalization becomes an entirely unreal projection and extrapolation of social relations, alienation, and science fiction. Even diffusionist transplantation is no longer relevant.

We must turn now equally briefly to what has been understood not by modernization but by traditionalization. Of all the models to which African rural development policies in the 1960's related, that of "traditional society," to be reinstated or reinvigorated, was perhaps the most overgeneralized and selectively incomplete. Admittedly, "traditional" society came in for more direct investigation in public policy statements than did "modern" society, and social science continued (as it had in colonial times) to focus its attentions also on this aspect, but only on certain kinds of phenomena, selected at will. The similarity to precedents in an earlier period is indeed uncanny. Rather, however, than go back as far as some of the earliest European travellers' accounts of "Kaffir socialism" and the like, let us glance at planned group farming in Kenya 1947–1953 by way of illustration of theory and practice about what was deemed "traditional" society.

In 1947, public policy in Kenya declared ways and means of achieving economies of scale so as to control the agriculturally disadvantageous effects of inheritance, fragmentation, and the division of individual holdings under customary law, the effects of which had worsened as population pressure had built up. The aim, then as more recently, was to facilitate mechanization. In 1947, the Department of Agriculture resolved that ". . . while this involves a change from the modern trend towards individualization, it is in accord with former indigenous methods of land usage and social custom." It was supposed that the social group concerned would be kin — planistration fondly imagined that the mutual trust essential to the outcome of the project would be automatically forthcoming between kinsmen (MacArthur 1968).

Whatever (and whenever) the "former" African tradition was that the 1947 resolution referred to, the land tenure and use sysem actually known and practiced by African farmers in Kenya at the end of the 1940's (and subsequently) reflected much more an intensive individualism than any extended family communalism — as can be seen in the demand for individual small holdings that government policy in the following two decades recognized and sought in various ways to meet. There was, however, also a political aspect during the colonial period, inasmuch as the peasant belief then prevailed that behind the interest of planistrators in consolidation and improvement was simply the ulterior European motive of stealing African land. As the ALDEV (African Land Development) report on Kenya in 1946–1955 said, while

... official doctrines on livestock and pasture have developed slowly in Kenya ... agriculture is liable to bewildering shifts. But seldom has a principle been so widely accepted and so quickly discarded as that of Cooperative Farming (African Land Development n.d.).[16]

Colonial administrators and others looked back, with varying degrees of romance and conspiracy, to yeomanry (Rigby 1969) and other long-past European antiquities as auguries for the future in Africa. When the fantasy reached its height and sought one single cure-all, it was above all to Rochdale that it turned. At least two assumptions prevailed: one was that, somewhere in the past, one ideal or pure form "of cooperation" had existed, and the other that this had manifested itself most evidently among the "Rochdale pioneers" in Britain in the nineteenth century. The story of the theories and practices of cooperation as manifested at Rochdale can be traced back *ad nauseam*. Thus, debate about the

---

[16]   It is always possible, of course, that had the group farming approach been implemented in, say, the Central Province, the results might have been different; in any event, it is an achievement in itself that unified drainage systems were laid out on the group farms.

originality or nonoriginality of the Rochdale venture can go on and on
without coming to any firm conclusion. For their parallels in African
studies, however, it is the theories and practice linked especially with
the name of Dr. William King (who started cooperatives in Brighton
in the second decade of the nineteenth century) that are particularly
instructive to examine (Mercer 1922). Dr. King, like other "originators"
and "leaders" of voluntary associations aiming at social reform for the
benefit of an economically-poor population, was himself of a liberal
profession. Those he aimed to help were not the very poorest, but
people who he thought would react to his leadership. The formative
years of his life he idealized as having partaken of the "pure streams
of natural truth ... *in divina gloria ruris.*" [17] He wanted to bring the
benefit of this to the working-class tailors and grocers. Through the
beginnings of cooperative buying and consuming, he planned for an
"endless perfection of character and happiness" that would culminate
in the setting up of cooperative communities. These were conceptualized as simply civic extensions of the principles on which "the family"
and "brotherhood" were based, regardless of the enlarged social scale
and different social systems that they might represent.

King's journal, *The Cooperator*, which analyzed the recommended
cooperative principles, was known to Henry Pitman, the editor of the
Rochdale *Co-operator*, in the 1860's. One issue of *The Cooperator*
(March 1, 1829), under the title "In cooperation capital is income,"
examined the means by which the workman can and should become
a (reconstituted) capitalist himself. Another issue (April 1, 1829) contained penetrating criticism of friendly societies. The fund of a friendly
society set up by an employer was described as simply one "which, in
sickness and old age, when the man is worn out in the service of the
capitalist, ... save[s] the capitalist from any further expense." Though
King considered friendly societies to be the first and feeble efforts of a
form of cooperativeness, "they relieve the capitalist even more than
they do the workman." An earlier issue (July 3, 1828) had explored
the important theme that the working classes had little if any idea of
the real value of their labor, and that it was especially mistaken of
them or anyone else to equate this real value with wages — another
issue with obvious implications for social planning today with regard,
for instance, to wages policies in development planning. The only
people in distress, it observed, "... are those and those only who

[17] This and subsequent quotations are from the issues of *The Cooperator*
reprinted in Mercer (1922).

produce all the food, clothes and houses of the world . . . all the non-working classes have plenty." The latter do not depend on wages for their wealth. Only through an approach to profit, capital, and independence on their own account could and would the workers rid themselves of their own poverty. Higher wages — indeed wages in any respect, it was asserted — had little to do with solving the problem of poverty.

William Lovett of the Chartists was one who criticized *The Cooperator* for its apology for the competitive system, and for advising workers that it was necessary to find a patron if they wanted to advance their cause. Rochdale differed from its Brighton beginnings in the different methods of cooperation it recommended, although its objections to profit were not extended to interest as well. Despite the relatively restricted aims of the Rochdale cooperative venture compared with the more utopian Owenism, it was the developments at Rochdale especially that were to bear the larger interpretation of "a cooperative movement" toward "social democracy" based on "social ownership." While trade unions did and should aim essentially to serve the material interests of their members, the emphasis in the cooperatives was different. It was to enable their members to participate in "direct functional democracy," from which grass-roots political participation the working classes at that time were excluded — *de facto*, if not *de jure*, as well.

In Britain in the nineteenth century, acute processes of social class formation were under way, this being one of the forms taken by national development. Insofar as the cooperative appeared to its members to offer them their one social solution to an economic problem within a sociopolitical system with which they did not have and could not have much positive identification (let alone control), the cooperative seemed to offer a means that, at that social level, was at the same time an end in itself. Certainly at the beginning, to the ordinary members of the cooperatives as well as to the originators and leaders, "the cooperative movement" was not without evangelical or ideological zeal or zealots. Far from it. Proselytizing in various forms was there at the beginning, and it continued to be one of the driving forces. In remarks as exiguous as these, one may only hint at the possibility that working-class organizations may have more evangelical overtones than similar movements in other social classes. In any event, most social organizations, as they become institutionalized, show a complex of social, economic, religious, and political aspects which may be tied very closely together. Cooperation in Britain, as elsewhere, provided no exception to this.

Now let us return to eastern Africa in the 1960's and affirmations of belief in traditional society and cooperatives. The classical source, "Ujamaa: *the basis of African socialism,*" is the policy statement by President Julius Nyerere (1962) which eloquently upholds ideals of socialism for the future development of his country. It affirms, for instance, that in "traditional" society

... the African's right to land was simply the right to use it; he had no other right to it, nor did it occur to him to try and claim one. ... the individuals or the families within a tribe [were] "rich" or "poor" according to whether the whole tribe was rich or poor. If the tribe prospered all the members of the tribe shared in its prosperity.

The same author's *Socialism and rural development* (1967) stated that:

The traditional African family lived according to the basic principles of ujamaa. Its members did this unconsciously and without any conception of what they were doing in political terms ... they lived together and worked together, and the result of their joint labour was the prosperity of the family as a whole (i.e. the extended family) ... social equality ... was at the basis of the communal life.

Other and similar writings were at pains to point out that so closely knit and so given to consensus was communal life in old Africa that traditionally there were no politics in Africa at all — least of all organized opposition, despite the fact that in practice not all ideals were realized. It was, for example, recognized that traditions varied as between sedentary cultivators and nomadic herdsmen, that economic equality was often only at a poverty level, and that in theory as well as in practice there were discriminations of various kinds against women.

While no analogy can actually be very exact, some analogies are much less exact than others. As I have frequently adverted to the "African traditional society" model earlier (Apthorpe 1972b: 47–52),[18] I will not rehearse its shortcomings again here. I have long considered the "one-party" political system (sometimes, indeed, called the no-party system) to owe its actual provenance more to the theory (especially Fabian) and practice of the colonial state in the colony than to indigenous African systems of politics. Otherwise, why, for example, were single parties so uncommon in African independence movements? This is not to say, however, that Ngoni indirect rule in the nineteenth century was systematically different from British overrule in all respects. And direct rule the world over has many common features. In African ideologies, the "traditional African society" model of a social system

[18]   For an analytical critique of exceptional clarity, see Kopytoff (1964). For an incisive historical critique see Argyle (1968).

was a travesty of social science (social-anthropological) contributions to social knowledge. It was, in turn, a travesty that ideology for applied social science (especially political science) should have incorporated this model, as so plainly did happen, especially in Tanzania in the middle 1960's. Of course, to theorists who held that society everywhere was like an organism, the model had its uses. For planistration purposes, it defined people as groups rather than as individuals, and it allocated specialization of functions hierarchically rather than horizontally.

The political kingdom that was sought and eventually formed as a result of independence was indeed a kingly kind of institution. I suspect that the figure cut by the late Sir Andrew Cohen as a colonial governor in Uganda, for instance, provided the reference model for a president in eastern Africa in the 1960's to a greater extent than did anyone or anything African. This, of course, is only what any historian of postcolonial times would expect.

Public policy in each country in eastern Africa in the later 1960's came to put less emphasis on the transformationalist kind of development administration that was represented, for example, by land settlement schemes. This was not always for the same reasons, but there were some common features. For one thing, in politics as well as in social science, the concept of economic performance itself was being reviewed. Also, it was to be more fully appreciated just how counterproductive initial planning decisions themselves could be of the effects they were intended to bring about.

Second, the earlier social-anthropological inquiries into the nature of cultural reality at the local level (Balandier 1970) took on a new importance. In the mid-1960's, criticisms of the notions of communalism (that were supposed to be favored by African tradition in general more than the individualism that planning and politics had redeveloped at the time of independence and immediately afterwards) came increasingly from Makerere social science in two respects. First, as already mentioned, it was argued that whatever the nature of traditional society was or might have been, surely this particular component in the overall situation was less significant than the nature and extent of administrative and other inputs from outside, in view of the social fact itself of independence and the departure of the colonial power. Second, it was pointed out that even if there were strong signs of communalization in one regard (in, say, kinship matters), this did not necessarily mean that, even in the "same" society, economic activities would be characterized by individualism rather than communalism. Both -ISMS coexisted in African society, as in any other society. But if there were any sum-total of -ISTS or -ISMS to be perceived, it would be safer to assume (especially as regards land) that rural life in Africa was and had remained more individualist than communalist.

Again, it was not only planning for the cooperative sector that was affected. The spiritual socialism behind the *ujamaa* idea that was so prominent in Tanzania especially in the mid-1960's was the inspiration for many government projects at that time. Theories of "African social-ism" in various forms were expounded in Uganda, Zambia, and even Kenya. The extent to which this "socialism" found its fullest expres-sion in the planning of cooperatives in our region can indeed perhaps be illustrated by an example from Kenya. The romantic notions about African communalism that had lingered on in rural development think-ing[19] were, on the whole, reinforced rather than undermined by the Kenyanization of planning and administration and United States aid, especially to the office of then Minister Tom Mboya. Despite the fact, for instance, that even the new settlers were to be selected on a quota basis from overpopulated areas elsewhere (a process that, if it had been implemented, would have resulted altogether in virtually ONLY total strangers moving on to the new land), it was wishfully hoped that the new life of these settlers would immediately flow from an activation or reactivation of latent and "traditional" communalism — paradoxically in the form of "modern" marketing cooperatives.

In the concluding section of this paper some critical reflections have been offered on the two-term straitjacket of the "traditional" and the "modern." Clearly any meaningful secondary or comparative analysis of social change is impossible within the confines of this dichotomy, especially when what is seen from the outside by planistrators as TRADITIONAL is seen from within by peasants as TRADITIONALIST. Modernization may be perceived as an active primary social force. Traditionalization, however, may equally be perceived as such — as when, for example, contrary to their inventors' intentions, new devel-opment plans succeed only in activating or reactivating old traditions. Of course, as ethics for change, rather than models of change, while ideals and -isms may elude or defy "evaluation" (as in "project evalu-ation"), they do express and contribute to the will to change. As such they are of essential importance.

What has been discussed in this paper are some ways of conceptual-izing social change for secondary studies that are analytically unpro-ductive. More important than ever in the case of policy studies by third

[19]   *African socialism* (1965) is a case in point.

parties are all the difficulties involving the value-positions of the observers, as well as of the observed. No framework for comparative
analysis can afford to assume that change for the better is necessarily
always change coming from an urban source. And especially where the
discontinuities (in social distance, political communications, etc.) between the local and national levels are deeply etched, there is no reason
whatsoever to assume that downward and outward from the center to
the periphery (whether gradualist or transformalist) is necessarily the
best development policy.

The task for secondary social science especially is to find analytical
points of view that are not necessarily so closely aligned with the
public policies under construction or under review that commitment
on the part of the analyst always gets the better of relevance, or that
concern for comparability of research results is always at the cost of
their significance. For this point of view it would be difficult to find a
better example than the theory and practice of positive nonalignment
that African international relations had the distinction of introducing
into internationalism in the 1960's.

REFERENCES

AFRICAN LAND DEVELOPMENT
n.d.   *African land development in Kenya 1946–1955.* African Land
        Development (ALDEV) Report.
APTHORPE, RAYMOND
1960   The introduction of bureaucracy into African politics. *Journal of
        African Administration* (July).
1968a   "The golden eggs of cooperation." Paper read at an Institute of
        Development Studies Conference, University of Sussex, May.
1968b   "Does tribalism matter?" *Transition* 38 (October). Kampala.
1969   Peasants and planistrators. *Bulletin of the Institute of Develop-
        ment Studies* 3.
1971   "Some evaluative problems for cooperatives studies with special
        reference for primary societies in highland Kenya," in *Coopera-
        tives and rural development in eastern Africa.* Edited by C. G.
        Widstrand. Uppsala: Scandinavia Institute of African Studies.
1972a   "Some evaluative problems for cooperatives studies with special
        reference for primary societies in highland Kenya," in *Two
        blades of grass.* Edited by P. Worsley. Manchester: Manchester
        University Press.
1972b   *Plural cooperatives and planned change in Africa: an analytical
        overview.* Geneva: United Nations Research Institute for Social
        Development (UNRISD).

1972c "Peasants and planistrators in northern Africa 1960–1970." Mimeograph.

ARGYLE, W. J.
1968 The concept of African collectivism. *Mawazo* 1(4):37–42.

BALANDIER, G.
1970 *La sociologie actuelle de l'Afrique Noire* [translated as *The sociology of black Africa*]. London: André Deutsch.

BARTH, F.
1967 On the study of social change. *American Anthropologist* 69(6): 661–669.

BOUDON, R.
1969 Secondary analysis and survey research. *Social Sciences Information* 8(6):7–32.

BRETT, E. A.
1967 "National objectives, marketing organization and cooperative development in Uganda." Departments of Political Science and Sociology, Makerere. Mimeograph.
1968 "Development policy in East Africa between the wars." Unpublished doctoral dissertation, University of London.
1970 "Problems of cooperative development in Uganda," in *Rural cooperatives and planned change in Africa: case materials*. Edited by R. Apthorpe. Geneva: United Nations Research Institute for Social Development (UNRISD).

ECONOMIC COMMISSION FOR LATIN AMERICA
1966 Social development and social planning: a survey of conceptual and practical problems. *Economic Bulletin for Latin America* 9(1):42–70.

ENGHOLM, G. F.
1967 "Immigrant influence on development policy in Uganda 1900–1952." Unpublished doctoral dissertation, University of London.

FABIAN BUREAU
1945 *Cooperation in colonies*. London: Fabian Bureau.

FALLERS, L.
1958 *Bantu bureaucracy*. Cambridge: Heffer.

GUTKIND, P. G.
1960 *The royal capital of Buganda*. The Hague: Mouton.

HOROWITZ, I. L.
1966 *Three worlds of development*. New York: Oxford University Press.

HYDEN, G., E. KARANJA
1970 "Cooperatives and rural development in Kenya," in *Rural cooperatives and planned change in Africa: case materials*. Edited by R. Apthorpe. Geneva: United Nations Research Institute for Social Development (UNRISD).

KENYA GOVERNMENT
1965 *African socialism*. Sessional paper 10. Nairobi: Government Printer.

KOPYTOFF, IGOR
1964 Article in *African socialism*. Edited by W. Friedland and C. Rosberg. London: Oxford University Press.

LEACH, E. R.
1961 *Rethinking anthropology*. London: Athlone.
LIPTON, M.
1968 The optimising peasant. *Journal of Development Studies* 1 (April).
LOPREATO, J., L. ALSTON
1967 Ideal types and the idealization strategy. *American Sociological Review* (April): 88–96.
MAC ARTHUR, JOHN
1968 "The group farming experience." Department of Agricultural Economics, The University of Wales. Mimeograph.
MAGUIRE, G.
1969 *Toward* uhuru *in Tanzania: the politics of participation*. Cambridge: Cambridge University Press.
MERCER, T. W.
1922 *Dr. W. King and the* The Cooperator, *1828–1839*. Manchester: The Cooperative Union.
NYERERE, JULIUS
1962 Ujamaa: *the basis of African socialism*. Dar es Salaam: TANU.
1967 *Socialism and rural development*. Dar es Salaam: Government Printer.
1969 *Essays on socialism*. London: Oxford University Press.
OBERSCHALL, A.
1969a Rising expectations and political turmoil. *Journal of Development Studies* 2.
1969b Communications, information and aspirations in rural Uganda. *Journal of Asian and African Studies* 4(1):30–50.
PEARSON, L.
1969 *Partners in development: report of the Commission on International Development*. New York, London: Praeger.
PITT, D. C.
1976 *Social dynamics of development*. Oxford: Pergamon.
RIGBY, PETER
1969 "Kongwa," in *Society and social change*. Edited by P. Rigby and R. Apthorpe. Kampala: Nkanga Editions 4.
RUTHENBERG, HANS
1964 *Agricultural development in Tanganyika*. Berlin: Springer.
Tanganyika Standard
n.d. *The cooperative movement in Tanganyika: Vyama vya ushirika Tanganyika*, with a foreword by P. Bomani. Dar es Salaam: *Tanganyika Standard*.
TILLION, G.
1961 *France and Algeria: complementary enemies*. New York: Knopf.
VAN ARCADIE, BRIAN
1969 "Tanzania: crisis in planning." Crisis in Planning Conference Papers. Institute of Development Studies, University of Sussex. Mimeograph.
WIDSTRAND, C. G., *editor*
1971 *Cooperatives and rural development in eastern Africa*. Uppsala: Scandinavia Institute of African Studies.

WILLIAMS, R., *editor*
  1968   *The May Day manifesto.* London: Penguin Books.
WOLF, E.
  1969   On peasant rebellions. *International Social Science Journal* 21: 286–293.
WORSLEY, P., *editor*
  1972   *Two blades of grass.* Manchester: Manchester University Press.
ZGHAL, A.
  1967   Système de parenté et système coopératif. *Revue Tunisienne des Sciences Sociales* (2):94–108, at. 98.

The Perils of Unconventional Anthropology

G. COCHRANE

After writing *Development anthropology* I entered a period of professional melancholia. There seemed to be something almost dishonest in continuing to teach and write in the area of development anthropology if one knew that students and readers could expect no better fate than in the past. Moreover, I was disturbed by many letters received from students who shared my impatience and who wondered whether there was any point in trying to train for a nonexistent career.

Why not return, I thought, to public service? It was appealing, but at the same time obviously escapist. It would have left me having conceded for all time that there is a wide gap between anthropology in public and academic life. But I knew that just as my experience in administration had fostered an uneasiness with conventional anthropology, so, too, a return to conventional administration would, in time, prove barren. This is the human dilemma faced by the development anthropologist: unless and until there is a recognized viable career structure, he or she will always be alone, whether in academic or in public life. Not only alone, but also a second-class citizen.

At this point — September 1970 — I decided to do what I had been recommending. I decided to try to demonstrate to some important developmental entity that anthropology could be useful, that it should be given a chance, and that the discipline could, given encouragement, supply a class of persons qualified to work in development. I chose the World Bank, because it enjoyed preeminent standing in the development community and because it had not been embroiled in anthropological squabblings.[1] It had the added advantage that it was an inter-

[1] The World Bank is now dispersing in loan funds around three billion dollars annually. For a detailed report of its activities see various of its *Annual reports*.

national institution, and therefore could not be thought the preserve of any single national association of anthropologists.

My first enquiry was addressed literally to "Dear World Bank." It elicited a polite reply, whereupon I went to visit the Bank and to explain what was in my mind. As time and visits and correspondence passed, I gradually got to know a few of the officials. During this period my own ideas about how to go about the task I had set myself began to form.

I felt the time was ripe for anthropology, because the Bank's own pattern of lending was beginning to change from institutional lending in the fields of power and communications toward agriculture, education, and population (World Bank 1971–1972). This meant that the need for behavioral assessments was increasing. I felt that my own administrative experience would be useful. I had always behaved myself in government and was not therefore likely, in the Bank's eyes, to misuse confidential information. Nor, obviously, do I intend to do so now. What I shall say will rely largely on material already published on the World Bank. My purpose is not to analyze what kinds of anthropology I did at the Bank, but to give a sense of how anthropologists might, even with no resources, approach the problem of introducing anthropology to an institution.

It is not always vital to publish all the details of one's involvement with institutions of size and importance. The routine competent practice of anthropology does not have to be published any more than every surgeon must write up every appendectomy. The ordinary pedestrian anthropology that I had being doing involved nothing new that would have been useful to publish. What was new in this endeavor was the viewing of anthropology as a component of institutional policy, and it is this that I am now prepared to publish.

Eventually, in February 1972, the Bank agreed that I could do a study of their project operations to see where anthropology might be useful. The then Deputy Director of Projects offered me office space and said that cooperation would be arranged. I submitted a detailed proposal, and it was accepted. Because the Bank did not at that time see the worth of the discipline, it could not fund the study, though they offered to endorse the idea to foundations if asked to do so. I anticipated no problems, and contacted a number of foundations.

Unfortunately, I could not persuade any foundations that the study was worthwhile. It seemed difficult for them to appreciate what such a study might do for the discipline of anthropology — that this and other similar kinds of studies might open up vast employment prospects, to say nothing of the opportunities for anthropologists to put their ideas about development into practice. When funds are tight, research projects must become more academic rather than more practical. It had taken much work to get to this point. I plunged once more into gloom, wondering what could be done. If I gave up, I thought it likely that I should always ask myself, "But what if . . ." A certain "bloody-mindedness" developed, not in me, but in those I love, saying "Do it."

Though not personally wealthy, and far from being highly paid, I decided to go ahead and try to bear the costs myself, borrowing when necessary. It was a logical continuation of my work that I could not deny; it did not seem that it could happen otherwise. With that prospect before me, I could not return to conventional anthropology. If I were not willing to take such a risk, could I ask students to invest thousands of dollars in an academic career whose future was so uncertain?

There were severe dangers. In the first place, I suspected that whatever I might do could in all probability not be published because of the confidential nature of the Bank's work. This proved, indeed, to be the case. In the second place, no matter how hard things went one could never complain, because, in a sense, one would be representing an entire discipline, and one could not spoil things for others in it. Finally, one might fail utterly and give the discipline such a bad name in the institution that it would take years to repair the damage. After weighing all the factors carefully, I decided nevertheless to go ahead with the study.

A student of mine, Raymond Noronha, who had just finished his doctorate, then decided to assist in the study, notwithstanding the lack of support, being willing also to bear his own expenses. My plan was to spend fifteen months on the work, with Dr. Noronha in Washington. I would stay in Washington in the summer and after that commute from Syracuse. I walked into the Bank with Dr. Noronha on June 1, 1972 and began work.

That summer in Washington was hot and muggy, sometimes depressing, sometimes very hopeful, but always I had a sense of purpose and a conviction that in the end I would succeed. Some friends helped and encouraged me in the work.

There had been some anthropologists occasionally engaged as consultants by the Bank, but my work did not, in fact, threaten any of them. My position had been that contacts with single individuals in isolated projects did not help the institution to reach a decision about the place of the discipline in all of its operations. The keynote of my position was anthropology as policy and the advantages that would accrue from a coordinated approach. This meant identifying the types of projects where the discipline could help, and devising suitable methods to achieve these inputs while conforming to existing operational standards in terms of time and personnel.

The first step was to learn about the institution to a point where one could do the work of an ordinary staff member. I felt that only then would it be possible to begin to talk about anthropology. Things were going well when the Bank underwent a major reorganization in July 1972, and the object of study fragmented itself before my very eyes. But the essential functioning of the institution remained unaltered, and it was thus possible to adjust my research design quite rapidly.

As an anthropologist, one had very little status and everything depended on the strength of one's personal contacts. These were slowly and very painfully made. Scores of offices had to be visited, my *spiel* had to be pared to a minimum because people were very busy. I had to make my points quickly and well. This usually meant doing my homework on the man's operations well before going to see him, listening around to learn what kinds of problems he had experienced, and just praying.

It was painfully tiresome at times to do five or ten of these meetings in a day; to do even one of them well left me pretty tired. I talked to large groups of staff members, sometimes as many as a hundred at a time. Gradually the work became known and the "don't call us, we'll call you" syndrome was surmounted.

At one point it occurred to me that it would be hilarious and appropriate to write a breathless account "from the field," in the manner of early anthropologists, detailing the problems of settling in, the difficulties of learning the language and communicating, and the ingenious ways in which rapport was established. Although the foundations might not agree, it seemed to me that this kind of work was potentially as important as studying the Trobrianders. Having reached the second Trobriand age, I began to look more closely at the trading partners in this new fun Kula Ring.

At that time the Bank was divided into geographical regions — Asia, the Pacific, Africa (East and West), South America, and the Caribbean. The area departments were staffed by loan officers who were personally responsible for the appropriateness of the projects for each country or region. Projects were mounted dealing with population, education, power, agriculture, tourism, highways, irrigation, and so on. The projects staff (specializing in power, education, etc.) was a separate entity, and there seemed to be a number of differences between projects staff and area staff (specializing in the geographical regions).

Projects covering all sectors went through what was called a cycle (Baum 1970; King 1967; Chadenet and King 1972). The first step in a country was to identify a project; then came the process of preparing the project; next it was appraised to see what the rate of return on investment and the benefit to the country would be; then it was negotiated between the representatives of the country and the Bank; and, finally, the project would be supervised as funds were disbursed. The project format is quite simple, and over the years the Bank has greatly refined its techniques. Project staff tended to be concerned with making sure they had a good project, while area people were concerned with how the project would make a contribution to the overall economic picture. Both points of view are essential but, unfortunately, they cannot always be completely reconciled (Overseas Development Institute 1967: 19–21).

The Bank is forbidden by its Articles of Agreement to concern itself with the political affairs of any of its member governments. Obviously, much could be made of the fact that it is impossible on occasion to separate economic matters from political matters, but the stipulation has been sensibly honored. This has been so because of the evolution of what is known as the "collaborative style," a process whereby the Bank seeks to ensure that the government asking for a loan does certain things, while the government in turn makes its wishes known, until agreement is reached. In this negotiation, the two parties are considered as equals (Meagher 1970).

Each of these separate steps in the project cycle usually meant a mission leaving Washington for the country concerned, because the Bank has only a limited number of resident missions overseas. In addition to these special project missions, there were basic economic missions which dealt with the general economic picture and overall prospects of the country concerned.

This emphasis on mission techniques seemed to me to be yet another reason why the Bank could do with some anthropology. The danger of mission methods is that on occasion, because of the constraints of time and protocol, very little opportunity may exist to gather information at the local level. Officials in the LDC's do not, of course, always have the opportunity to know what is happening in the villages.

The Bank itself can be regarded as a specialized agency of the United Nations. Its five hundred or so staff members come from most of the member countries (now over one hundred and thirty in number). Decisions on the making of loans are on the recommendation of the president to the board of directors. The executive directors, who stay full time in the Bank, are appointed by their governments, and it is they who decide in their meetings which projects shall be carried out.

What is called the World Bank Group is really a composite of three organizations — the International Bank for Reconstruction and Development (IBRD), the International Finance Corporation (IFC), and the International Development Association (IDA). The World Bank itself was founded at Bretton Woods in 1944, at the same time as the International Monetary Fund. As its name indicates, it was established to rebuild a war-torn Europe; its role has now changed from reconstructing what was already in existence to actually building economic strength. The IFC gives loans to corporate endeavors in the LDC's. The IDA lends money on what are called concessionary terms, that is, they lend money at a little above the cost of its procurement. However, much of the money used for IDA financing comes from the subscriptions of member governments. Although there are three organizations, the same staff members do the basic operations in each entity (Reid 1965). The major share of work time is spent on IBRD project loans to governments, loans which are for development and for which funds are lent at terms above the cost of procurement.

The Bank must raise its capital for IBRD and IFC operations on the world markets, where its bonds now enjoy considerable confidence. There are those who point to the fact that its policies must first be sold on Wall Street, but it cannot be denied that the Bank is promoting genuine growth, which is supported strongly by the LDC's themselves. Unlike lending by individual countries, which often has strings attached, the Bank is not pursuing selfish interests, and its operations are therefore greatly appreciated by the LDC's. At a time when many international organizations are foundering, the Bank is thriving; profits made by it are lent out again, usually in the form of IDA financing. Lord Keynes thought the Bank would be a failure unless it disbursed all its funds within a matter of years. This has not happened and, if anything, the danger is that the Bank has been too successful. It is constantly being asked to do more and more.

In its early days the Bank was mainly interested in large construction schemes. The rate of return on investment from such schemes was good, and the risks were relatively easy to calculate; also, conventional economic-development theory of the day suggested that these were the right investment decisions. But it soon became apparent that if genuine growth was to be achieved, new fields such as agriculture, education, nutrition, and population control were key investment areas. The benefits of economic growth did not trickle down — the rich were getting richer and the poor poorer: "marginal men" were discovered.

It was against this background of growing dissatisfaction with conventional development measures that I began work to show why anthropology was relevant. There was very little high-powered economic analysis as such in projects (Price-Gittinger 1972). My economist friends would remark that we should not be despondent about the prospects of introducing anthropology into the Bank because economists were still trying to do the same thing. But it was readily apparent that economists had made the progress they had made largely because they were able to supply hard data on which investment decisions could be based. I did not meet any staff member who would deny that social issues must be more effectively dealt with through using more insights from the noneconomic social sciences. But the problem was how much, and in what form?

And, obviously, although the Bank can give advice when asked, the Bank cannot dictate (even if answers were known) how social issues are to be dealt with. Many countries do not agree with the Bank concerning which priorities for investment are most urgent and feel that it is better to concentrate a critical amount of resources in certain key areas in the hope that the effects will ripple through the entire economy. These local decisions must be respected. Many countries have elites who have no intention whatever of undermining their own power base by attacking social issues. Alleviation of human distress and suffering requires more than good intentions on the part of donors — it requires economic diplomacy (Reid 1965: 47).

Staff members in the Bank were concerned with some five hundred projects in countries all over the world at various stages of the project cycle. Obviously, I could not examine all of these. Obviously, time would not permit me to see a project through its entire cycle.

There was also an awesome policy question to be faced. If I were to operate on a global basis, looking at projects in a particular sector (say education) no matter where they were located in the world, then it would be hard to inject the insight of special local knowledge, long considered a strong point of anthropology. But if, on the other hand, I were to concentrate on one geographical area (say the Pacific), then, with the resources I had at my command, data on which a policy decision for the entire institution might be based would not be forthcoming. I decided that a project approach was the only feasible way to proceed. It was not ideal but. . . .

Inasmuch as I wanted to make policy recommendations for the entire institution, a first step was to see what kinds of things I could do and how much work this would entail. After the number of projects had been estimated by sectors (based on past performance and projected trends), it was possible to make a rough estimate of the number needed for purposes of demonstration. The idea was to take each of the sectors and then to demonstrate what anthropology could do — to estimate the usual amount of time required and, then on the basis of what was known of the discipline, work out the future manpower that would be needed. But before being able to say how many anthropologists would be needed and what kinds of training they would require, I had first to demonstrate that they actually were needed.

I offered our services to staff members at each of the meetings where the object of the study was explained. They then brought forward projects at various stages of the project cycle. Not all the projects could be accepted; to be accepted a project had to be representative of a general class of problems encountered in that sector. Gradually a sample was put together that included projects for all sectors and had represented in it all the Bank's area departments.

My feeling had been that no matter where a project was located, the discipline would have useful data. The idea was to scan the project initially to see what needed to be done. Often there was little to be done from the point of view of the discipline. Often enough was known to be helpful even though the project was not in an area with which I was familiar. Sometimes I would identify the problems and recommend that an area specialist be engaged. With a few exceptions the strategy worked.

Where anthropology is concerned with bilateral and multilateral agencies, there must, I think, be more widespread recognition of the need for a two-tier system — that is, a system for very large institutions with widespread geographical and cultural responsibilities that would permit initial scanning or monitoring by generalists, who would then decide whether more specialist advice was required. Those anthropologists who doggedly stick to the single-tier traditional community system are in effect suggesting that an institution like the Bank, or UNESCO (United Nations Educational, Scientific, and Cultural Organization), or FAO (Food and Agriculture Organization) would have to have hundreds of anthropologists. But generalists can keep abreast of both policy and academic developments. They can also brief adequately and translate the work of anthropological consultants into institutional terms.

The basic strength of the scheme was as a demonstration. I was prepared to take the same projects as a staff member, to accept the same constraints of time, and to attempt to inject into that process something that the organization could not itself supply and that staff members admitted was important. I did not make claims that could not be backed up, nor did I imply that every mission or every project needed an anthropologist. In fact, I rejected a number of projects in instances where it was clear that there was little that anthropologists could do.

A number of things about the staff members with whom I dealt were very impressive. They worked hard and for extremely long periods of time. Their knowledge about development around the world was immense. They had a pragmatism that appeared to make it easy for them to get right to the heart of problems in such a way that they could quickly expose the strengths and the weaknesses of anthropology. I learned a great deal.

I had an immense amount to learn because, although it was my object to have anthropologists work as staff members, it was necessary that such people also OPERATE as staff members. This could be achieved by getting anthropologists involved as early as possible in the project cycle.

At the beginning of my stint there was a certain courtesy accorded to me as a member of the academy and as a visitor, a certain curiosity as to what on earth anthropologists were really like, a certain delight in pointing out that the LDC's were sovereign, as were their problems. I learned to recognize and sympathize with the problems of the man whose main concern was to transfer hundreds of millions of dollars from the Bank to an area; the man who believed that the key to successful irrigation was good engineering; the man who believed that when economists had hard data concerning family budgets for the whole world, problems would decrease; the man who believed that if incentives to participate in development were sufficiently high, then culture did not matter. All these points of view had a place; I began to think that mine did too.

But for the very reason that there was no settled policy toward the discipline of anthropology in the Bank, the use made of anthropology was dependent on the experience and attitude of individual staff members. There was no system, no method that would require the application of anthropological techniques where the discipline could be of use. Unless a policy toward the discipline was adopted — and the weakness of individual project consultations was that they could not achieve this — this situation would continue.

I made a point of demonstrating a concern not with the use of anthropology but with better projects. I made a point of getting right to the essentials of a project in such a way that the anthropology was incorporated in it, rather than extruding as some kind of afterthought. I began to grow very fond of the institution and its staff. Of course, there were minor problems and irritations, but when one considered the odd genesis of what I was doing, and the demands placed on senior staff in terms of time and patience before they could discover that I had anything of value to say, the fact that the work was done at all was no inconsiderable achievement.

It was evident that the success of the Bank in international development was causing severe strains. The institution was being asked to do more and more, to lend for additional categories of projects, to give advice, to plan, and to coordinate, without there being commensurate increases in staff.

Under these circumstances, the idea of adding an anthropological dimension to the projects might seem an additional burden, unwarranted on the basis of past successes and unwise in view of the demand for more staff when the effectiveness of the staff on hand had already been established. What did one say to the man who admitted the worth of the proposed addition, but who maintained that at present he did not have sufficient staff to carry out work already in hand? One replied that it was not a question of comparing the utility of different kinds of staff but of ensuring that an important missing element — anthropology — was added, so that the quality of the projects could be improved.

This was indeed what a number of the project analyses achieved. They were not overly elegant or exhaustive, because time did not permit optimum replies. But the analyses did manage in some cases to convince hardheaded projects people that the discipline was useful. Although several anthropologists who had worked as consultants for the Bank had done good work on individual projects, in some important ways doing good work at the project level was one of the least important elements in the problem of having anthropologists introduced into the Bank on a career basis. It may be instructive to state why this was so.

It could have been claimed that the good work done by anthropologists was no more important than that which could have been done by demographers, ecologists, rural development experts. The Bank could not take on all the different kinds of people who might be of use in a development situation whose discipline or profession is not presently utilized — so the point was not simply to have a case, but to make sure that it was stated in a relevant way.

It was important to appreciate the delicate dynamic balance between the various functional entities in the Bank, the ways in which changes were proposed and implemented, the ways in which such proposals were likely to be received. At this point, the public-administration animal in me took over.

The addition of a number of anthropologists on a career basis could disturb the existing balance of power, and for that reason might be unpopular with some elements in the institution who might feel that their claims for new staff were being overlooked. Therefore, the addition had to complement or supplement the existing balance of power without altering it significantly. To appreciate the difficulties involved, it is crucial to appreciate the difference between where one "stands" on an issue and where one "sits" in the organization when that position is adopted.

Had I been formally attached to an area department at the outset, when I commenced my work, it is unlikely that an institutional point of view could have been developed. Also, it is likely that the proposals would have been resisted by other area departments, to say nothing of the reaction of projects people.

A major problem was that my research design had been set up prior to the reorganization of the World Bank Group in July-August 1972. That reorganization was designed to split up the projects departments, which had been centralized and had been growing in power, so that it was felt by some that individual area departments had insufficient countervailing authority. The reorganization was to provide for a regionalization of projects departments (Thomas 1972). Each area then had its own projects staff, under the control of a regional vice-president. What was left of the old projects central staff was regrouped to provide advice and support to area departments in keeping up the quality of projects.

As a result of the reorganization, I found myself attached to the new central projects departments, the "rump" as it were. From being in a completely operational environment, I had moved into an advice-giving setting. If I wished to have the institution adopt a policy toward the discipline, my basic structural problem was, as it had always been, to surmount the hiatus between projects and area staffs. The reorganization did not solve that problem — it merely regionalized the hiatus.

What is important about this structure, designed to facilitate the Bank's business (which it did successfully), is that there was no organizational point at which I could attach the research where the study would not be identified with either projects people or area people. The similarity between this situation and that of the anthropological field-worker moving between Brahmins and untouchables in an Indian village will be apparent.

The question whether anthropologists should be attached to projects departments, area departments, or both, although vital to resolve, was difficult to address. It was important to avoid a few token appointments. It was also important to avoid appointments which did not offer a career commensurate with ability and experience.

What, then, was the danger of making recommendation from the new central projects department? I might appear to be running against the whole trend and logic behind the reorganization of 1972. That reorganization had sought to restore the balance between area and projects interests which some felt had been going in favor of projects. Would my proposals coming from this new department appear to be somewhat phoenix-like? For this reason would they be resisted?

There was obviously no foolproof method of proceeding, nor was the example of other recent innovations in the Bank's history (in nutrition, education, population) very helpful. These innovations had all come down from top management. I was working upwards in the organization. In any event, I was satisfied that the case could not be made more effectively than I was making it.

But to continue the narrative. By October 1972, the worth of the study had been recognized, and I was requested to submit a report as soon as possible, rather than at the end of the fifteen-month period as had been planned. Cognizant of the many potential pitfalls, I drafted my report as carefully as I could. I took care to attach no criticism, nor did I attempt to be overly wise after the event. I stuck to the facts and tried to make recommendations that would be of use to all sections. After having the preliminary reactions of a wide spectrum of interests in the institution, I submitted a final draft in March of 1973.

There were some happy developments. The Bank made a generous *ex gratia* payment that partially helped to defray the costs of the project. In February, Dr. Noronha went to Indonesia as a regular consultant on a tourism mission for the Bank and a week or so later went on to Iran for six months as part of a rural development task force. I finished my year's teaching with a sense of satisfaction, knowing that the kind of anthropology I believed in was useful and that it could be done. It is much too early to say what the final results will be, but I am confident that permanent appointments will eventually be made which would not have been made had the study not been undertaken.

This approach of evaluating anthropology at a policy level within the framework of the needs of an entire institution can and should be used in other institutions. Doing anthropology instead of writing about it for an audience may be unconventional, costly, and risky, and may carry with it few of the conventional professional rewards, but it is very worthwhile personally. It is, to my mind, the only effective way to introduce an anthropological dimension into the operations of multilateral and bilateral institutions.

REFERENCES

BAUM, WARREN C.
1970   The project cycle. *Finance and Development* 7(2).
CHADENET, BERNARD, JOHN A. KING
1972   What is a World Bank project? *Finance and Development* (September).
KING, JOHN A.
1967   *Economic development projects and their appraisal.* Baltimore: Johns Hopkins Press.
MEAGHER, ROBERT F.
1970   "The World Bank and non-economic aspects of development: some questions posed." AID (Agency for International Development) Research paper. Washington.
OVERSEAS DEVELOPMENT INSTITUTE
1967   *Effective aid.* London: Overseas Development Institute.
PRICE-GITTINGER, J.
1972   *The economic analysis of agricultural projects.* Baltimore: Johns Hopkins Press.
REID, ESCOTT
1965   *The future of the World Bank.* Washington: International Bank for Reconstruction and Development.
THOMAS, ANTHONY
1972   Article in *The Times.* June 8. London.
WORLD BANK
1971–1972   *Annual reports.*

Use of Anthropologists in Project Appraisal by the World Bank

TARIQ HUSAIN

With the objective of introducing the World Bank, I have tried to structure this paper around the words in the title: "World Bank," "project appraisal," and "use of anthropologists." The background of the institution is dealt with in Section 1. Section 2 describes the Bank's experience with the use of anthropology, and Section 3 discusses some of the possibilities for further use of anthropology in the Bank as I see them. Finally, I describe two personal experiences with anthropologists in projects in Kenya and Tanzania.

1. THE WORLD BANK GROUP

The World Bank Group comprises three institutions: International Bank for Reconstruction and Development (IBRD), International Development Association (IDA), and International Finance Corporation (IFC). IBRD is generally known as the World Bank whose purpose is to stimulate economic growth and to help raise the quality of life in the developing countries of this world. The Bank (IBRD) is owned jointly by 122 nations and attempts to meet its ambitious goals in all its member countries by lending money to finance a wide variety of projects in those countries. Projects financed by the Bank include a whole range of activities: road systems, power plants, urban water supply and sewerage, irrigation net-works, family planning, tourism, rural development, technical assistance, research, education, and telecommunication. IDA is the soft loan window of the Bank Group and lends for the same type of projects as the Bank but at softer financial terms. IFC mainly focuses on the private sector and encourages the flow of domestic and foreign capital and expertise into productive private investments in developing member countries.

Origin of the Bank

The International Bank for Reconstruction and Development was created in 1945 as a result of agreements reached the year before at the United Nations Monetary and Financial Conference held in Bretton Woods, New Hampshire. Financial experts from the forty-four allied governments had realized during the Second World War that the post-war world would need international cooperative agreements on monetary, economic, and reconstruction problems. The International Monetary Fund (dealing with balance of payments, exchange rates, and other monetary relationships) and the IBRD were created to tackle the post-war problems of development and reconstruction. The Bank began operations in 1946.

The Bank was created as a cooperative institution and governments, in joining the Bank, agreed to subscribe capital shares to it. The number of shares subscribed by a government was based on each government's wealth and position in world trade. Thus the risks in the operations of the Bank were, and still are, shared on a proportional basis by all its members. In 1973 the Bank had 122 members including Rumania and Yugoslavia.

Lending by the Bank

By 1948 the Bank had lent almost one-half billion dollars for the reconstruction of four countries in war-torn Europe. However, with the advent of the Marshall Plan for the economic recovery of Europe in 1948, the Bank was enabled to turn to its second, and as it turned out more difficult, responsibility implicit in its formal name: development.

When a government joins the Bank, it agrees to subscribe ten percent of its shares in cash or demand notes. The remaining ninety percent is not paid-in but serves as a guarantee of the Bank's credit worthiness against debts incurred from borrowing in the capital markets of the world. Since 1951, the Bank has raised the larger part of its needed money through the sales of its bonds and other borrowings in financial centers around the world. By 1972 the Bank had borrowed about twelve billion dollars around the world. The Bank's authorized capital is about twenty-seven billion dollars and its cumulative loans till June 30, 1973 were about twenty-six billion dollars. Table 1 summarizes the loans made by Bank and IDA by purpose for the period 1969 to 1973.

The Bank gives loans or credits after reviewing proposed projects through a process which may be defined as a project cycle which begins with a comprehensive economic survey of all sectors of a country's economy, goes through more detailed review of individual sectors and feasibility studies of individual proposed projects, and ends with an appraisal of the project to be financed. The process is a continuing one, and the thoroughness of the reviews has improved with the passage of time. It is the potential for further improvement in the review process that concerns us today when we discuss the use of anthropology and anthropologists in project appraisal at the Bank, and I shall concentrate on this aspect.

2. THE BANK'S EXPERIENCE WITH ANTHROPOLOGY

The Bank has made limited use of professional anthropologists in the past and has relied on the general experience of its professional staff for the anthropological aspects of projects. A significant number of Bank staff have had overseas resident experience as technical specialists and/ or administrators. Consequently, they brought with them a deep knowledge of the customs, traditions, taboos, and values of the communities with which they had associated. With the increasing complexity of its projects, the Bank began to recognize the need for a more professional consideration of anthropological aspects. So far, about six anthropologists have been employed by the Bank on a consultant basis for the appraisal of agricultural projects: Dyson-Hudson in livestock projects in Kenya (1967 and 1972 respectively); Reining in a livestock project in Tanzania (1972); and others in agricultural projects in Nigeria, Lesotho, and the Mekong during the last two years. The appraisal of a livestock project in Kenya in 1967 was the first time an anthropologist was involved. The project in Kenya had two objectives: (1) to obtain better utilization of Kenya's rangeland and (2) the transition of traditional pastoralists from a subsistence to a market-oriented pattern of production. The latter objective required that judgements be made about the response of pastoralists to alternative methods of modifying their relationships with land and cattle. This was a new problem for the Bank, and so the skills of an anthropologist were imported. This first use of

Table 1.   Cumulative bank loans and IDA credits listed by purpose

	1969 as percent of total	1969	1970	1971	1972	1973	1973 as percent of total	Growth rate/year in percent 1969–73
		in million of U.S. dollars						
Electric power	29.1	4,279.2	4,805.0	5,284.0	5,908.8	6,230.3	23.7	9.8
Transportation	31.3	4,601.3	5,252.1	5,876.9	6,794.9	7,499.8	28.6	13.0
Telecommunications	2.0	299.6	379.7	575.2	645.3	900.4	3.4	32.0
Agriculture	10.3	1,508.1	1,919.1	2,347.7	2,739.6	3,726.6	14.2	26.0
Industry	13.5	1,977.7	2,269.8	2,517.3	3,166.7	3,546.7	13.5	15.7
Education	1.7	243.8	323.7	424.4	612.0	905.5	3.4	39.0
Water supply and sewerage	1.0	142.9	175.1	328.7	440.6	739.6	2.8	50.0
Tourism				10.0	80.2	80.2	0.3	—
Urbanization			2.0	9.8	15.7	51.7	0.2	—
Population					44.2	65.7	0.3	—
Post war reconstruction	3.4	496.8	496.8	496.8	496.8	496.8	1.9	—
Program loans	7.6	1,143.4	1,224.9	1,338.8	1,736.1	1,986.3	7.6	14.7
Technical assistance					10.0	24.0	0.1	—
Total	100	14,692.8	16,848.2	19,209.3	22,690.7	26,243.7	100	15.7
Incremental		1,784	2,155	2,361	3,481	3,553		
Number of operations (number)								
Bank		84	70	80	74	74		
IDA		38	56	53	74	91		
Net income (U.S.$ million)		171	213	212	183	—		

an anthropologist was subsequently found advantageous, and the precedent was set. However, no additional consultations with anthropologists were attempted for the next four years, partly because the process was not institutionalized and partly because Bank lending in the intervening period did not require anthropological inputs. With hindsight, one may argue that anthropological inputs could have been used advantageously in a number of projects in agriculture, as well as other sectors.

An anthropologist was used for the second time in February, 1972 in the appraisal of the Second Livestock Project in Tanzania. Dr. P. Reining accompanied the appraisal mission, and she worked within the framework of evaluating the anthropological aspects of organizing pastoral people into *ujamaa* villages. The third time was in November, 1972 with Dr. N. Dyson-Hudson accompanying an appraisal mission to Kenya to review another livestock project — an extension of sorts of the original 1967 livestock project. His assignment was similar to Reining's: the organization of the production activities of the Masai. At that time, and subsequently, anthropological inputs were being sought in other agricultural projects involving settlement, introduction of cash crops in subsistence societies, and introduction of modern inputs like fertilizer, pesticides, and credit. Anthropological inputs have not been sought in other sectors.

3. POSSIBLE USE OF ANTHROPOLOGY IN THE FUTURE

The first formal step the Bank took to assess the contribution that anthropology can make in Bank work was to invite Dr. Cochrane to spend six months in the Bank (1972–1973) and advise on what could be done and why. Cochrane reviewed Bank experience and gave three reasons for the limited use of anthropology in Bank work:
1.   lack of familiarity of Bank staff with anthropology, and the attendant problems of how to recruit anthropologists and how to interpret and use their recommendations;
2.   lack of an institutional basis for use of anthropologists; and
3.   absence of in-house capacity.
The limited use may be largely attributed to the lack of an institutional basis which led to only incidental consideration of the desirability of anthropological inputs; and the given unfamiliarity with the discipline led to the observed sporadic use. The absence of in-house capacity meant that no internal reminders were present to encourage a more

widespread and systematic use of the discipline. Cochrane went on to include anthropologists themselves as being partly responsible for their sporadic use by the Bank. The Bank is not well known to anthropologists so they are not aware of the Bank's broad needs nor of how their advice may be used to improve the Bank's evaluation procedures.

Dr. Cochrane suggested that the Bank should systematize the inclusion of the social dimension in its project work. He also recommended that the Bank employ anthropologists as permanent staff members and that the process be gradual; these recommendations are under review in the Bank. It is unlikely that major changes in staffing will occur overnight, but the direction seems to be clear. The Bank is increasingly emphasizing the need to put resources towards improving the living conditions of the poorest segment (bottom 40 percent in income) of the human population. Thus, the Bank has been increasing its lending to agriculture, population (family planning), and education as may be seen from Table 1. From 1969 to 1973 loans to agriculture increased at the substantial rate of 26 percent per annum; to education at 16 percent per annum; and population projects were added to the Bank's roster. An increasingly large share of Bank lending is going into projects with larger social dimensions. The increased emphasis on rural development, income distribution, and poverty and its redressal means that the Bank will have to enhance its expertise in the evaluation of the social impact of projects. This follows the general pattern of the Bank's evolution — from straightforward infrastructure projects like dams and power plants to complex projects like changing the life-style of pastoralists in Kenya, resettling the farmers in Colombia and Brazil, or modernizing the irrigated agriculture in Yemen. The Bank's interest in family planning, nutrition, ecology, and health is relatively recent, and each new step required the expansion of the skill base of the Bank.

The relatively global concern with the social aspects of projects is expected to induce the Bank to expand its skill base further by the inclusion of anthropological skills. Possibly the starting point could be to have one or two general anthropologists centrally located having two essentially interrelated objectives: (1) to develop a roster of anthropologists with identification of their geographic or other specialization, and (2) to promote a systematic evaluation of the need for including or excluding an anthropologist on different appraisal missions. The need for taking some such steps is generally recognized.

4. TWO EXPERIENCES WITH ANTHROPOLOGISTS

It may be of interest to relate the relevant aspects of two Bank projects in which anthropologists participated. Both are livestock projects in East Africa: Tanzania Livestock Project and Kenya Livestock Project.

Tanzania Livestock Project

The project is a broadly based program for developing beef ranching in Tanzania. The novel element in this project is the attempt to develop *ujamaa* ranches. *Ujamaa* is a Swahili word meaning familyhood. An *ujamaa* ranch is a socioeconomic reorganization of pastoralists. The objective is to modify the relationship between pastoralists and their herds which is at present intermittently market oriented, where animals are sold only sporadically to meet cash needs, to one which is generally commercial in which cattle become a vehicle for income creation. Introducing *ujamaa* ranching to different habitats required judgments on what was feasible and, among the feasible approaches, which one was best. Dr. P. Reining, who had experience in the northwest of Tanzania, was requested to participate in the appraisal mission. Her specific terms of reference required her to make judgements about:
1. the social suitability of *ujamaa* ranching in the various locations proposed under the project;
2. the need for structural differences among *ujamaa* ranches in different parts of the country;
3. the recruitment criteria for participants: how old? with what background? what should they contribute — labor, cattle? how much? what constitutes an incentive for the participant? what do they value most?
4. the respective roles of men, women and children and how should authority be structured?
5. the inheritance customs of the population and their effect on the organization of the ranch;
6. the basis for equitable sharing of costs and benefits;
7. the basis for cost sharing of public goods like education and health.
In a nutshell she had the rather difficult task of suggesting the set of feasible alternatives and structuring a reasonable system of criteria for selection, organization, and incentives.
   Difficult though the task was, she came up with a set of recommendations:
1. the basic framework for *ujamaa* ranches should be partnership

cattle ranching in which pastoralists could organize their cattle under skilled management provided by a public body;

2. the recruitment should be of relatively young men from families who own cattle;

3. livestock *ujamaas* should be established only in rural societies with well-established cattle keeping traditions, thus excluding a number of proposed areas with noncattle keeping traditions;

4. only areas with low population densities (up to fifteen per square mile) should be considered for ranch location;

5. each ranch should be large enough to accomodate about sixty families (approximately 300 persons);

6. the ranch areas should not be enclosed;

7. the aim should be to bring in essentially unused land rather than attempt to rework existing holdings in a new manner; at the same time such areas should be near the habitat of the cattle-owning people so as to avoid long-distance dislocations and enable participants to keep some contact with their friends and families;

8. each ranch should be governed by a constitution, jointly approved by the participants, which should clearly lay down (a) the economic rules of participation: cost sharing, repayment of loan, distribution of benefits and the like; and (b) the rules for social organization, procedures for joining and leaving the *ujamaa*, inheritance procedures, and roles and rights of men, women, and children.

On the basis of these recommendations, about twenty-two *ujamaa* ranches were selected out of a proposed one hundred. In addition, we (the other members of the team) learned about the multipurpose nature of the cattle herd from the viewpoint of the pastoralist: food from milking, butchering, and bleeding; power as draft animals; raw material for craft use; insurance against drought; payment and receipt in marriage and other social transactions; and status in the ownership. In a nutshell, cattle were seen to represent much more to the pastoralist than they do to a commercial rancher. The path to commercial ranching would, therefore, be long and tedious. It would be successful only if the proposed social/economic organization of the *ujamaa* could assure appropriate substitutes for the many purposes that cattle fulfilled.

It appears unlikely that the team, without an anthropologist, could have seen all of the ramifications of the changes the project was proposing. The anthropological input was significant; it added depth and understanding to our reasons for supporting *ujamaa*.

Kenya Livestock Project

This project also was concerned with introducing new relationships among pastoralists in Kenya. The bulk of the potential participants were the Masai who have special relationships with cattle and land. Dr. Dyson-Hudson accompanied the Bank team as a consultant working within a framework similar to that of Dr. Reining. The main anthropological issue in this project related to the organization of "group ranches" defined as enterprises in which Masai families would collectively hold title to land, maintain agreed stocking levels for cattle, market surplus cattle in rotation, herd their livestock as sex/age aggregates, and yet continue to OWN their livestock as individuals. This arrangement was proposed by Dyson-Hudson in 1967 in the first Kenya livestock project and retained for the second one. The arrangement is a mix of technical and social considerations. The technical considerations require that the grazing of rangeland should be controlled — that is, overgrazing is a high-cost activity. To control grazing it is necessary to introduce incentive elements which induce pastoralists not to overgraze. On communal land with wet and dry season grazing areas, the modal use of land would be overgrazing — as the grazers do not bear the cost of overgrazing. All they have to do is to move on. The government of Kenya is, therefore, trying to bring in land legislation to enable individuals or groups of individuals own land. It is hoped that land ownership would induce pastoralists to restrain from overgrazing. However, given the limited carrying capacity of the rangeland, and the animal and human populations that have to be accommodated, it would be necessary to prefer "group" ownership to "individual" ownership which would not be feasible as there is not enough land to be allocated to individuals.

Given the technical requirements for allocation and group ownership of land, the next question was one of social feasibility. Would Masai be willing to own land as a group? Would they be willing to give up individual ownership of cattle to enable the group ranch to benefit from large-scale economies? If the group ranch were to be operated as a single unit, how should it be organized and how should costs and benefits be shared? How should the authority hierarchy be structured? There are similar questions about values and incentives like those asked for the Tanzania livestock project.

Dyson-Hudson, building on previous work, suggested that group ownership of land would be acceptable, but group ownership of cattle would not. Consequently, the ranch structure should incorporate these two premises. The proposed structure of the group ranch included these important aspects, and the project included sixty group ranches.

A secondary anthropological aspect of this project was the interaction between group ranches and individual ranches. An individual ranch is a conventional commercial ranch owned by one individual, although located on previously communal land. The first livestock project (1967) included a number of such individual ranches with the intention of using these as "demonstration ranches" to induce group ranches to accept the newly introduced management techniques of controlled grazing, dipping, and emphasis on income creation through cattle sales rather than maximization of cattle numbers. Experience with the first project, however, indicated that individual ranches in the neighborhood of group ranches had a negative demonstration effect. That is, they induced members of group ranches to desire ownership of individual ranches and thus led to (1) lack of enthusiasm in the development of the group ranches and (2) a substantial dropout rate from membership in group ranches.

In the second project, therefore, the suggestion was to eliminate individual ranches from the project in order to give group ranches a better chance of success. An additional technical reason for doing so was that individual ranches were usually owned by rich and/or powerful city-based individuals who could, through their influence, manage to get the best parts of the arid rangeland. This led to the reduction of available grazing resources for the group ranches and resulted in either allocation of too little area for a group ranch, making it internally unviable, and/or migration of members of one group ranch into another group ranch for dry season grazing. This was usually self-defeating as it made nonsense of allocation and the entire concept of careful resource utilization through ownership of the resource.

As in the Tanzania livestock project, the anthropological aspects were quite revealing. The concept of the group ranch and the interaction between group and individual ranches had significant anthropological dimensions. It is unlikely that these dimensions could have been explored as well as they were without assistance from an anthropologist familiar with the Masai.

The above description of two projects in which anthropological inputs were needed and found useful is perhaps too brief, and I am hoping that the professional treatment will be forthcoming from Dr. Dyson-Hudson and Dr. P. Reining themselves. I have only sought to outline the general implications as seen by an economist.

CONCLUSION

The Bank has made limited use of professional anthropologists in the past. It has relied on what may be called generalist inputs of experience to supplement its evaluation of projects. A significant number of Bank staff with overseas experience have a deep knowledge of the customs, traditions, taboos, and values of the communities with which they have associated. This knowledge partly compensated for the Bank's limited use of anthropologists. But with the Bank Group's increasing involvement with social development projects, more professional anthropological inputs were deemed necessary. So far, over the past six years, about six projects have been evaluated by a team which included an anthropologist. In the future a more systematic use would be necessary due to the Bank's increasing emphasis on rural development, income distribution, and poverty and its redressal.

REFERENCES

KENYA LIVESTOCK DEVELOPMENT PROJECT
   1973   Appraisal report of Second Livestock Development Project in Kenya, June 26, 1973.
TANZANIA LIVESTOCK DEVELOPMENT PROJECT
   1973   Appraisal report of Second Livestock Project in Tanzania, March 19, 1973.

Thoughts on the Relevance of Social Anthropology for Development Planning: The Case of Nepal

B.-E. BORGSTRÖM

THE CONTRIBUTION OF SOCIAL ANTHROPOLOGY[1]

In discussing the contribution of social anthropology as a discipline there seem to be many who are content to define it simply as a method, that is to say, the way data is gathered defines the subject. In this sense the questions asked during fieldwork and the problems raised are considered secondary and are not seen to affect the basic unity. Anthropology becomes in this way region- rather than problem-oriented.

The method of anthropology is based on the study of rather small groups of people through direct contact effected by living among them for extended periods of time. In this way the anthropologist gets a thorough knowledge of most aspects of their social life, and it gives him the possibility of checking his conclusions against constantly changing data as well as discussing them with the subjects of his research. The disadvantage of the method is related to the fact that there are only rather small geographical areas and a rather small number of people that can be covered by one researcher and in this respect the results may be specific rather than general.

This method is important not only to the collector of descriptive data, but to the more theoretically inclined anthropologist as well. To a

My stay in Nepal was made possible through grants from Humanistiska forskningsrådet, Stockholm and Kungafonden, Stockholm.
[1] For the sake of brevity I shall use "anthropology" and "anthropologist" instead of the more cumbersome "social anthropology" and "social anthropologist" in the rest of the paper.

certain extent the method shapes the theory since it gives the researcher access to social data ranging from hard economic facts to intangible ideological patterns. But the closest collaborators for a problem-oriented anthropologist may not necessarily be other anthropologists working in the same area; they also may be drawn from other disciplines within the social sciences. Here, anthropology becomes a method for eliciting data about a social reality as well as a way of "thinking" about social life from a point of departure offering as complete a knowledge of the society in question as possible. In this manner the anthropologist comes to see the different activities in the society as statements of something more general; statements which should not be reified, but are always referable to a basis of the most important kinds of social relations defining the structure of the society.

Although the field of the social anthropologist is the local community, he cannot in the world of today look away from the things that take place at much higher levels, national or even international. These developments and their possible effects on the microcosm he is studying must always be in the back of his mind. When he describes the formal setup in the local community and the attitudes and beliefs of the people he works with, he should also be aware of the plans that are being made higher up in the administrative hierarchy and which may radically alter the situation at the local level. With his knowledge of local conditions the anthropologist should be able to make some fruitful predictions as to the likely results of such changes and these could furnish the basis for further research.[2] But this approach does not mean that everything that exists in the local community is good and that everything coming from the outside is bad. The way people in a remote area experience the world and the feelings they have towards the society in which they live will change once they are integrated into a wider society. Many of the local institutions will be swept away whether the integration is planned or not. It is of course good if existing institutions can be built on when development projects on a large scale are being introduced, but since they more often than not tend to favor local elites it may sometimes be desirable from a social-justice point of view that they should not be used as a foundation. For better or worse

---

[2] The anthropologist's problem is to a certain extent the reverse of, say, the historian's when dealing with development and planning. The latter tries to get at people's minds AFTER the event and he is concerned with how these people experienced the world they lived in. The anthropologist must try to find out how people will react to the world they do not yet live in; an anthropologist often does his research BEFORE the event.

the social relations envisaged to go with development and integration mean that local conditions will have to give way.

The wills of the planners and the power-holding groups at the center are going to prevail. The problem, then, is not how to make this change as gradual and nondisruptive to traditional ways of life as possible, but how to make all groups able to take a meaningful part in the new reality that is being created. One has to go from the bigger to the smaller.

So far this paper has been concerned with what anthropology should be concerned with, but, as noted above, one single anthropologist cannot do everything, and especially when working in a complex society, he will probably have to shed some of his "holistic" commitments in the face of a social life too complicated for one person to handle. He will have to concentrate on specific issues and problems. Here the discussion is limited to the relevance of anthropology for developmental planning, with Nepal as the unit of illustration.

There are many academic disciplines represented in development planning — most of them contributing specialized knowledge directly applicable to the solving of a particular problem. Anthropology is not among them. The role of this discipline has to be concerned with the overall implementation of planning with regard to the consequences on social relations on the ground, not in the sense of looking at a project here or there, but investigating plan implementation from a processual angle. "Social relations" would then be taken to mean those relations which reveal the "consumption pattern" of newly introduced institutions and how this changes over time. This has to be done on such a level that meaningful patterns of changed social interaction can be discerned over wider geographical areas and in large strata of the population. This means, in turn, that one single anthropologist is not enough. There has to be a conscious buildup of bigger programs over rather long periods of time, and anthropology would be mainly concerned with studying stratification and the continuities of social groupings, as well as changes in these. With regard to Nepal this would fit in well with the oft-quoted concern for social justice that is part of the planning but often vaguely expressed when it comes to concrete measures. Here is the field where anthropology can provide something that other disciplines do not furnish, or furnish only to a small degree.

THE "ANTHROPOLOGIZATION" OF PLANNERS

When anthropological work is being discussed one thinks of a trained anthropologist going into the field, carrying out a piece of research, and coming back to write up the material, after which those interested can make use of the results, if these are relevant to the work or the research that they are doing. This is doubtless a picture which is in harmony with what normally takes place and will doubtless be so even in the future. But this is not all that anthropology could or should be. It is desirable that anthropological education and ways of thinking should be part of every planner's mental equipment, that is to say, that he should be aware of the further social complications and unintended consequences that may be caused by the implementation of development planning. He should not be content with the fact that a project has been carried out in the technological sense. He has to be alert to the advantages and disadvantages that go with it and how these are distributed over the population. In fact, the planner must be able to anticipate, correct things that go wrong while the project is in progress, and follow up the wider implications once it is completed. This is in no way different from the role that has been suggested for anthropologists working with planning for development (Foster 1965: 218–240; Barth 1971: 252). It is not necessary for the planner to go out to the field himself and find out the relevant anthropological factors for each and every project that is to be carried out within his area of competence. Rather, it is desirable that the planners higher up have a theoretical knowledge of the interrelationships within a culture and an idea of how these may interact. Then, in addition, they should have specific knowledge of various culture areas in Nepal so that they can apply their theoretical knowledge in particular cases. Here there is ample scope within which ethnographers can work and help increase the so far rather scanty material available to the interested professional or layman. But, up to a time when such specialized anthropological knowledge comes into existence, an awareness on the part of the planners at different levels of the possibility of unexpected consequences of development projects will no doubt increase their preproject planning performance and make them look for effects of social relevance that are outside the purely formal working of the new institution they are creating. The day-to-day local studies will probably still be carried out by anthropologists as they have always been.

Such an "anthropologization" of the planners would perhaps also contribute to a more integrated view of development planning. As it is now many projects which are financed with foreign money tend to come under the authority of the donor rather than under the Nepali recipients, and they are not integrated into the overall plan (Rana

1971: 5–6). These projects tend to become islands with no connections between them (Rana 1972: 10), and this is obviously not in the interest of an approach to planning that stresses the social sphere as much as it stresses technological goal-fulfillment. Perhaps the "anthropologized" planner will look more to the social dynamics of development and be prepared to appraise projects not only for pragmatic reasons but also with a view to how their long-term social effects will turn out. It is clear that this means that the local expert, as a representative of an aid-giving agency, will have to convince it of the necessity for considerations other than the immediate pay-off of a project, and to hope to achieve this may of course be utopian. Still, such a change of approach will be necessary if development planning is to be tied directly to transformations of a thoroughgoing nature on the social level.

It is obvious that anthropological awareness along the lines discussed above would be of immense benefit to the foreign expert working in Nepal in improving his understanding of the general situation and ridding him of ethnocentric ideas. The situation today in this respect is not encouraging. They are in Nepal (most often in Kathmandu) to do a specialized job and that is exactly what they do. Their relations with the Nepalis are almost solely professional and economic, most of their time outside the work situation being spent with other foreigners. They go on inspection tours, but only for limited periods of time and then only to check up on a project from a technological point of view. If these experts are to become more integrated into Nepalese society in order to broaden their approach to the developmental problems of Nepal, there has to be a lot of rethinking both by the experts themselves and by those who send them to Nepal.

The case is probably easier with regard to the Nepali planners. They already have a good knowledge of their country, but, being in many cases educated abroad and in the tradition of Western ideals of specialization, they too need to get rid of their expert role and to approach planning on a more integrated basis. That such training is necessary is also indicated in the literature on recruitment of higher administrators in Nepal. They are almost exclusively Brahmans, Chettris, or Shresthas. Thus, the incumbents of posts at the levels of undersecretary or above are up to 90 percent recruited from these castes (Rana 1971: 8–9). In addition, their families come mostly from Kathmandu, and individuals not belonging to these castes and coming from outside the Kathmandu Valley have difficulty in obtaining posts in the administration and getting promoted later on (Rose and Fisher 1970: 70).

These facts show that those who wield power in Nepal come from a small minority; they are high caste and economically privileged. Belonging to "different realities" as a result of the division of society into castes (cf. Berreman 1967: 355, 358), people have scanty knowledge of the ways in which individuals in other castes view the world. In the case of the higher administrators in Nepal this is aggravated by the fact that they belong to a class vastly superior to that to which most of the people belong, and since this generally goes with residence in Kathmandu the separation from the common Nepali is made even greater. They tend to become specialists in their fields with a social life restricted to a great extent to their equals.

But there is not only the question of what the high-caste individuals know about other castes. There is also the problem of knowledge about the Mongoloid peoples of the hills. They are very badly represented at the seats of power in Kathmandu and the gulf between them and the high-caste administrators is great indeed. It would seem, then, that even the Nepali policy makers are to some extent in the same position as the foreign experts. They are in many ways cut off from local-level reality and have become specialists in their fields. If they are to become something more and achieve a view of development that is based on a transformation of opportunity structure, they too will have to "anthropologize" their outlook.

THE PRACTICE OF ANTHROPOLOGY IN PLANNING

If the "anthropologization" of the planners in Nepal could be achieved it is reasonable to assume that they would take a more serious look at the "human costs" of a project, and perhaps they would be able to gauge this cost in advance and to decide whether the project would be worth going through with. With regard to legislation they would be able to anticipate how different strata of the population at the local level will be affected and what consequences new laws will have. As a result of this they would be able to build in safety devices against malpractices by the local elites. A case in point is the Land Reform Act of 1964 which apparently lacked such devices and thus at least parts of it did not work out favorably for the weaker sections of agricultural society (Pant and Jain 1972: 51–52).

The appropriation of institutions brought in by development planning is not something that occurs by default. There are a number of such cases taking place in areas like political representation, education, agricultural facilities, recruitment to salaried jobs, and so on. All these tend to follow class and caste lines closely. Here the question of distribution comes to the fore and a planner with a knowledge of local conditions will be able to anticipate to a great extent what will happen when a new institution or a new law pertaining to planning is introduced. The anthropologist could also play a role here by checking how development projects actually work out on the ground, and much would be gained if anthropologists, maybe with interests of their own far removed from the problems of developmental planning, still devoted some of their time in the field to questions like these. The gain in coverage relevant to problems of development for Nepal would be immense, especially since the topography of the country happens to be such that generalizations over wider geographical areas are difficult and thus a planner has problems in obtaining information as to what is happening in different parts of it. Anthropologists spread out over Nepal would facilitate things for the planner and make it easier for him to arrive at decisions with at least some hope that they might be relevant to and not go against the interests of the people concerned. The information gained in this way could then be used to secure a more just distribution of services to the people. It is difficult to envisage a system of scheduled castes or tribes in Nepal, since probably a majority of the population would come within these categories. However, some kind of enforcement agencies may well have to be set up as parts of the planning effort to ensure that everybody gets a fair share.

The philosophy of the panchayat system is attuned to a society free of exploitation and this may well be an area where the greatest achievements can be made. In order to investigate how planned development transforms the opportunity structure and how new, formerly disadvantaged groups gain access to new resources, anthropologists should select key areas of social life which could be studied over time with changes noted. In this way it would be possible both to assess the rate of change for different categories and the direction of this change. The most important key area would be that of political representation. Local panchayats are supposed to carry out their own development projects and in this respect the political influence of different sections within the panchayat will be of importance. Political representation is also an arena where one can "read off" the headway that democratization is making by looking into the caste and class background of those elected and following the changes of these over time. The same procedure should be followed with regard to representation on the different class organizations which are part of the panchayat system.

The political process can also be studied at election campaigns. The way that candidates approach their prospective supporters is important. Some of the latter will be treated as equals while others will be regarded as dependants who can be bullied into voting for the candidate. Here a diachronic perspective is necessary, and the anthropologist has to investigate how the politicians' attitudes towards different categories of the electorate change over time. This approach can be profitably tied to an analysis of the individuals involved.

In anthropology the phenomenon of the broker has been known for a long time, and in Nepal it is also common for people with connections in the administration and knowing urban ways to help less fortunate individuals who have to fight a court case or look for a job in town. These brokers do of course exert a certain influence over their dependents which may be made apparent at various times, say, at an election. With the advance of a true transformation of the opportunity structure, these disadvantaged groups can be expected to be able to help themselves and the institution of brokerage can be expected to decrease.

Another important key area consists of the field of education. As formal education becomes available to more children one would expect that former illiterate segments of the society would be drawn into the education process. The anthropologist can follow this progress by examining the social background of the children who do and do not go to school. Often the children from poorer families and from strata with no tradition of schooling will take their children away from school after a few years for economic reasons or because they simply do not see the point of continued schooling. A changing picture in this regard would say something about changing material possibilities as well as indicating changing attitudes to schooling, signaling a change in the way people perceive their place in society and their possibilities of playing new roles.

Changes in the key areas mentioned above will not just furnish data relevant to the progress of planned development. They will also indicate a change in psychology on the part of those involved, and this will be very important in carrying the transformation further where initiatives from the recipients of planned projects today may become important. Nepal obviously has a long way to go before this can be turned into reality, but it must be the ultimate aim of planning for development.

The term "key groups" could be given to those groups which respond favorably to planning and which change their behavior in accordance with new possibilities in the opportunity structure brought about both by intentional planning and the largely unintentional consequences of Nepal's growing involvement in an international economy. Such key groups merit the same attention as the key areas discussed above. Key groups would be expected to exist or emerge in these key areas, but the concept is also applicable outside these. They are made up of people who operate institutions as a traditional elite or as newly formed groups resulting from changes in the structure of society. They have experienced changes and have a commitment that goes beyond the local community. Their group of reference is often urban in nature (Pearse 1971: 74). These groups are similar to those discussed by Wolf in his article on the social integration of Mexico (1971: 50–51). The appropriate focus of the study of the key groups would be to look at the process whereby they emerge from their rural background while pursuing activities like commerce, cash cropping, carving out careers in the administration or in politics, and so on. One important variable would be the progressive change of consciousness as to where they feel themselves to belong. Here one would perhaps find a difference between, say, those who do wage work or salaried work while continuing their subsistence farming and those who turn their land into growing cash crops. One could expect the latter to be more prepared to shed the customary duties to their kinsmen since the actual ground on which they all live is turned into an enterprise (cf. Long 1968). As mentioned above, special care should be taken to look into the background of the emergent strata to determine whether it is the old elite making use of new opportunities or whether it is a genuine transformation of relations between different categories of people. If the previous discussion was centered on institutions in the broadest sense, the interest is now concentrated on those who operate these institutions formally or informally.

One powerful inducement to change which may well merit study by anthropologists is the effect of tourism on the social landscape. Nepal is committed to a rapid increase in tourism, reaching 180,000 by 1974-1975 (*Fourth plan* 1970: XVIII [4]), as one of the sources to obtain foreign exchange. Tourism will have its largest impact in only a few selected areas with the Kathmandu Valley as the center. In these places the service sector of the economy will probably grow at a rather fast rate as more people are needed to staff the hotels and so on. This would be one dimension of the study, viz. an investigation of the recruitment to the industry both from a caste and class and from a geographical point of view. In addition, the workings of the trade have to be researched. There is no doubt that in such a fast-growing industry there will be many out to earn quick money, and one interesting aspect of the key area/key group complex would be to study these. This should include an interest in the socialization and further careers of those working in the tourist industry as a whole.

The other dimension of studying tourism would be concerned with its impact on the social level. There has already been some discussion about the influence of hippies on Nepali youth, and with the trend of visiting foreigners increasing at the speed envisaged in the plan this question is bound to be raised again and again. It is obvious that this is of vital interest to the possibilities of a planned social development in the areas concerned.

CONCLUSION

Anthropology, when used in development planning, should attempt to integrate the activities of other disciplines, with the aim of achieving social progress. It should be used both at the national level and at the local level. At the national level it should be concerned with coordination, preventing different projects from becoming discrete units. This broad approach to planning could be carried out by the planners themselves as outlined above.

Such a stress on the "social usefulness" of a project may well create conflicts when the relief it may bring to some people from the technological angle must be measured against social consequences which might thought harmful. If there are no questions of life and death importance involved, one could argue that considerations of social progress in a desired direction should take precedence, since it is this kind of integrated development that will in the long run make social development self-sustaining.

As was mentioned earlier, one of the problems here is to make foreign donors realize the importance of social progress. They may achieve good economic results but the social impact of their work may be only partially relevant to social planning or it may even go against the desired direction of change. If this is the case, anthropology should be used at the local level to help remedy the situation. This, again, may generate conflicts. It is quite possible that social developments emanating from such a project may have far-reaching consequences, especially in the economic sphere, and that control of these activities may adversely affect the categories of people whom the experts and the administrators favorably regard as providing the initiative for a more rapid increase in production and general prosperity. There is no clear-cut answer as to what should be done in such a situation, but it is obvious that, again, the desire for a just distribution of the fruits of development comes up against the wish for rapid economic development.

REFERENCES

BARTH, F.
1971   *Socialantropologiska problem.* Uppsala: Prisma/Verdandidebatt.

BERREMAN, G. D.
1967   Caste as social process. *Southwestern Journal of Anthropology* 23:351–370.

CHAUHAN, R. S.
1971   *The political development in Nepal 1950–1970.* New Delhi: Associated Publishing House.

FOSTER, G. M.
1965   *Traditional cultures: and the impact of technological change* (first reprint edition). London: Harper and Row.

Fourth plan (1970–1975)
1970   Kathmandu: HMG Press.

LONG, N.
1968   *Social change and the individual.* Manchester: Manchester University Press.

PANT, Y. P., S. C. JAIN
1972   *Long term planning for agriculture in Nepal.* Delhi: Vikas Publications.

PEARSE, A.
1971   "Metropolis and peasant: the expansion of the urban-industrial complex and the changing rural structure," in *Peasants and peasant society.* Edited by T. Shanin, 69–80. Harmondsworth: Penguin Modern Sociology Readings.

RANA, P. S. J. B.
1971   *Nepal's fourth plan: a critique.* Kathmandu: Yeti Pocket Books.
1972   "Role of foreign aid and trade in economic reconstruction during King Mahendra's reign." Mimeographed.

ROSE, L. E., M. W. FISHER
1970   *The politics of Nepal.* Ithaca and London: Cornell University Press.

WOLF, E.
1971   "Aspects of group relations in a complex society: Mexico," in *Peasants and peasant society.* Edited by T. Shanin, 50–68. Harmondsworth: Penguin Modern Sociology Readings.

POSTSCRIPT

The Limits of Planning

In this paper arguments have been presented, perhaps naively, for a vital reorganization of some of the features of development planning in Nepal. It seems that most of the planning is geared to economic development pure and simple. This is not surprising considering the extreme poverty of the country. There are, however, references to social considerations in the plans, and what strikes a reader is the difference in effort going into the two kinds of planning. The economic side is detailed while the human aspect is treated as something that has to be included in a plan, but not necessarily anything that merits a lot of thinking: references are general in the extreme and there is no mention of how the goals of social justice and all-round development are going to be effected. It is possible that these omissions are more than accidental. Some reasons are related to Nepal's international situation and have been touched on in the paper: more or less complete dependence on the aid-giving agencies of other countries, loans and trade-terms with many strings attached. These facts put severe restrictions on the choices available to the Nepali planners. Sometimes they will have to accept package deals, which may even include foreign labor (Rana 1971: 55).

There are also conditions peculiar to Nepal which go a long way toward explaining why social development is so incompletely spelled out in the plans. Power-holding groups in a country do not want the kind of development that jeopardizes their control of the center, or, put differently, they adopt the kind of development strategy that seems to them to be most suited to the needs of the country as they perceive them. New groups, both from the class and ethnic points of view, might upset the balance, and these differences might turn into antagonism once avenues to equal possibilities, and hence competition, are open. The caste associations of India are cases in point.

As has been seen in the paper, the castes of Brahmans, Chettris, and Shresthas are the most powerful groups in Kathmandu and they seem to have the same hold locally in different parts of the country (Chauhan 1971: 243–250). These local power holders are characterized as mainly indulging in traditional professions (1971: 245), while being rather untouched by modern education (1971: 245).

Both these facts militate against encouraging new groups with new economic outlooks and with a national commitment. And to the extent that the elite in Kathmandu is dependent on these local elites, it will have to concern itself with other things than displacing these groups and, ultimately, perhaps itself from the seats of power. To this extent the ideas presented in this paper are obviously utopian, and it is likely that development in Nepal will continue to mean trying to lift everybody without changing the order between the groups. However, there is always the hope that planning will change towards a more "anthropological" approach, and it is only then that anthropology will be able to make an important contribution.

Social Science, Food, and Nutrition

ADEL P. DEN HARTOG and ANNIKA BORNSTEIN-JOHANSSON

After some trials (and errors), nutritionists working both in the industrialized countries and the developing world have realized that problems of malnutrition cannot be solved in isolation. The food supply available to a community, the food distribution system, purchasing power, and the prevailing social system, all have their influence on the diet of the community. It is surprising that until quite recently only a few nutritionists asked the assistance of the social sciences in order to help them find a solution for malnutrition. On the other hand, only a few workers from the social sciences have spontaneously approached nutritionists to point out that they have something useful to offer. The aim of this paper is to focus attention on the relation between social sciences and nutrition and its practical implications in programs to improve the nutritional situation of the community.

NUTRITION AND SOCIAL SCIENCES

The science of nutrition, as Magnus Pyke (1968) points out, "is the fruit of a century of revolutionary intellectual activity. In the nineteenth century, during the industrial revolution, Western people suddenly got the idea of combining scientific principles with technology resulting in the biochemical and physiological understanding of what food meant for man." An interesting account of the sequence of ideas in investigations of nutrition is given by McCollum (1957). Some of the early investigators had a keen interest in the social implications of nutrition for man. Mulder, for example, introduced the term "proteins" into the nutrition sciences and wrote in 1847 that "the meagre diet is one of the causes of the lack of physical and intellectual strength of the labourers (in the Netherlands). Specially children need our attention. Those who do not die carry the results of their miserable youth with them" (quoted by Verdoorn 1965). This was a very enlightened point of view in the context of the nineteenth century. Mulder also urged that nutrition education should be included in the school curriculum, advice which was not taken into account.

In 1905, the actual era of the discovery of vitamins started with Pekelharing's demonstration of the existence of unidentified nutrients (McCollum 1957); several of these investigators had an open eye for the social aspects of nutrition as they were dealing with deficiency diseases.

War has always been a potent cause of nutritional diseases. As a result of World War I nutrition got wide attention and nutritionists were con-sulted by various governments. In the United States and Canada people were instructed about food in relation to health and, consequently, dietary habits altered (to a certain extent) for the better (McCollum 1960). In Great Britain nutritionists advised the government on food rationing.

There has been no nutritional study which caused such alarm as that of Lord Boyd Orr (1936) on the relation between food, health, and income in Great Britain. About 4.5 million people or 10 percent of the British population were living on poor diets. Due to poverty, 10 percent of the population was underfed, while the overall food supply was satisfactory! In the dependent overseas territories of Europe and the United States, thanks to pioneer efforts of nutritionists, administrations gradually be-came aware that forms of malnutrition existed. The League of Nations got interested and Britain and France, for instance, published extensive reports on food and nutrition in their overseas territories (*Nutrition in the colonial empire* 1939; Hardy, Richet, and Vassal 1933).

So far, what has been the interest of the social sciences in food and nutrition? Some social scientists have dealt with the problem but most studies have been made for purely scientific reasons, with no direct practical purpose in mind. Thomas R. Malthus's pessimistic view was of no help in solving practical problems of nutrition. Robert Owen, although strictly not belonging to the social sciences, had a more realistic approach to nutrition and he may be regarded as the father of modern industrial catering (Curtis-Bennett 1949). Karl Marx and Friedrich Engels realized the importance of food for society, but did not suggest the means for an immediate solution to the nutritional misery of the working classes (apart from the expected collapse of capitalism).

The statistician Ernst Engel was much concerned with the place of food expenditure in the household budget, his "Engel's Law" being a great contribution to both the social and nutritional sciences (1895 [1857]). Charles Booth, the English reformer, was a practical surveyor who took food into account to a certain extent in his classic study *Life and labour of the people of London* (1889–1897).

It was towards the end of the 1930's that some social scientists became interested in the practical application of the social sciences to food and nutrition problems. One of the first was Audrey Richards, a student of Malinowski. In 1939, the International African Institute made a special issue on problems of African native diet. The dietary study in north eastern Rhodesia by Richards and Widdowson (1936) is one of the first examples of cooperation between a social scientist and a nutritionist. Audrey Richards published her study '*Land, labour and diet in Northern Rhodesia*' in 1939.

It seems that only a calamity like World War II was able to stimulate the cooperation between different disciplines which culminated in the establishment of the Committee on Food Habits in the United States. Of the activities carried on by this committee, the study "Forces behind food habits and methods of change" by Kurt Lewin (1943) and the *Manual for the study of food habits* by Carl Guthe and Margaret Mead (1945) are still of great value for their practical application.

After World War II, nutrition problems as revealed by nutritionists, especially those in the developing countries, got more and more attention from the general public and the social scientists. In France, Chombart de Lauwe (1956) in his study on living conditions of laborers in Paris showed a great understanding of the sociological aspects of nutrition in daily life. For nutritionists working in field programs, two early publications (Murdoch, et al. 1950; *Notes and queries on anthropology* 1954) on anthropological research are still of practical value as they give detailed attention to food supply, food processing, and consumption.

In 1949 the International Geographical Union set up a World Land Use Survey, which concentrated mainly on developing countries. On several occasions the nutritionists and social geographers worked together. A good example is the study of Uboma in Nigeria by Oluwasanmi, et al. (1966). The International Conference on Malnutrition and Food Habits held in 1960 in Cuernavaca, Mexico tried to bring nutrition research workers and the social scientists to cooperate more closely (Burgess and Dean 1962). Social researches such as Pierre Gourou (1966), Yves LaCoste (1960), and Margaret Read (1966) deal with practical aspects of food and nutrition in developing countries. The study of José de Castro (*A geography of hunger* 1952), had a strong influence on public opinion, although one may challenge some of his ideas. From the time it was established in 1963, the Ethiopian Nutrition Institute used the services of both nutritionists and social scientists in studying the dietary problems of the Ethiopian community (Knutsson and Vahlquist 1968; Knutsson and Mellbin 1969; Knutsson and Selinus 1970). Another example of social scientists and nutritionists working together are the studies carried out in Peru and Mexico using rating techniques (Mintz and van Veen, 1968; Chassey, van Veen, and Young 1967; Sanjur, Cravioto, and van Veen 1970). An interesting account of the sociological aspects of the nutritional situation of a Colombian rural community is given by Avila (1971).

Some university departments of nutrition, such as Queen Elizabeth College of the University of London and the Agricultural University of Wageningen, have now employed social research workers. Also, on a very modest scale, the Food Policy and Nutrition Division of FAO has some social scientists in its service.

Although this section does not pretend to give an exhaustive list of works in the field of social science dealing with practical aspects of food and nutrition, we use these examples to show that until quite recently few nutritionists and social scientists have worked together on problems of malnutrition. It is hoped that the International Committee on Food Habits established at the VIIIth International Congress of Anthropological and Ethnological Sciences in Tokyo will stimulate a more frequent cooperation between these two different disciplines.

SOCIOECONOMIC AND CULTURAL ASPECTS OF FOOD AND THEIR IMPLICATIONS FOR NUTRITION

Food Habits and Ecology

It is sometimes forgotten by nutritionists, especially by those working in the field of nutrition education, that man does not think of his food in terms of calories and nutrients. Lévi-Strauss points out that animals, in contrast to man, just eat food and food is anything available which their instincts place in the category "edible" (Leach 1970). It is the convention of the society which decrees what is food and what is not food (see, for example, den Hartog and de Vos 1973) and what kind of food shall be eaten and on what occasions. And since most occasions are social ones, there must be some kind of homology between the kinds of food on the one hand and the social occasion on the other (Leach 1970). A better knowledge of the social aspects of eating is therefore of great importance to understand the nutritional situation of a group of people. The definition given by Guthe and Mead (1945) on food habits is clear and of a practical nature: "Food habits are the ways in which individuals or groups of persons, in response to social and cultural pressures, choose, consume and make use of available foods." Food habits are influenced by a large range of environmental variables as is illustrated in Figure 1.

Land tenure	Cultural pattern
Food production system	Urban/rural
Marketing	Artefacts
Purchasing power	(Roads, dwelling, utensils)

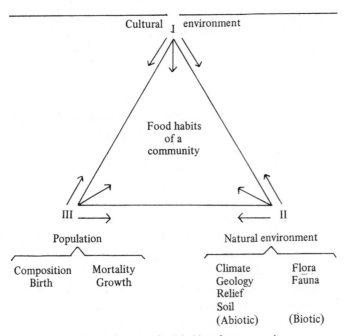

Figure 1.   Main variables influencing food habits of a community

To choose and make use of available food means that food habits have an ecological component. This is not a plea for an old-fashioned geographical determinism; however, the regional studies carried out by the *Indicative World Plan for agricultural development* of FAO (1970) show a close relationship between the diet of a community and the ecological zone where it is situated.

Domestication of plants in response to natural ecosystems has led to two generalized agricultural systems: (1) seed agriculture, dependent primarily upon seed reproduced crop plants and (2) root and tuber agriculture or vegeculture, dependent mainly upon vegetative reproduction (Harris 1969). Seed agriculture appears to represent the indigenous mode of agriculture in the drier tropics and subtropics of the Old and New Worlds. Root and tuber agriculture is most highly developed as an indigenous agriculture in the humid tropical lowlands of America, Southeast Asia, and Africa. In the highlands of the Andes with their cool, temperate climate, root and tuber agriculture is based on potatoes and some minor root crops. Domestication of plants and animals initiated major changes in human ecology, leading to larger settled communities and ultimately to the amenities of urban life. Plant domestication can also lead to an overemphasis on a single staple, such as rice, maize, cassava, or plantain. If this staple is poor in certain nutrients, vitamin deficiency or disease may result. In the forest zones of tropical Africa with their root and tuber agriculture, the diet is characterized by a deficiency of proteins and riboflavin. In the savanna zones of West Africa, deficiencies of riboflavin and vitamins A and C are common during the long, dry season when vegetables are in short supply. Animal production is also limited due to scarcity of pasture and other animal fodder. The content of these nutrients in the staple cereals millet and sorghum is not sufficient to compensate for these periodic shortages of other foods.

According to Oomen (1971), man can be considered as part of an ecosystem in a state of dynamic equilibrium which has not been disturbed even in large population groups. Taking an example from the New Guinean population he shows that the traditional New Guinean diets of the root and tuber farmers rarely create malnutrition problems. Although communities situated in the same ecological zone usually have a similar dietary pattern, this does not mean that all their food habits are the same. Differences may be found between various communities of the same ecological zones, e.g. in food distribution systems, food avoidance, and infant feeding practices. The age-old balance of the community with its environment is now being disturbed by external factors.

Geertz (1963) describes how the two types of ecosystems in Indonesia, swidden agricultural ecosystem (shifting cultivation) and *sawah* or wet rice agricultural ecosystem, were broken up as a result of external interference. It seems that three main forces have deteriorating effects on a balanced ecosystem and the food habits of the community. These are (1) population growth, (2) orientation away from subsistence towards cash crop farming, and (3) urbanization.

Food Habits of Rural Communities

ORIENTATION FROM SUBSISTENCE FARMING TO CASH-CROP FARMING. Despite the fact that subsistence farming in its pure state can only be found in very remote areas, the foods consumed in many rural communities are derived mainly from the consumers' own farms. The vast majority of the Asian population still live on foods which they produce themselves. The FAO *Indicative World Plan* estimated from available food consumption data that 64 percent of the food consumed in Africa south of the Sahara is derived from subsistence farming.

With the economic development of rural areas, agriculture is directed towards cash crops and marketing. From many points of view this process is necessary as it gives the country the needed resources for economic development and it allows the farmer the possibility of raising the standard of living for himself and his family. However, from the nutritional point of view, this process may have some harmful side effects: (1) substitution of labor-intensive food crops by less labor-intensive food crops which are nutritionally inferior but have a high calorie yield per hectare; (2) substitution of food crops by nonfood crops; and (3) the cash income is generally not used to compensate for the lost nutritive value.

A cash crop may be either a food or a nonfood crop. In many areas a tendency can be observed to abandon the cultivation of those food crops which necessitate a lot of work for less time-consuming foods such as cassava or maize with a high calorie yield per hectare. In Africa south of the Sahara, there is a tendency to replace yam, millet, and sorghum with cassava, maize, or rice (see Table 1).

Table 1.　Food crop substitution in tropical Africa

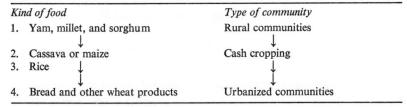

Kind of food	*Type of community*
1. Yam, millet, and sorghum ↓	Rural communities ↓
2. Cassava or maize	Cash cropping
3. Rice ↓	↓
4. Bread and other wheat products	Urbanized communities

Other regions of the world show similar trends, e.g. Mexico and Central America where there is a tendency to replace maize with bread and rice.

Everywhere in the world where people have the opportunity, there seems to be a tendency to replace the traditional unrefined, dark cereal flours with refined, white wheat flour or polished white rice for reasons of taste, convenience, and prestige. This most often results, however, in a nutritional loss.

Another result of this change towards cash crop farming is that the cash income of the family is generally not used to compensate for the lost nutritive value of the former diet by purchasing additional foods. Investigations in a settlement with irrigated farming in Kenya revealed that the improvement of the general living standards did not coincide with an improvement in the nutritional status (Kraut and Cremer 1969). Apparently, other needs such as better clothing, a radio, or a bicycle had to be satisfied at this stage.

URBAN INFLUENCE ON FOOD HABITS IN THE RURAL AREAS.   Urbanization is a two-part process; it is not only movement towards urban areas and the development of urban life, but also the outward movement of urban influence into the rural areas (Anderson 1964). This means that urbanization is influencing the food habits of both city dwellers and rural communities.

Urbanization has a strong influence in the rural areas, not only in the migration of people from the rural areas to the cities and the absorbing of villages into urban areas, but also in the spreading of the urban way of life to the countryside. We may thus speak of both:
1.   physical urbanization of the rural areas, by bringing the urban amenities like better housing, good roads, etc. to the villages, and
2.   mental urbanization of the rural areas, by bringing some aspects of the urban way of life to the rural communities.

The urban influence on the food habits of the rural communities may go in the following directions:
a.   Migration of labor force to the town will cause the absence of able-bodied men in agriculture and thus the food economy will be endangered; the increased work load of rural women when the men are absent will cause a deterioration of the quality of child care and feeding and also of the cohesion and stability of family life.
b.   A greater orientation towards food cash crops for the urban market occurs.
c.   New urban food habits and foods developed in the towns, such as the eating of bread in non-wheat-producing countries, are most likely to spread in the rural areas; modern infant feeding practices, such as bottle feeding, are a typical sequel of urban influence.

Food Habits and Urbanization

Urbanization, in the sense of migration from rural to urban areas, is a widespread phenomenon. In the preindustrial era, urbanization was primarily a tendency of the rural population to agglomerate towards the large towns with good administrative and commercial facilities, while retaining their farming activities. In modern cities the agricultural element is negligible. The definitions of what constitutes an urban area are many, and we need not go into them here. In the context of our topic, we understand "urban" to mean an area with a sizeable population (e.g. in Ghana the lower limit is set at 5,000 inhabitants) where the large majority are nonfood producers and depend on the market for their food supply.

Many of the urban dwellers are newcomers and are, as Southall and Gutkind (1957) said for Kampala, "townsmen in the making." Urban growth is not only caused by migration, however, but also by the natural growth of many cities in the developing countries (Arriaga 1968).

The migrant coming to the town is faced with many problems: the change from a rural to an urban environment and way of life, finding employment and housing, and the social experience of being separated from his family in the case where the family remains in the village. The new urban environment will have its effects on the food habits and dietary pattern (Freedman 1973). The migrant is confronted with the fact that in a big town all foods have to be bought. The supply of local traditional commodities is often inadequate and there is not always sufficient time for lengthy food preparation. In the town the family loses several important economic functions, e.g. the production and preservation of foods, and handicrafts such as weaving, making clothes, etc. All these factors cause the towndweller to be particularly receptive to new foods (bread, sugar, rice), that are quick and easy to prepare and attractively packaged, and to all kinds of preserved foods.

Food habits in the towns are focused on two points (de Garine 1969):
1. Food habits at home remain traditional. Several changes may have taken place but, in many cases, they are still quite strong. In Accra it was found that new foods were used, but much adapted to the traditional culinary techniques (den Hartog 1973a).
2. New influences were received during the working period in canteens, restaurants, or small roadside cafes.

What is the dietary pattern of the urban dweller like compared to that of his rural counterpart? In Japan, reports of the National Institute of Nutrition show that the urban diet is superior to that in the rural areas.

The reports indicate that in the towns more milk and milk products were consumed, together with more meat and fish (see *Annual report* 1971). However, with the rapid economic development of Japan, differences are becoming less.

Mbabane, the capital of Swaziland, has a better dietary pattern compared with the rural areas as is shown by a study carried out in 1963 (see Table 2).

In spite of urban problems such as insufficient employment, over-crowding, inadequate cooking facilities, and increasing housing expenses, many studies show that, compared with rural populations, the town dweller

Table 2. Percentage of dietary calories derived from protein and fat in urban and rural areas of Swaziland (after Jones 1963)

Locality	Average calories per head per day	gr.	Protein Percentage of total calories	gr.	Fats Percentage of total calories
Urban Mbabane	2011	75	15	46	21
Peri-urban	1253	42	13	20	14
Rural areas (mean value)	1672	54	13	27	15

(1) has more varied food, including fruit and vegetables; (2) has a higher consumption of animal protein; and (3) has less seasonal influence in his diet (Bornstein-Johansson 1974; de Garine 1969; Dema and den Hartog 1969; Santos 1967).

However, this general picture should be qualified as the situation may differ from country to country and also within the different socioeconomic groups of the town.

Among the urban population, especially in the bigger cities, there are often large marginal groups of under- or unemployed, with very low and irregular incomes. The problems of the poor urban groups are different from those of the traditional rural community. The farmers have certain advantages which the citizens of a cash-crop society have to a large extent lost. Within their very limited physical resources the farmers have, through ages of experience, achieved a kind of social and ecological balance; they are able to foresee seasonal food shortages, hazards of climate, and other environmental difficulties, and they have built up a defence against them. In the urban society, the flow of resources is completely beyond the control of the majority. Unforeseen problems arise which cannot be coped with by experience. For example, developing countries experience inflatory price increases of foodstuffs, which hit the urban consumer much harder than the rural one who depends partly on his own production. This may be illustrated by what a Sisala migrant in Accra, Ghana, said: "When I was living with my father my food was free, my room was free. At home I worked hard on the farm but I never had to worry. Here in Mamobi (Accra) everything costs money. If you can't find work, you will starve and nobody cares" (Grindal 1973). In a village community there is usually a system of mutual aid to help members in distress and prevent individuals from starving. In Yemeni villages, for example, there is a tradition for families who have milk animals to regularly distribute free skimmed milk to poor neighbors who have no animals (Bornstein-Johansson 1974). With the weakening social ties in urban areas this system of protection against misfortune is getting weaker and the individual is more vulnerable, both socially and nutritionally.

Food Habits of Socioeconomic Groups

In the urban areas one may distinguish three main socioeconomic groups, which can be subdivided into more refined groups. Each particular group has common characteristics in their food habits and nutrition. This is summarized in Table 3.

Table 3. Some characteristics of food habits among socioeconomic groups in urban areas in developing countries

Socioeconomic groups	Food habits
1) High socioeconomic groups (Traditional aristocracy, high-ranking civil servants, modern managers)	1) High consumption of calories, proteins, fats, and sugars. Some members have unbalanced diets due to overeating. Large consumption of imported foods; large consumption of convenience foods.
2) Middle socioeconomic groups (Professional, lower civil servants)	2) Have elements of both (1) and (3). Strong tendency to copy food habits of the high socioeconomic groups.
3) Low socioeconomic groups (Laborers, proletariat, in some cities 40–80 percent of the population)	3) Lower consumption of calories, proteins fats, and sugars. Unbalanced diet due to lack of monetary resources. Low consumption of imported foods.

Although middle and high socioeconomic groups are small in size compared with the great masses of the population, their food habits have strong economic consequences, especially their demand for imported foods. Food importations are for many countries a heavy drain on foreign exchange which otherwise could be used for investment purposes.

As yet there is little information available on the diets of the unestablished newcomers to urban areas who live in the shanty towns or *bidonvilles*. In a Caracas shantytown it was found that fresh meat, green vegetables, and milk are unknown commodities. The food consumed resembles that of the countryside, but chicken and fresh fruit are no longer eaten (Brisseau 1963).

In general, the shantytowns which have sprung up on the edges of large cities are widely regarded as being "sinks of social disorganization," but studies such as one in Peru, for example, discovered that in the squatter settlements or *barriadas* the opposite was true (Mangin 1967). In comparison, these people are better off than the population of the city slums; although poor, they do not live a life of squalor and hopelessness.

In Africa migrants have formed organizations of mutual assistance. In Kinshasa, for example, *zone de squatting* has many good points; here also more problems are found in the slums of the city. In the shanty towns, there are positive attitudes toward working in the field of nutrition education, while in the slums, which are in fact old urban areas in decay, the social situation is much more difficult.

A lively account of food habits in a classic slum of the first quarter of this century in England is given by Roberts (1973) and shows how, due to the return of the ex-serviceman of World War I, food habits changed to a more diverse dietary pattern.

When dealing with the impact of income rise on improvement of nutrition of the low socioeconomic groups, it is, according to Walter (1973), necessary to make a distinction between two types of poverty, i.e. those groups who became poor due to external factors and those who have been born into the "culture of poverty." For the group born into poverty Walter found no correlation between income and diets among the urban youth of Trujillo, Peru. A good diet is something that is carried over time. Such a time concept is not congenial to the culture of poverty and nutrition cannot be expected to improve automatically with an increase in income.

Much of the schematic presentation of the characteristics of food habits among socioeconomic groups in urban areas applies also to rural areas with distinct social classes. This does not generally apply to traditional rural tropical Africa. In general, due to the limited nature of technology, the sufficient availability of land, and the low differentiation in terms of levels of consumption, it seems that standards of living, as measured by the usual criteria, were not markedly different (Goody 1971). In those regions with a highly developed cash economy, such as the cocoa-growing areas of West Africa, some differences may be found.

In this respect the situation in most of rural Latin America and Asia is quite different. According to Huizer (1973), after the land reform of 1952 in Bolivia the improvement in living conditions, particularly the nourishment of the peasantry, was so marked that the average size of the army recruits increased notably in the years after the land distribution. The peasants simply ate a good deal better, which was also one of the reasons for the temporary decrease in marketed agricultural produce in the first postreform years.

This does not mean that any agrarian reform will automatically have a beneficial influence on the food and nutrition of the farmer.

Food Distribution at Household Level and Infant Feeding

FOOD DISTRIBUTION. Food available in a country, whether locally produced or imported, is not equally distributed among the population. Unequal distribution of food is found between different regions of a country, rural and urban areas, different socioeconomic groups, and members of the household.

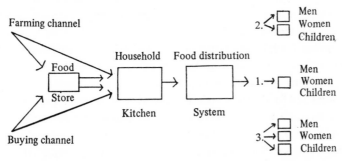

Figure 2. A simplified model showing supply and distribution of food at household level in a rural situation (after den Hartog 1973b)

The supply and distribution of food for a rural household is summarized in Figure 2 which is inspired by Lewin's Channel theory. It is of importance to know which members of the household (the husband, wife, or domestic personnel) control the various channels. In some societies the housewife is responsible for the buying channel and the husband for the farming channel. The women may control the farming channel as far as vegetables are concerned and the men may control the staple foods, as in various parts of tropical Africa. Or, for example, in Yemen, as in most traditional Moslem societies, it is usually the men who buy the food and who control the household budget (Bornstein-Johansson 1972).

The members of the household will not always eat together "around the same table" as is mainly the case in Western societies. In other parts of the world members of the household may eat in separate groups and not all at the same time. It may be as in Indonesia, where the men eat first and the women and children later, or as in parts of Africa where we sometimes have three eating groups: the men, the women and very young children, and the other children under the guidance of an older sister.

It is important to know which group receives the food first and who is responsible for the distribution of the food both as a whole and in the various eating groups.

The distribution of food within a household has both a physiological and sociocultural basis. Important sociocultural factors influencing the food distribution are (1) the social position of the member of the household who has the first choice of the food and the sequence in which meals are served; (2) prevailing attitudes about food; and (3) the social function of food, especially food as an expression of prestige and an obligation of hospitality. In male-dominated societies it is common that meat, to a certain extent, is regarded as belonging to the men and as a means for a man to reinforce his prestige (den Hartog 1973b).

In many cultures food sharing and food gifts have a strong social and religious significance. In Islam eating is considered to be a matter of worshipping God, like praying, fasting, and other religious practices. It is said that the quantity of food for one person is always enough for two, and the quantity for two is enough for four; it is unthinkable that a person should eat his food alone without sharing it with other people present. Food gifts are a way of showing one's friendship and appreciation of a person or compassion for the poor. The sharing of meat during the Islamic Feast of Sacrifice is an example of this practice (Bornstein-Johansson 1974).

Food avoidance and taboos as part of the prevailing attitudes about food may also influence distribution of food within the household (de Garine 1967; Simoons 1962). Of particular importance are the so-called temporary food avoidances which apply to individuals during certain periods within the life cycle. Temporary food avoidances are mainly concerned with the vulnerable categories: women during pregnancy and lactation and children during the weaning period, infancy, and puberty. The importance for nutrition has been somewhat overstressed compared with other aspects of food habits. Food regulations and avoidances during these periods are unfortunately often the kind which bar the individuals from the nutritionally most valuable foods, i.e. mainly animal proteins.

INFANT FEEDING PRACTICES.   The most important form of malnutrition in all developing countries is the protein-calorie malnutrition of early childhood (PCM). This can occur in several clinical appearances, from mild forms shown by slight growth retardation to the severe forms known as *kwashiorkor* and marasmus (Jelliffe 1968). The term PCM is used for this group of conditions because all of them are due to a diet low in protein but with different levels of intake of carbohydrate calories. The underlying cause of PCM is almost always a combination of dietary inadequacies and chronic or repeated acute infections. Behind these two factors are a number of conditioning factors which are related to and influence each other, as illustrated in Figure 3.

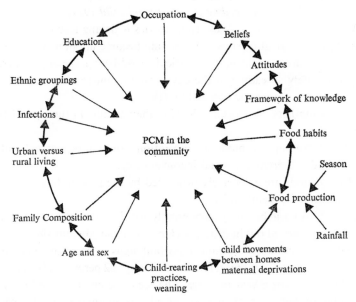

Figure 3.   Factors related to the rate of malnutrition in the community (from King 1966)

To tackle the problem of PCM in any given community, the main causative factor or factors must be clearly identified. In one area the main factor may be polluted water and poor hygiene, resulting in chronic or acute infections in the infants; in another it may be periodic or permanent shortages of certain essential nutrients, e.g. lack of animal milk during the dry seasons; in a third area, the main reason for infant malnutrition may be the parents' lack of knowledge of how to utilize available foods in the weaning diet or a harmful food avoidance during this period. Usually several of these factors combine and result in the state of malnutrition.

A common reason for infant malnutrition, especially in urbanizing areas, is the growing tendency to replace breast feeding with artificial feeding at too early an age. Infants receiving sufficient breast milk run no risk of protein-calorie malnutrition up to the age of about six months, provided that no complications set in; for up to two years the breast milk continues to represent an important part of the diet. Prolonged breast feeding is still the common practice among lower socioeconomic groups in rural areas of the developing countries. Among these groups there is no satisfactory alternative to breast feeding. Milk substitutes are either in short supply or too expensive and the poor hygienic conditions make artificial feeding, especially bottle feeding, extremely hazardous for the health of the baby (see *Feeding the pre-school child* 1971).

While breast feeding in Western countries is having a renaissance (for mainly psychological reasons, after having become unpopular already in the seventeenth and eighteenth centuries [Wood 1955]), the opposite trend is unfortunately spreading in the developing countries. The reasons for this have been summarized by Jelliffe (1968):

1. Many mothers are working, leaving their infants in the care of relatives.
2. Breast feeding by modern conventions should be carried out in privacy and is therefore a social inconvenience.
3. Infant foods are extensively promoted by the food industry.
4. Lactation frequently fails.

Breast-feeding habits may vary greatly within a country, as shown by three studies carried out in Ethiopia (Knutsson and Mellbin 1969). In one agricultural community without important signs of economic and social change, the duration of breast feeding was long: 92 percent of the children were breast fed for a year or more. The second community followed the same pattern, but where changes occurred in economic sectors, the period of breast feeding was shorter. In the third community studied, an active weaning of infants took place in order to increase the number of children borne by a woman during her fertile years. In some societies sexual intercourse is not permitted during lactation and the waning of polygamy has led to a decrease in the period of breast feeding.

Several studies have shown the decline in breast feeding in urbanizing areas. In Chile breast feeding at one year of age has fallen from 95 percent to 6 percent in the past 20 years (Mönckeberg 1966). In Yemen a sample of women working at a factory stopped breast feeding completely at an average age of eight months, many of them after the second month, while in rural areas one and one-half to two years is the common age. The working women used bottle feeding in 85 percent of the cases, whereas this is still uncommon in villages (Bornstein-Johansson 1974).

Although the influence of advertizing on behavior patterns may be somewhat overestimated in industrial countries (McKenzie 1964), the situation in developing countries is quite different. Here the consumer is much more unprotected and receptive to persuasion to use "modern" items and methods. In a paper on the decline of breast feeding in Nigeria

(Wennen van der Mey 1969), the author describes how milk firms initially behaved well by satisfying only the demand of the upper classes and refraining from exploiting the unsophisticated market of the low income groups. Nowadays, however, the low income groups are being reached through efficient sales promotion; this results in a spread of bottle feeding with the consequent vicious circle of infections (diarrhea — malnutrition — infection) known as the "bottle disease."

The weaning period has become identified with the overwhelming problems of PCM and other deficiency diseases (Cameron and Hofvander 1971). The culturally prescribed weaning foods among uneducated populations are usually soft, carbohydrate foods. Animal products, vegetables, and fruits play an insignificant role, although these may be available and consumed by the other family members. Nutrition education has an important role to play in the area of improved weaning diets. But before attempts are made to modify the feeding practices, like any other aspects of food habits, the actual practices, as well as the underlying economic and sociocultural reasons for them, must be fully understood, (Bornstein-Johansson and Kreysler 1972).

Numerous schemes for protein food enrichment have been carried out in developing countries with varying degree of success (see E. Orr 1972). Apart from problems such as distribution and low purchasing power, it must be realized that the position of children in Western society is rather different from that in non-Western societies. In Western society the child does not belong to the adult world and hardly participates in or shares duties in the activities of the adults. In non-Western and basically rural societies children form a part of the world of adults. At a very young age they have responsibilities for the basic daily needs of life, such as production and preparation of food and the care of younger brothers and sisters. This may be one of the reasons why in most developing countries, after breast feeding, children are introduced to the diet of the adults as soon as possible.

THE DYNAMICS OF FOOD HABITS AND INDUCED CHANGE

Changes in Food Habits

The food habits and dietary pattern of a society are never static but change with the changes in the socioeconomic system of which they form a part. A very important aspect of the dynamics of food habits is the diffusion and acceptance of food crops and animals over the world. Trade, wars, and mass migration have contributed in part to new foods. In the past 400 years the transference of different foods from one people to another has been very extensive.

From the American continent, maize, "Irish" potatoes, sweet potatoes, cassava, cocoa, tomatoes, lima beans, ground nuts, and "turkeys" went to Europe, Africa, and Asia. Products like rice, tea, sugarcane, and many fruits spread from South to Southeast Asia and to other tropical and semi-tropical areas of the world. It is interesting to note that in many countries these imported foods are so deeply rooted that the people consider them as indigenous and not foreign. With regard to Africa, Schnell (1957) estimated that 50 percent of the food crops originated from the American continent.

The new foods have had a considerable influence on the societies where they have been accepted. Cassava, with its high caloric output per hectare has, despite its low protein content, saved populations from famine on many occasions. In Indonesia and parts of East Africa the cultivation of cassava was promoted as a hunger crop at the expense of rice and sorghum. The potato has played a similar role in Europe. According to Salaman (1949) it enabled the laborers to survive on the lowest possible wage when foods such as bread, meat, and milk became beyond the reach of the low economic classes of the society.

When maize was brought across the Atlantic it became very well established in several countries around the Mediterranean, replacing wheat to some extent. Maize is a more drought-resistant crop and gives a higher yield per hectare. Until quite recently it was the food of the poorer sections of society in the Mediterranean (Chick 1968).

Another aspect of the dynamics of food behavior is the acceptance of bread in nonwheat producing areas of Africa and Asia. The history of the production of wheat and of bread consumption is very old, but, with some exceptions, the acceptance of bread in nonwheat producing areas is recent. For instance, in tropical West Africa in Ghana, Bosman (1704) wrote that bread was available at the local market of Elmina (see also Kilby 1965; Youngs 1973). In southern and eastern Asia where rice is the predominant-tly preferred cereal, bread is increasingly accepted (see Table 4). In a sense the two cereals do not compete with each other, since rice remains the center of the diet and wheat products are supplementary foods suited to urban conditions (Aykroyd and Doughty 1970).

In Mexico, Central America, and northern parts of South America where the traditional diets of the indigenous people are based on maize and beans, one may observe a swing towards bread and rice; the same

Table 4.   Wheat import trends in the Far East and Africa (after Aykroyd and Doughty 1970)

Region	Average Pre-war (millions of tons)	Average 1953-57 (millions of tons)	1965 (millions of tons)
Far East (excluding Mainland China)	1.01	5.66	14.51
Africa	0.28	0.87	1.79

applies for parts of Brazil and in some of the tropical regions of Andean countries where cassava is a staple food.

Also in tropical Africa bread and other wheat products such as biscuits are increasingly consumed. Several factors have led to this development, some of which are:

1.   urbanization and the need for time-saving foods;
2.   the presence of large groups of expatriates with bread-eating habits;
3.   in certain countries wheat has served as a substitute for rice in periods of hunger (for instance Ceylon); and
4.   repatriation of soldiers who acquired a taste for bread while serving abroad.

In the industrialized countries of Europe, North America, and Oceania a contrary trend has taken place, i.e. a decline in the consumption of bread. A general increase in purchasing power and the greater diversity of foods other than wheat products has led step by step to the adoption of a diet containing large amounts of meat and other foods of animal origin and a high proportion of fat as well as vegetables and fruit.

The Role of the Social Scientists in Nutrition Programs

We hope to have shown in this paper something of the dynamism of food habits and their close interrelation with other sociocultural and economic features of society. Food habits are changing constantly, for the better or for the worse, as a result of external influences or modifications from within the social system itself. The question we should be asking, as Margaret Mead observed (1962:51–52), is not "How do we change food habits?" but "How do food habits change?" It is only with a knowledge of existing trends and interrelations of the food habits and dietary patterns with other development trends that one can hope to introduce those changes which, from a nutritional point of view, are desirable and necessary.

The induced change of food habits is, generally speaking, caused by two primary agencies of change, each with its own objectives and methods:

1.   Governmental institutions (Department of Health and Agriculture, Applied Nutrition Programs) and voluntary welfare organizations promote good food habits for a better nutrition, generally through extension and nutrition education.

2.   Commercial companies and agricultural marketing boards (both private and state-owned) sell foodstuffs, therefore needing to change food habits through advertising.

Often the interests of these two agencies of change do not coincide but may lead to conflicting situations, such as the already mentioned example of promotion of artificial feeding by commercial companies.

To avoid such situations it is necessary to integrate the aims and methods of the agencies of change into a coordinated nutrition policy, so that they will not compete with but rather complement each other. Unfortunately, such an approach is still wishful thinking in most countries, both industrialized and developing.

Generally, as observed by Colby (1964), there is a tendency in non-commercial research to be more concerned, at least in the initial stages, with analyzing the problems rather than with finding a solution to them. On the other hand, commercial research may pursue a rapid path to solutions, with inadequate analysis of the situation. In order to induce desirable changes or modifications, both sides have much to learn from each other.

Social scientists should participate both in the formulation and the implementation of a food and nutrition policy, either through a nutrition program itself or a component of a broader development program.

The general role of the social scientist in such programs as we see it is (1) *to analyze objectively the sociocultural and economic context of nutrition of the target group and identify the socioeconomic variables contributing to malnutrition.* Such an analysis is an important part in program planning and implies that the social scientist must be actively involved right from the beginning in the planning of the program. Too often they are invited only if something "goes wrong," which might have been avoided if they had been consulted in the planning and (2) *to assist in the actual execution of the programs and in their periodic and final evaluation.* We think that the main role of the social scientist in both the planning and execution stages of a program should be to voice the opinion of the people on what they see as their priority problems and needs. He should suggest ways to promote forms of cooperation and communication between the local groups and the national government or development agency and help in their implementation (see Salisbury this volume).

Nutrition programs are generally carried out by extension workers. The effectiveness or failure of such programs depends on the readiness of the population concerned to accept the program and cooperate in its execution. An often heard complaint from nutrition workers trying to influence a community to modify its feeding practices and consumption patterns is that the people are conservative, backward, and "resistant to change." The conception of rural communities as fatalistic and conservative is a diehard image among scholars and development workers alike. This theory has been many times disproved, however (see e.g. Huizer 1973), and reflects more of the attitudes and approaches of the development workers than of the behavior of the local people. If people are unwilling to listen to and follow advice from outside, they usually have their good reasons, although to a nutritionist they may seem irrelevant and mistaken. One reason may be that the extension worker is identified with the ruling elite which makes communication very difficult (see Bantje 1972).

Too often nutrition projects are imposed on the communities from above, without asking about the wishes and ideas of the people concerned or recognizing their own efforts and endeavors. There is much talk nowadays in development agencies about self-help programs, participation of the local people, etc. and it is recognized that no real change can take place without the active involvement of the community. But such programs are difficult to realize and the easier "do as you are told and you'll see the results" approach is often resorted to (see Pitt's article [this volume] on "Development from below"). It is of interest to note that those nutrition programs which have been most successful were all well established in the administration of the country and received good support from the population involved.

One crucial point remains: what can the social scientist do if the policy makers and planners of a country do not have a genuine interest in the welfare of the population. Often public administrators must be looked at as powerful and self-interested. Redistribution of national resources would mean a sacrifice for just those who are supposed to be carrying it out (Schaffer 1973). This is a factor all development programs must take into account.

The social scientist who sees his task as making a diagnosis of the problems of malnutrition may feel the dilemma of working within an unfavorable political framework less strongly than the one who is also concerned with the implementation of the program. In such circumstances we see the role of the social scientist as most useful at the grass-roots level. His presence as an outsider, with contacts and access to information from both sides, may help the people to analyze and understand their own situation in relation to the wider context of the society and to act accordingly.

REFERENCES

ANDERSON, N.
1964   *The urban community, a world perspective*. New York: Holt, Rinehart and Winston.
ARRIAGA, E. E.
1968   Components of city growth in selected Latin-American countries. *Milbank Memorial Fund, Quarterly* 47 (2): 237–252.
AVILA, A.
1971   *Sociología del Hombre*. Barranquilla: Ediciónes Universidad del Atlántico.
AYKROYD, W. R.
1970   *Conquest of deficiency diseases, achievement and prospects*. Geneva: WHO.
AYKROYD, W. R., J. D. DOUGHTY
1970   *Wheat in human nutrition*. Rome: FAO.
BANTJE, H. F. W.
1972   "Sociological aspects of the Lambs River Project, Jamaica." Rome: FAO. (Mimeographed.)
BOOTH, C.
1889–1897   *Life and labour of the people of London, 1889–1891*, seventeen volumes. London: Macmillan.
BORNSTEIN-JOHANSSON, A.
1972   Some observations on Yemeni food habits. *FAO Nutrition Newsletter* 10(3):1–9.
1974   *Food and society in the Yemen Arab Republic*: Rome. FAO.
BORNSTEIN-JOHANSSON, A., J. KREYSLER
1972   Social factors influencing the attendance in "Under Fives' Clinics." *Journal of Tropical Pediatrics and Environmental Child Health* 18(2): 150–158.
BOSMAN, W.
1704   *Naukeurige Beschryving van de Guinese Goud-, Tand-, en Slave-Kust, nevens alle desselfslanden, koningryken en gemenebesten*. Utrecht. [A New and Accurate Description of the Coast of Guinea. London. 1705.]
BRISSEAU, J.
1963   Les "barrios" de Patare, faubourgs populaires d'une banlieue de Caracas. *Les Cahiers d'Outremer* 16(61):5–42.
BURGESS, A., R. F. A. DEAN
1962   *Malnutrition and food habits, report of an international and inter-professional conference*. London: Tavistock Publications.

CAMERON, M., Y. HOFVANDER
1971 *Manual on feeding infants and young children*. New York: Protein Advisory Group of the United Nations System.

CHASSEY, J. P., A. G. VAN VEEN, F. W. YOUNG
1967 The application of social science research methods to the study of food habits and food consumption in an industrializing area. *The American Journal of Clinical Nutrition* 20(1):56–64.

CHOMBART DE LAUWE, P.
1956 *La vie quotidienne des familles ouvrières. Recherche sur les comportements sociaux de consommation*. Paris: Centre Nationale de la Recherche Scientifique.

CHICK, H.
1968 *Maize and maize diets*. Rome: FAO.

COLBY, C. W.
1964 "The role of the experimental psychologist," in *Changing food habits*. Edited by J. Yudkin and J. C. McKenzie. London: Macgibbon and Kee.

CURTIS-BENNETT, N.
1949 *The food of the people, the history of industrial feeding*. London: Faber and Faber.

DE CASTRO, J.
1952 *Géopolitique de la faim*. Paris: Les Editions Ouvrières. (Reprinted and revised in 1971.)

DE GARINE, I.
1967 Aspects socio-culturels des comportements alimentaires. Essai de classification des interdits alimentaires. *Maroc Médical* 47(508):764–773.
1969 Food, nutrition and urbanization. *FAO Nutrition Newsletter* 7(1):1–19.

DEMA, I. S., A. P. DEN HARTOG
1969 Urbanization and dietary change in tropical Africa. *Food and Nutrition in Africa* 7:31–63.

DEN HARTOG, A. P.
1973a Dietary habits of northern migrant labourers in Accra, Ghana. *Voeding, Netherlands Journal of Nutrition* 34(6):282–299.
1973b Unequal distribution of food within the household, a somewhat neglected aspect of food behaviour. *FAO Nutrition Newsletter* 10(4):8–17.

DEN HARTOG, A. P., A. DE VOS
1973 The use of rodents as food in tropical Africa. *FAO Nutrition Newsletter* 11(2):1–14.

ENGEL, ERNST
1895 [1857] *Die Production und Consumtionsverhältnisse des Königreiches Sachsen*. International Statistical Institute, Bulletin 9(1), supplement 1.

Feeding the pre-school child
1971 *Report of a PAG Ad Hoc Working Group*. New York: FAO/WHO/UNICEF Protein Advisory Group.

Food habits in Calcutta
1972 *A study of food habits in Calcutta*. Calcutta: Hindustan Thompson. (Published under the auspices of USAID.)

FREEDMAN, R. L.
1973   Nutrition problems and adaptation of migrants in a new cultural environment. *International Migration* 1(1–2):15–31.

GEERTZ, C.
1963   *Agricultural involution: the process of ecological change in Indonesia.* Berkeley: University of California Press.

GOODY, J.
1971   *Technology, tradition and the state of Africa.* London: Oxford University Press.

GOUROU, P.
1966   *Les pays tropicaux: principes d'une géographie humaine et economique* Paris: Presses Universitaires de France. (Also published in English. *The tropical world.* Longmans. 1959.)

GRINDAL, B. I.
1973   Islamic affiliations and urban adaptation: the Sisala migrant in Accra, Ghana. *Africa* 43(4):333–346.

GUTHE, C. E., M. MEAD
1945   *Manual for the study of food habits. Report of the Committee on Food Habits.* Bulletin of the National Research Council 3. Washington: National Academy of Sciences.

GYÖRGY, P., KLINE, O. L.
1970   Malnutrition is a problem of ecology. *Bibliotheca Nutritio et Dieta* 14. Basel: Karger.

HARDY, G., CH. RICHET FILS, J. VASSAL
1933   *L'alimentation indigène dans les colonies françaises.* Paris: Vigot Frères.

HARRIS, D. R.
1969   "Agricultural systems, ecosystems and the origin of agriculture," in *The domestication and exploitation of plants and animals.* Edited by P. J. Ucko and G. M. Dimbleby. London: Duckworth.

HUIZER, G.
1973   *Peasant rebellion in Latin America.* Harmondsworth, Middlesex: Penguin Books.

Indicative World Plan (IWP) for agricultural development
1970   *Indicative World Plan (IWP) for agricultural development. A synthesis and analysis of factors relevant to world, regional and national agricultural development.* Rome: FAO.

JELLIFFE, D. B.
1968   *Infant nutrition in the sub-tropic and tropics.* Geneva: WHO.

JONES, S. M.
1963   *A study of Swazi nutrition.* Durban: Institute of Social Research, University of Natal.

KILBY, P.
1965   Patterns of bread consumption in Nigeria. *Food Research Institute Studies* 5(1):3–18.

KING, M.
1966   *Medical care in developing countries.* London: Oxford University Press.

KNUTSSON, K. E., T. MELLBIN
1969   Breastfeeding habits and cultural context. *Journal of Tropical Pediatrics* 15(2):40–49.

KNUTSSON, K. E., R. SELINUS
  1970   Fasting in Ethiopia, an anthropological and nutritional study. *American Journal of Clinical Nutrition* 23(7):956–969.

KNUTSSON, K. E., B. VAHLQUIST
  1968   Medicine and social anthropology, some notes on a joint attack on nutrition problems in Ethiopia. *Acta Universitas Upsaliensis* 17:376–390.

KRAUT, H., H. D. CREMER
  1969   *Investigations into health and nutrition in East Africa.* Afrika Studien 42. Munich: IFO.

LA COSTE, Y.
  1960   *Les pays sous-développés.* Paris: Presses Universitaires de France.

LEACH, E.
  1970   *Lévi-Strauss.* London: Fontana.

LEWIN, K.
  1943   "Forces behind food habits and methods of change," in *The problem of changing food habits. Report of the Committee on Food Habits.* Edited by C. Guthe and M. Mead. Bulletin of the National Research Council 108. Washington: National Academy of Sciences.

MANGIN, W.
  1967   Squatter settlements. *Scientific American* 217(14):21–29.

MC COLLUM, E. V.
  1957   *A history of nutrition.* Boston: Houghton Mifflin.
  1960   "From Hopkins to the present," in *Human nutrition historic and scientific.* Edited by I. Galdston, 111–142. New York: International University Press.

MC KENZIE, J. C.
  1964   "Food trends: the dynamics of accomplished change," in *Changing food habits.* Edited by J. Yudkin and J. C. McKenzie. London: Macgibbon and Kee.

MEAD, M.
  1962   "Culture change in relation to nutrition," in *Malnutrition and food habits. Report of an international and interprofessional conference.* Edited by A. Burgess and R. F. A. Dean. London: Tavistock.

MINTZ, AHMED J. J., A. G. VAN VEEN
  1968   A sociological approach to a dietary survey and food habits survey and food habits study in an Andean community. *Tropical Geographical Medicine* 20(8):88–100.

MÖNCKEBERG, F.
  1966   "Programs for combatting malnutrition in the pre-school child in Chile," in *Pre-school child malnutrition, primary deterrent to human progress.* Washington: National Academy of Sciences, National Research Council.

MURDOCH, C. P., C. S. FORD, A. E. HUDSON, R. KENNEDY, L. W. SIMMONS, J. W. M. WHITING
  1950   *Outline of cultural materials.* New Haven: Human Relations Area Files.

Notes and queries on anthropology
1954   (revised and rewritten by a Committee of the Royal Anthropological Institute of Great Britain and Ireland). London: Routledge and Kegan Paul.

NATIONAL INSTITUTE OF NUTRITION
1971   *Annual report.* Tokyo.

Nutrition in the colonial empire
1939   *Nutrition in the colonial empire.* London: H. M. S. O.

OLUWASANMI, H. A., *et al.*
1966   *Uboma, the world land-use survey.* Occasional Paper 6. Berkamstead, Herts.: Geographical Publications.

OOMEN, H. P. A. C.
1971   Ecology of human nutrition in nutrition. *Ecology of Food and Nutrition* 1(1):3–18.

ORR, E.
1972   *The use of protein-rich foods for the relief of malnutrition in developing countries: an analysis of experience.* London: Tropical Products Institute.

ORR, J. B.
1936   *Food, health and income.* London: Macmillan.

PYKE, M.
1968   *Food and society.* London: John Murray.

READ, M.
1966   *Culture, health and disease.* London: Tavistock Publications.

RICHARDS, A. I.
1939   *Land, labour and diet in Northern Rhodesia.* London: Oxford University Press.

RICHARDS, A. I., E. M. WIDDOWSON
1936   A dietary study in N.E. Rhodesia. *Africa* 9(2):166–196.

ROBERTS, R.
1973   *The classic slum, Salford life in the first quarter of the century.* Harmondsworth, Middlesex: Penguin Books.

SALAMAN, R. N.
1949   *The history and social influence of the potato.* Cambridge: University Press.

SANJUR, D., J. I. CRAVIOTO, A. G. VAN VEEN
1970   Infant nutrition and sociocultural influences in a village in Central Mexico. *Tropical Geographical Medicine* 22:443–451.

SANTOS, M.
1967   L'Alimentation des populations urbaines des pays sous-dévelopés. *Revue Tiermonde* 8(31):605–116.

SCHAFFER, B. B.
1973   Comments on problems in studies of development administration. *Administrative Science Quarterly* 18(1):109–116.

SCHNELL, R.
1957   *Plantes alimentaires et vie agricole de l'Afrique noire.* Paris: Larose.

SIMOONS, F. J.
1962   *Eat not this flesh, food avoidances in the Old World.* Wisconsin: Madison University Press.

SOUTHALL, A. W., P. C. W. GUTKIND
  1957   *Townsmen in the making.* Kampala: East African Institute.
VERDOORN, J. A.
  1965   *Volksgezondheid en sociale ontwikkeling* [Public health and social development]. Utrecht: Het Spectrum.
WALTER, J. P.
  1973   Internal-external poverty and nutritional determinants of urban slum youth. *Ecology of Food and Nutrition* 2(1):3–10.
WENNEN VAN DER MEY, C. A. M.
  1969   The decline of breast-feeding in Nigeria. *Tropical Geographical Medicine* 21:93–96.
WOOD, A. I.
  1955   The history of artificial feeding of infants. *Journal of the American Dietetic Association* 31(5):474–482.
YOUNGS, A. J.
  1973   Wheat flour and bread consumption in West Africa: a review with special reference to Ghana. *Tropical Science* 14(3):235–244.

Anthropology, Government, and Developmental Planning in India

H. M. MATHUR

In India, government interest in the contribution of anthropology to development problems has grown noticeably over the past few years. In delivering the chairman's address to a seminar on "The tribal situation in India" held at Simla recently, M. N. Srinivas (1972: 27) observed:

From the little I know of the Government of India and its functioning I find today sharply increased awareness of the importance and urgency of associating sociologists and anthropologists in the solution of the many complex and baffling problems which confront the country today.

And a British anthropologist, F. G. Bailey (1962: 254) finds that

... at the present time anthropologists in India whether Indian or foreign are considered an asset by the Administration and their books are read and their point of view considered even by their fellow intellectuals in other disciplines. No research team is complete without someone to put the anthropological point of view, and no welfare organization feels itself properly constituted unless it has someone carrying on social research for the purposes of planning or evaluation.

This should be a matter of no small satisfaction to the anthropologists when considered alongside the fact that in many newly-emerging nations, particularly in Africa, their colleagues are not thought of so highly.[1]

India, in fact, has had a long tradition of utilizing anthropological knowledge in administrative actions and policies directed toward improving the living conditions of its aboriginal peoples. In the pre-

---

[1] In this connection, see Onwuachi and Wolfe (1966).

independence era, administrators found anthropology of considerable use to them in implementing several government programs, and a few among them (including Risley, Dalton, Ibbetson, Crooke, Thurston, Russell, Mills, and Hutton) even carried out extensive ethnographic researches on their own. All this has also helped, to an extent, to make today's planners and administrators more receptive to the contributions of anthropology.

There are, in addition, some other factors that would seem to be particularly conducive to the utilization of anthropology in government-directed developmental activity. In the first place, planning for economic growth and social change presupposes a thorough understanding of the sociocultural profile of the country. In India, with its sharply contrasting ethnic, linguistic, religious, and other sizable heterogenous population groups, the need for planners to have the necessary facts at their command becomes even more urgent. Anthropologists who make studies in these areas can evidently be relied upon to provide this material for the planners. Secondly, the planning effort that seeks to achieve rapid economic and sociocultural modernization of all peoples (with special emphasis on the development of tribal areas) surely requires expertise that derives directly from anthropological researches into the problems of sociocultural dynamics. Moreover, planned development in India has fascinated many anthropologists, and the fast-proliferating literature on change in India's tribal and village life should very much interest the planners and administrators. And lastly, anthropology in India has matured into a fairly well-established discipline now, so that the anthropologists who could be trained to work for development are not in short supply.

What, in the face of these apparently abundant opportunities, have anthropologists contributed to the process of planned development initiated in India by the government over the past two decades? In what ways can the contribution of anthropology to development now be made more purposeful? How is this participation in development viewed by the anthropologists themselves? These are questions that should interest the anthropologist as much as the planner. It should surely be worthwhile to examine them.

But there is another aspect to this problem, to wit, the role of the government in promoting the use of anthropological knowledge in its development programs. In order to have a clear perspective on the issues concerning the role of anthropology in development, it would be useful first to review briefly all that the government has been doing to involve anthropologists in this process.

RESEARCH IN AID OF PLANNING

Since the dawn of planning, development planners in India have pursued the policy of encouraging social research, the results of which it was hoped might facilitate and help to accelerate the adjustments to new conditions arising in the rural and tribal areas in the wake of changes implanted in their traditional concepts and practices — in community and cooperative organization, education, nutrition, family pattern, medicine, and public health. As part of this policy, they have therefore given new directions to the activities of the research institutions already existing and have set up others specifically for conducting research of an applied nature. Some of the institutions are briefly described below.

1. THE CENSUS OF INDIA   This is the oldest organization providing useful sociological data. It celebrated its centenary in 1971. Keeping the planner's interest in view, the census of India has now considerably expanded its research operations. Following the last decennial census in 1961, the census organization employed some anthropologically-trained researchers specifically for producing a series of village studies. Irma Adelman and George Dalton (1971) recently used these data in a highly sophisticated study of microdevelopment in India. George Dalton (1971: 7) made this comment on their utility:

We hope that the result is judged to be sufficiently promising to encourage departments of planning and statistics in Third World countries to emulate the Government of India in collecting hard data series on village communities.

2. ANTHROPOLOGICAL SURVEY OF INDIA   Established in 1948 on a permanent basis, the Anthropological Survey of India has functioned in one form or another, with interruptions, for some time. The inception of this institution actually goes back to 1905, when an ethnographic survey was launched under the direction of Risley.[2] Today the Anthropological Survey is the largest government-supported anthropological research organization of its kind in the world. Its wide-ranging publications include many that should be of particular interest to the planners.

3. TRIBAL RESEARCH INSTITUTES   A prerequisite for executing the development schemes successfully in the tribal areas is a thorough under-

---

[2]   A fuller account will be found in Majumdar (1948).

standing of the tribal way of life. With the purpose of sharpening this understanding for planning purposes, in the course of the past fifteen years or so a chain of tribal research institutes has been set up in all states that have pockets of tribal concentration. These research centers (located in Assam, Bihar, Gujerat, Madhya Pradesh, Maharashtra, Nagaland, NEFA [North East Frontier Agency], Orissa, Rajasthan, and West Bengal) occasionally bring out, in addition to their regular bulletins, useful research publications on various aspects of tribal life.

4.   NATIONAL INSTITUTE OF COMMUNITY DEVELOPMENT   The planned programs of change in village life which began in 1952 had need of sociological research support. The National Institute of Community Development (NICD) was created to meet exactly this specific need. Action-oriented research conducted here on a wide range of development problems has the primary aim of discovering ways by which rural populations might be persuaded to accept the recommended innovations. In recent years the Institute has been bringing out useful publications on the strategy of promoting change in agricultural practices, family planning methods, and other aspects of rural life. It also publishes a quarterly journal, *Behavioural Sciences and Community Development.*

5.   RESEARCH PROGRAMMES COMMITTEE   Over a period of about twenty years, this committee of the government of India's Planning Commission has contributed importantly to the production of valuable research by funding several research projects of the anthropologists attached to the universities and other institutions of higher learning. Without this financial backing, the academic centers would perhaps not have been able to undertake many of their useful research schemes.

6.   INDIAN COUNCIL OF SOCIAL SCIENCE RESEARCH   These functions of the Research Programmes Committe (RPC) were taken over by the Indian Council of Social Science Research (ICSSR) when it came into existence in 1968. The ICSSR has recently sponsored a large research project involving study of the development needs of tribal populations in various states. The results of these studies are expected to provide material for formulating programs of development in the tribal areas during the period of India's fifth Five-Year Plan (1974–1979).

UTILIZATION OF ANTHROPOLOGY

Government support to anthropological studies has the simple objective of making it possible to plan and implement the development programs in the light of research experience. The ways in which it is sought to achieve this objective are several, and by now are clearly identifiable.

First, the development administration is well served by the results of anthropological researches made available by the institutions created specifically for this purpose. The planners are additionally benefited by the researches conducted by (a) the Programme Evaluation Organization (PEO) attached to the Planning Commission and (b) the anthropologists on their own, as part of their study of the sociocultural change process.

Sometimes, government specially consults the anthropologists for their expert advice on particular development problems. A case in point is the study by Oscar Lewis (1954) of factionalism in a north Indian village. Reports made by visiting missions[3] that include anthropologists also provide useful information to the planners.

Anthropologists are often included in the working groups set up by the Planning Commission to recommend policy measures and plans of action for tribal areas, development of rural areas, forestry, cooperatives, etc. The planning process also profits a good deal from associating anthropologists with special commissions set up periodically for suggesting improvements in the implementation of particular development programs. A committee appointed to examine the functioning of the Special Multipurpose Tribal Blocks was headed by a noted anthropologist, Verrier Elwin (1960). He was also associated with the Scheduled Areas and Scheduled Tribes Commission which was appointed under Article 339 of the Indian Constitution.[4] Currently Sachidananda, an anthropologist, is a member of the panel of sociologists attached to the Indian National Commission on Agriculture.

Anthropologists are also represented on the Central Advisory Board for Tribal Affairs, which came into existence in 1958. This is a forum in which their participation can and does influence governmental thinking on policy and action aspects of tribal development.

Development administration is further helped by the fact that a large number of anthropologists are employed in several training institutions and program-executing agencies. In fact, the prerequisite for qualifying for jobs in several agencies (for example, in the office of the Commissioner for Scheduled Castes and Scheduled Tribes) is a degree in anthropology.

[3]   An example is Adams, Foster, and Taylor (1955).
[4]   This Commission (1960–1961) submitted its *Report* in 1961 (1962).

IMPACT ON THE DEVELOPMENT PROCESS

It is obvious that government has done a good deal both to assist the production of anthropological research and to ensure its effective utilization in the development process. The question that arises now is: what has been the impact on the development process of the anthropologists' participation? Have they been able to help the planners and administrators materially to speed the achievement of the planned socio-cultural and economic changes?

The question of the eventual outcome of the anthropologists' involvement in the development endeavor has indeed much to do with the considerations that go into the decision making. It is important to note that in determining any development goal or planning strategy anthropology can be only one among the several interacting factors. Quite obviously it is not the only determinant of the policy line or course of action. Despite this constraint, anthropology in India has been able to add some dimension to development policy and action.

Role in the Policy Making

On the basis of his researches among the Baigas, a tribe inhabiting central India, Verrier Elwin (1939) once suggested that to ensure development of these people it was essential to insulate them temporarily against contact with outsiders, who all along had been exploiting them in various ways. This observation gave rise to a heated debate. Branding the anthropologists as a group intent on keeping the tribal people tribal for the sake of their researches, many, including some social scientists,[5] then proposed that the tribal peoples instead be totally assimilated into the Indian society. Though the isolation-versus-assimilation controversy is now over and anthropologists are no longer accused of wanting to keep the tribal people in a zoo, the controversy gave anthropology a great setback. For a long time anthropologists were thought not fit to be consulted on tribal matters.

It is to the anthropologists' credit that not only have they since regained the ground lost, but they have also made some positive advances. The government policy toward the tribal people laid down by the late Prime Minister of India, Nehru,[6] was to a great extent influ-

[5] G. S. Ghurye, a sociologist, in his book *The aborigines so-called and their future* (1943), argues for the complete assimilation of tribal groups in the Indian society. This book has now reappeared under the title, *The scheduled tribes.*
[6] The principles that should guide development in tribal areas were spelled out by Nehru in the second edition of Elwin's *A philosophy for NEFA* (1959).

enced by the views of an anthropologist, Verrier Elwin. Referring to the influence of Elwin on his thinking concerning this subject, Nehru (1957) confessed that:

I have learnt much from him, for he is both an expert on this subject with great experience of tribal life and my own views, vague as they were, have developed under the impact of certain circumstances and of Verrier Elwin's own writings.

But apart from tribal life, there is no other major sphere where anthropology could contribute very significantly to policy formation. With their studies of the changing rural scene, anthropologists might have been in a good position to help shape development policy for rural areas, but they do not seem to have done much.

Effect on the Implementation Side

In the execution of the development plans, the contribution of anthropology has not been very notable. It is true that many anthropologists are employed in the government, but a large number of officials who are supposed to carry out the policy at the grass-roots level are not adequately equipped for the job. The critical importance of training in anthropology and social sciences is still not appreciated at all levels. Naturally such unawareness results in faulty implementation of otherwise wisely-formulated plans. Speaking of the community development program in the tribal areas, von Fürer-Haimendorf (1967) has pointed out how, in the absence of knowledge of local conditions, things could go awry:

Thus, houses were built but people would not live in them, roads were built only to be washed away in the rainy season, basketry centres started where there were no bamboos, and bee-keeping [was] established where there were no flowers . . .

In his view, the implementation of development, on the whole, does not receive as much attention as its planning:

It would appear that the provisions for the welfare of the tribes are strong on the constitutional and planning sides, but weak on the executive side. The concern of the Government of India and of Parliament for the rights and progress of the tribes is admirable, but by the time measures decided upon at the centre have filtered down to state and district level, their impact is often weakened or outright lost. In all the reports of the Commissioner for Scheduled Castes and Scheduled Tribes, the Planning Commission, and other bodies concerned with tribal affairs, there is the repeated complaint that the staff and administrative machinery provided by the states is not adequate to carry out the policy of the centre, even if the necessary funds are voted by Parliament (von Fürer-Haimendorf 1967).

In states where implementation is given due importance, things have been moving as they should. When he revisited NEFA recently after some years, von Fürer-Haimendorf found the development policy for the tribal people there to be helping them greatly in the manner intended.[7]

Overall, this account of the anthropological contribution to developmental planning in India does not look very impressive. It is possible that the involvement of anthropologists in all decisions affecting agriculture, education, population control problems, communication, medicine, and public health may not have been thought so very vital. But the fact must be faced that anthropology in the present stage of its development in India does not have much to offer. Anthropologists themselves are realizing that, owing partly to their own inadequacies, they have not been able to accomplish all that they had set out to achieve. S. C. Dube (1971: 89–90), who has had a long association with the government developmental planning machinery, is perhaps correct in his estimation that:

As an organized profession they have done little more than pass platitudinous resolutions making claims for their disciplines which were never demonstrated in the shape of concrete accomplishments. They did take up a number of sponsored research projects, some of which yielded valuable data and adequate analysis, but a large number of these exercises were carried out in a mechanical way and their results were uninspiring. The operational suggestions they contained were all too often simplistic or trite. The strategy of policy-oriented research lacked focus and coordination, and the low prestige assigned to it by the academics resulted in much inferior work. With imaginative direction there could have been much better utilization of available resources.

NEEDED CHANGES IN GOVERNMENT

The difficulties of implementing policies with staff who are not fully

---

[7]   Christoph von Fürer-Haimendorf (1972), reporting his experiences in Nagaland and NEFA, says, "I should like to conclude this account of my impressions ... by expressing my admiration for the spirit of understanding and service which I found among all the officials engaged in the administration of these regions. It is undoubtedly due to their efforts and motivation that the situation of the people of Nagaland and NEFA is far better than that of the tribal population of any other region of India of which I have personal knowledge."

equipped are all known very well. Von Fürer-Haimendorf (1967) says:

The Planning Commission has clearly recognised the problem of finding suitable personnel for tribal development work, and in the Third Five Year Plan the suggestion has been put forward that the Central Government and state governments should cooperate in forming a special cadre comprising technical and other personnel for work in Scheduled Areas. The most significant aspect of such a policy would be that a body of trained persons would spend their entire period of service among the tribal people, so that their knowledge, experience and sense of identification would become a vital factor in assuring rapid and uninterrupted service.

A similar proposal was also made in the fourth Five-Year Plan. But the trouble is that such ideas do not get translated into action, as a former member of the Planning Commission, V. K. R. V. Rao rightly thought "because of apprehensions that members of the cadre, particularly the officials, may not like to be tied down to tribal areas for the entire life-time" (1969: 198). The start in this direction, which has long been overdue, is therefore not being made. About the doubts of those to be included in this cadre, possibly something can be done. As V. K. R. V. Rao (1969: 198–199) himself put it:

It should be possible to allay the fears by restricting the period of direct service in tribal areas to a limited period of five to seven years, widening the area for recruitment, and providing sufficient incentives for attracting persons of good calibre and right spirit. Since tribal development has ceased to be a mere localised effort, officials who have done their tenure in tribal areas could be assigned supervisory, administrative and planning positions at the Central and State levels. This might help to offset what is felt as the hardship of service in tribal areas and promote better recruitment to the special cadre for service in tribal areas. It could also lead to better planning of tribal development at the central and state levels because of the presence of officers with first-hand knowledge and experience of having served in the tribal areas.

For anthropologists seeking jobs in the government, career opportunities are thus very limited. Those who value academic freedom do not feel encouraged to join the government service. In fact, government jobs are not usually preferred by them. Quoting from the report of the Commissioner for Scheduled Castes and Scheduled Tribes, Stephen Fuchs (1969: 71) says:

The Commissioner for Scheduled Castes and Scheduled Tribes, in his Report for 1963–64, complains that "there is a dearth of properly qualified and experienced persons for manning the newly created posts." ... This scarcity of trained personnel is, however, due not to the unavailability of trained anthropologists in India but, as the Commissioner himself pointed out in his Report, to the fact "that pay-scales offered are not attractive enough...." Such factors deter competent anthropologists from joining these institutes, and they prefer more lucrative congenial posts elsewhere.

Surely something needs to be done to improve matters here.

Changes desired in development administration would also come about more rapidly if the training capability of the National Institute of Community Development and the various tribal research institutes were improved. There are two things that need to be done first in this connection. One, more officials must become sensitive to the human aspects of development at these centers than has been the case so far. Two, the quality of training must be greatly improved. Of course, the development agencies would then ensure that none of their trained staff who were competent were shifted to jobs elsewhere.

Also, government would get higher returns from expenditure on research conducted through its own organizations if all agencies were to coordinate their efforts more meaningfully. It would be futile, for example, to mount research on the same problems at all the institutes. Also, effort must be directed toward wider dissemination of research findings among the officials and development agencies concerned.

Finally, things would improve very considerably if the anthropologists were more closely associated with the decision-making process at the highest levels of the government.

MAKING ANTHROPOLOGY MORE RELEVANT

These suggested changes in the government would not by themselves bring about overall improvement in the situation. There have to be corresponding changes in the profession of anthropology also. Anthropology can genuinely help to accelerate the development process only if attention is devoted to some of the following aspects:

1.   In the first place, action-oriented research need not be regarded by the academics as something not worthy of their attention. At the present moment, for most of them developmental planning still seems to hold little or no attraction, and, as Pocock (1968: 288–289) observes:

There is little sign that academic social anthropologists have recognised that their place is with the planner.... It is by no means required of the academic anthropologist that he approve the plan or even planning as such.

His precise opposition may well be as valuable as his collaboration; in my case it is collaboration. Academic social anthropology in India is not expected to work for this or that particular end of the plan, but it can be expected to take cognizance of it and to realize that planning is as much a part of Indian society as caste.

2.   Anthropologists in India tend to think of their action role in the context of tribal affairs only. Development actually must be seen to embrace all areas of human life. It is, in fact, necessary to identify relevant issues in development clearly if the research effort is to proceed in the right direction. The really challenging problems in India today are poverty, unemployment, inequality, high rate of population growth, and low productivity generally. But not all of these problems seem to be attracting much of the attention of the anthropologists. An understanding of the sociocultural dimensions of these problems can indeed be helpful in planning the programs more realistically.

3.   It is important for the anthropologists to try to communicate with development planners and administrators more frequently. By keeping aloof, anthropologists only render themselves less useful. Developmental planning is basically an interdisciplinary field. Anthropologists should therefore participate increasingly in projects involving sociologists, economists, public administration specialists, communication experts and others.

4.   Lastly, there should be an effort to present research findings in a language that the administrators may understand. If many of the books by anthropologists that have grown out of action research done at government expense are any indication, it is clear that anthropologists normally prefer to address themselves to their own professional colleagues. This should change.

COLLABORATION WITH DEVELOPMENT PLANNERS AND ADMINISTRATORS

But the proposal to give anthropology a further applied slant is not likely to be greeted with enthusiasm by anthropologists. There is already a strong feeling that the conduct of research through government funding not only jeopardizes academic freedom, but also makes a heavy demand on the scarce manpower available for investigating fundamental questions. M. N. Srinivas (1960) expressed his fears thus:

There is a danger here which must be pointed out if sociology and social anthropology are not to take a wrong direction. The Government of India has an understandable tendency to stress the need for sociological research that is directly related to planning and development. And it is the duty of sociologists as citizens that they should take part in such research. But there is a grave risk that "pure" or "fundamental" research might be sacrificed altogether. We are not so rich in our human resources that we can afford to have our few sociologists all doing applied research.

On the other hand, the development planners would naturally want more applied research done to facilitate their task. For them this obviously has the greatest importance. As Elwin (1964: 142) put it:

... in India at the present time, when, as a result of the great Five-Year Plans, the tribal people are being very rapidly changed and merged into ordinary society, I believe that we should put every possible anthropologist and sociologist into the work of guiding development and training its agents.

Their duty as citizens is certainly recognized by anthropologists. In a seminar on "Urgent research in social anthropology," Berreman, Dube, von Fürer-Haimendorf, Vidyarthi, Fuchs, and Edward Jay, among others, stressed the need to take the practical side into account, as when Berreman (1969: 43) said:

Ours is the science of man; it cannot ignore human relevance. I am simply making the point that in all of our research and writing and teaching we should exercise the sociological imagination to the limit of our abilities lest we become a science of man irrelevant to man.

The fact remains, however, that the research sponsored by the government for practical uses does result in the neglect of basic research on problems which for the anthropologist may be of crucial importance. Von Fürer-Haimendorf (1969: 78) stresses this point thus:

For the administrator and the politician many of the most primitive populations are of comparatively little interest. Their numbers are small and they are unlikely to cause any disturbances of which governments would have to take note. In this respect they differ greatly from such substantial tribal groups as Nagas, Mizos, or Santals. Those expected to apply anthropological knowledge to the solution of contemporary problems have therefore little incentive to spend much time and energy on the study of such small tribal communities. Yet, it is just the most primitive groups which most easily lose their individuality and are absorbed within more advanced ethnic groups. Their study is hence even more urgent than that of the bigger tribes which have a better chance to maintain at least some aspects of their traditional way of life.

The conflict between the anthropologist's role as citizen and as scientist should not, however, be altogether irreconcilable. Even in government-sponsored research there should be opportunities for the promotion of scientific objectives. On the other hand, the pursuit of anthropology for anthropology's sake cannot be the sole cherished goal of everybody who is attracted to the study of man. Indeed, the participation of anthropologists in the development endeavor should be useful both to them and to their country alike.

REFERENCES

ADAMS, H. S., G. M. FOSTER, R. P. S. TAYLOR
1955   *Report on community development programs in India, Pakistan, and the Philippines.*

ADELMAN, IRMA, GEORGE DALTON
1971   "A factor analysis of modernization in village India," in *Economic development and social change.* Edited by George Dalton. New York: Natural History Press.

BAILEY, F. G.
1962   "The scope of social anthropology in the study of Indian society," in *Indian anthropology.* Edited by T. N. Madan and Gopala Sarana. Bombay: Asia Publishing House.

BERREMAN, GERALD D.
1969   "Urgent anthropology in India," in *Urgent research in social anthropology.* Edited by Behari L. Abbi and Satish Saberwal. Simla: IIAS.

DALTON, GEORGE
1971   *Economic anthropology and development.* New York: Basic Books.

DUBE, S. C.
1971   *Explanation and management of change.* New Delhi: Tata McGraw-Hill.

ELWIN, VERRIER
1939   *The Baiga.* London: John Murray.
1959   *A philosophy for NEFA* (second edition). Shillong.
1960   *Report of the Committee on Special Multipurpose Tribal Blocks.* New Delhi: Ministry of Home Affairs.
1964   *The tribal world of Verrier Elwin.* Bombay: Oxford University Press.

FUCHS, STEPHEN
1969   "Urgent anthropological research in middle India," in *Urgent research in social anthropology.* Edited by Behari L. Abbi and Satish Saberwal. Simla: IIAS.

GHURYE, G. S.
1943   *The aborigines so-called and their future.* Bombay: Popular Book Depot.

LEWIS, OSCAR
  1954   *Group dynamics in a north Indian village.* New Dehli: Planning Commission, Government of India.
MAJUMDAR, N. D.
  1948   Department of Anthropology, Government of India. *American Anthropologist* 50:578–581.
NEHRU, JAWAHARLAL
  1957   "Foreword," in *A philosophy for NEFA.* By Verrier Elwin. Shillong.
ONWUACHI, P. CHIKE, ALVIN W. WOLFE
  1966   The place of anthropology in the future of Africa. *Human Organization* 25:93–95.
POCOCK, DAVID
  1968   "Social anthropology: its contribution to planning," in *The crisis of Indian planning.* Edited by Michael Lipton. London: Oxford University Press.
RAO, V. K. R. V.
  1969   "Social change and the tribal culture," in *Conflict, tension and cultural trend in India.* Edited by L. P. Vidyarthi. Calcutta: Punthi Pustak.
Scheduled Areas and Scheduled Tribes Commission
  1962   *Report of the Scheduled Areas and Scheduled Tribes Commission.* Delhi: Manager of Publications.
SRINIVAS, M. N.
  1960   "Editor's introduction," in *India's villages.* Edited by M. N. Srinivas. Bombay: Asia.
  1972   "Chairman's address," in *Tribal situation in India.* Edited by K. Suresh Singh, 25–27. Simla: IIAS.
VON FÜRER-HAIMENDORF, C.
  1967   "The position of tribal populations in modern India," in *India and Ceylon: unity and diversity.* Edited by Philip Mason, 182–222. New York: Oxford University Press.
  1969   "Fundamental research in Indian anthropology," in *Urgent research in social anthropology.* Edited by Behari L. Abbi and Satish Saberwal. Simla: IIAS.
  1972   Recent developments in Nagaland and NEFA. *Asian Affairs, Journal of the Royal Central Asian Society* 59 (February).

Rural Participation in Planning

CARL WIDSTRAND

TWO SCENES FROM A RURAL MILIEU

Scene One

It is a hot day at the end of the dry season. The scene is a small village, red-dusty, waiting for the minister and visitors, who were due to arrive at 9:30. It is now a quarter past four. Two men are sleeping under a tree. The resident anthropologist is sitting under another tree, reading Franz Fanon. Two boys are playing with a blue ball (a gift from UNICEF — United Nations Children's Fund). There is a faint smell of cashew nuts and stale beer. Nothing is really happening.

Suddenly a cloud of dust down the road; the cortege arrives. The two men wake up, the Peace Corps volunteer runs down the village street trying to organize the spontaneous reception. Three Land Rovers and two Mercedes arrive, bringing the minister (actually only the assistant) and the visitors, in well-polished, pointed shoes. After twenty minutes the school choir is assembled and some fifteen members of the village. Song, welcome speech, and delivery of forty-five shillings and sixty cents as the village contribution to the local Institute of Science and Technology (the minister has specially asked to have cash, as most of the checks so far presented have tended to bounce). Speech: work hard, don't be lazy, don't drink, the government will help you. Song. Departure. Everything is as before.

Scene Two

Fifty naked tribesmen, with beautiful headdresses of clay and ostrich plumes, are seated on small stools, their spears stuck in the earth beside them; lip plugs and nose-leaves of aluminum tinkle faintly; there is a slow humming of voices and a smell of cow dung, goats, and humanity. The district commissioner is having a *baraza* in his regalia of office — khaki uniform and sun helmet wrapped in the Kenyan colors. Speech in Swahili, translated by the chief (who had 4,000 acres under wheat last year and whom the breweries have talked into growing barley this year): Don't be lazy, you must pay taxes, stop raiding across the border, stay on this side of the river with your cattle — and, by the way, why don't you settle somewhere instead of running around with your cattle all over the place? Any questions? Long silence (the laity is really not expected to talk, nor even to listen, only to turn up and sit). Someone slowly says that the grazing during the month of hunger and the month of dust has always been on the other side of the river. The district commissioner responds: only during the month of the happy goats do we come back here. You must learn to obey your government and their regulations. Departure of Land Rovers in a cloud of dust and exhaust fumes. Tribesmen slowly assemble their herds and move across the river.

These meetings took place within the last year. I have chosen these examples so as to have a point of departure when talking about participation. Participation is, of course, one of those words universally revered throughout the Third World. (Like development, socialism, planning cooperation and nation building, they occupy a special place in the proclamations of developing countries.) PARTICIPATION, being the sweetest of all the words in that vocabulary of public policy, sugars many a pill and is put to a great variety of uses (closely followed by the word cooperation).

I would like to restrict my comments to local participation in planning, because I think that that is an area where the word is used very often and where indeed the participation is crucial: TO PARTICIPATE IN DECISIONS ABOUT ONE'S OWN FUTURE.

As may have been apparent from the examples, there is not much participation, or, indeed, INTELLIGIBLE COMMUNICATION between various groups. Their ways of looking at the same problem (productivity, overgrazing) may be so different as to make it difficult for each to grasp the substance or the importance of what the other is talking about. Yet we hear about participation and the necessity of participation in the development-planning process both from the people and from the various ranks of the leadership. But, for a variety of reasons, a lot of planning takes place without implementation. The planning comes from the top downwards; there is little contact between planners and local politicians. This is one aspect of the very difficult problem of communication BETWEEN THE CENTER AND THE PERIPHERY.

Another is the difficulty of the contact between planners and top-level administration and politicians, which is sometimes very time-consuming and laborious. Because so much effort and energy have gone into the planning and selling of a project to decision makers, there is a common tendency to conceive of a project as almost finished or implemented once the planning stage has been reached. Moreover, the middle-level administrators and, in Raymond Apthorpe's term, the "planistrators," who are supposed to implement the plans, are sometimes badly prepared to do that job, due to the legacy of the British Administrative Longhand and to outside pressures of various kinds from local interests on the administration.

We may look at this in another way and identify the reasons for nonimplementation as:

1. unrealistic target-setting (or overemphasis on comprehensive plans under conditions of comprehensive uncertainty);
2. fuzzy objectives and goals which make evaluation difficult and which create conflicting objectives, i.e. various parts of the plan are in conflict with each other. (Forced or increased sale of livestock may have negative effects on health and nutrition programs. To give an example: in the Kenyan rural-development program I was working with one of the stated goals is "to improve the quality of rural life." What does that mean? More fun? For whom? To make the elite stay? To make money? A new busline? To be able to get out of the place? More cows?);
3. regional overbidding in relation to available resources; and
4. planning documents and studies which stop short of detailed action proposals.

Another gap, which is of utmost importance to recognize, is in knowledge of local conditions. It is a technical problem, and not really a question of participation political or otherwise, and it should come much higher up in the planning process. Participation by the public and the administrators should take place in the context of knowledge of local conditions. Lack of such knowledge is very often the reason for the gap between the plan and the social/physical reality.

Let me continue with this last question and also look at THE STRUC-TURE in which the planning for rural development takes place.

Most ministries have some kind of gap somewhere in their hierarchy

— it is really only the administration (president, office of the president, regional commissioner, district commissioner, district officer, chief, subchief) that has an unbroken line of command all the way down to the local level. The ministry of finance and planning reaches down to the regional level (provincial planning officer, or PPO) and stops there. Central government institutions (e.g. agriculture, ministry of works) may serve as the prime initiators of innovations, while the PPO may do the effective planning, but neither is necessarily the most reliable participant. Central planning in Kenya is particularly difficult due to the wide variety of local and institutional environments within which the policy must function. The center in Nairobi also lacks a comprehensive intelligence system that can keep abreast of these conditions and the policies as they evolve (Holmquist 1970).

In order to have some kind of input at the other end, there has been created the district development committee (DDC), consisting of all the technical and administrative officers in the districts, as well as local politicians and members of the district council.

In some areas these committees function very well, but in most areas they seldom meet, and the principal members — the politicians — are likely not to attend. The DDC's were created to channel critical feedback and to generate legitimacy for planning by giving a voice to local politicians (which is as close as one can get to popular participation) and notables.

There are other reasons besides nonattendance by the politicians why the committees have not worked as well as had been hoped:
1.   There were no direct lines to Nairobi to clear up difficult questions.
2.   When efforts have been made to bridge the planning gap from the bottom this has sometimes been met by suspicion from the center (until the foreign donor representative, if there is a major project in the area, has used his leverage in Nairobi).
3.   Politicians have refused to attend because they were denied attendance and subsistence allowances.
4.   Politicians may prefer to criticize the decisions of administrators, and they would lose some ability to do this if they participated in these meetings.
5.   Politicians may have perceived, correctly or incorrectly, that the DDC's have very limited ability to influence the local decisions of the government. (For some of these points I am indebted to Robert Jackson 1970.)

Outside pressures on the DDC are another difficulty. Politicians naturally evaluate a policy in terms of what it may do for their constituencies. When the politics of resource allocation in an environment of scarcity has, as in many parts of Kenya, a strong kinship-geographical character, struggle is likely to be fairly intense, and this is also very apparent in the DDC meetings.

The COMPETENCE OF OFFICERS has already been mentioned. A contributing factor is often that they stay too short a time in any one district to learn its special features or problems. This is especially apparent in the outlying districts such as Turkana and West Pokot, and in the northeast. And whom do officers communicate with, "participate" with? In many cases, especially in self-help ventures, they cooperate with politicians and leaders — but politicians know that their financial contributions to self-help activities are important ways of purchasing political support at the local level by winning the respect and approval of those groups and communities which their contributions assist. The PATRON-CLIENT relationship forged by such contributions doubtless makes it very difficult for planners and other public officials to direct this facet of local self-help.

Another important group is that of the PROGRESSIVE FARMERS (with whom officers sometimes share a "niche"). And here we may identify another gap, that between the urban and the rural populations, namely the gap between the activists, the entrepreneurs, and the parochials at the local level.

To sum up, participation is rather nonexistent in Kenyan planning at the local level. Plans are civil servants' plans, and the inability to come to grips with the political nature of popular participation is obvious.

Thus, planning at the grass-roots level in Kenya is still largely a formal exercise which has not yet involved local citizens to any great extent or significantly affected local development activities, which take place in spite of planning. And this situation is not likely to change until planners themselves gain greater influence in the allocation of public goods and services in rural areas and elicit the preferences of local groups to guide allocation decisions. But this may open a Pandora's box of rural instability caused by excessive political claims and too few public goods and services to satisfy these claims. Perhaps planners and other public officials know this, and perhaps this is why popular rural participation in planning and public decision making may not get beyond the stage of rhetoric in Kenya (Jackson 1970).

REFERENCES

HOLMQUIST, FRANK
  1970   "Implementing rural development projects," in *Development administration — the Kenyan experience*. Edited by G. Hyden, R. Jackson, and John Okumu. Nairobi.
JACKSON, ROBERT
  1970   "Planning, politics and — administration," in *Development administration — the Kenyan experience*. Edited by G. Hyden, R. Jackson, and John Okumu. Nairobi.

Why Interdisciplinary Studies?

PAUL STREETEN

There are three quite distinct reasons for interdisciplinary, multidisciplinary, or supradisciplinary work. Each has different methodological implications. First, a practical problem (improving nutrition, locating an airport, controlling population growth, planning a town) may call for the application of several disciplines. In the cooperative effort the disciplines are not transcended but brought together to solve a particular set of practical problems. The prevalence of planning at all levels has contributed to the cooperation between different disciplines. The planner has to draw on all relevant knowledge and skills. This practical need to bring all relevant methods, data, and information to bear on the solution of a specific problem does not affect the methods used in the contributing disciplines. On the contrary, it is just because they are specialists in their fields that each of the different members of the team has a contribution to make to an integrated solution. We might think of them as members of a royal commission investigating problems of conserving our environment or deciding upon the location of a new airport or planning a new town.

Second, it may be the case that certain assumptions, concepts, or methods, hitherto applied only to one sphere of activity, yield illuminating results when applied to another sphere previously analyzed in quite different ways. There has been some invasion by economic concepts and methods into the territory of political scientists and sociologists. Thus, the assumption of maximizing behavior has been fruitful in analyzing the behavior of consumers, firms, and farms. Its success has encouraged its application to political activities, such as voting and party formation. Calculations of economic returns have been extended from profit-making investments to education, health, birth control, and the allocation of leisure time. Occasionally, although much less frequently, concepts used in political theory have been applied to economic problems. Hirschman's use of "voice" as an alternative to "exit" is an interesting example (Hirschman 1970).

Third, it may turn out that for a particular time or region the justification for having a separate discipline does not hold. This justification for a discipline consists in the empirical fact that between the variables encompassed by this discipline and those treated by another there are few interactions and the effects of any existing interaction are weak and damped. Only then are we justified in analyzing causal sequences in one field without always and fully taking into account those in others. We may all agree that society is a system and that all social variables are related, but, with growing differentiation of functions and standards, some relationships are stronger than others. This justifies our separation of business responses, for instance, from family responses or of economics from anthropology.

There is a case for a merger of disciplines, if the interdependence among variables normally studied separately is strong; or, if, the reaction coefficients, although weak, are large; or, if, although small, they change size for moves above a critical level. This merger is sometimes called transforming parameters into dependent variables. Family ties and economic calculus, land tenure and responses to incentives, and religious beliefs and commercial motivation may in this way interact. Where interdependence of this kind occurs and where the interdependent variables belong to different disciplines, there is a case for interdisciplinary work.

It is possible to draw two quite different conclusions from such interaction. First, it might be said that what is called for are not interdisciplinary studies but a new discipline that constructs concepts and builds models appropriate to the conditions of underdeveloped societies. In this case, we should have to discard concepts like employment, unemployment, underemployment, income, savings, and investment, and construct altogether new terms.

Second and less radically, the existing concepts and models may continue to be used, but their content may have to be changed or their definitions modified.

The difference can be illustrated with the concepts "capital" and "investment." Conventionally, "investment" is defined as the addition of physical pieces of equipment, plant, or stocks in order to raise the future flow of products or services above what it otherwise would have been. "Capital" is the stock of these items that has resulted from past flows minus depreciation through use and obsolescence.

Now it is possible to enlarge this concept so as to cover all forms of expenditure that lead to a larger flow of future output, not only those that result in physical items of machinery, constructions, or inventories. This would include "investment in human capital," such as education, health, and, at some levels, nutrition; it might possibly include expenditures on birth control, if we are concerned with raising income per capita, or expenditures on institution building and shaping attitudes. All this can, in principle, be covered by an enlarged concept of "capital" and "investment," as long as one condition is fulfilled: there must be a fairly systematic connection between the devotion of current resources (that might otherwise be used for current consumption) and the resulting flow of extra output. These resources need not be the only condition for the enlarged flow of output, but they must be systematically linked to this output by a fixed technical coefficient or at least by a range that is not too wide.

But if the link between current resources and extra ouput is only tenuous, so that a given result can be achieved with widely varying inputs or the same inputs can lead to widely varying results; or if the results can be achieved without devoting any current inputs; or, if, in spite of large current inputs, no results ensue — then the notions of "capital" and "investment" become inapplicable, and we have to focus on those factors on which the outcome truly depends. The output of a factory may be, within wide limits, a function of the degree of capacity utilization which, in turn, will depend upon the quality of the management; the result of a family planning program may be only tenuously linked to the money spent on clinics, doctors, nurses, and contraceptives but may depend largely upon the economic, social, cultural, and religious attitudes of couples. The quality of the administration, the system of land tenure, the solidarity between different classes, the ethnic origin of the entrepreneurs, and/or the history of the country may be more important determinants than the amount of resources. If this is so, no new wine can be poured into old bottles; the bottles themselves have to be changed.

In either case, we may, in the process of analyzing social phenomena in underdeveloped countries, incidentally gain new insights into those in advanced industrial countries. Studies of the caste system may illuminate trade union behavior and demarcation (jurisdiction) disputes; scrutiny of the capital/output ratio may change our view of the production function; a wider concept of capital may throw new light on our own problems of industrial management. If this happens it will be a bonus over and above what we had bargained for.

How then does anthropology fit into all this? In the first case, for interdisciplinary work — the team approach — anthropologists will be used for their traditional training. If a land reform, a birth control program, or a tourist project is proposed, they will be able to point to "constraints" in the beliefs and mores of the people, or they will be able to point to beliefs or institutions which can be mobilized and on which the proposed reforms or projects can be built. Nothing new or radical is required here.

The second case is more interesting. I suspect that economic methods could illuminate some anthropological work and probably the reverse is true too. While I know of some cross-disciplinary work of this kind between economics and political science, I do not know of any between economics and anthropology.

The most interesting possibilities are opened up by the third case, whether in its reformist or radical version. It is quite clear, for example, that an agricultural production function in many underdeveloped countries should count among its inputs, not only land, labor, fertilizers, water, and power but also the levels of education of the farmers, nutritional standards, distance from town, health, and systems of land tenure and of family kinship. All these variables are likely, in some societies, to be systematically related to agricultural production.

Still, while we stick to the notion of a "production function," a status-conscious anthropologist will complain that he is being used only to provide fodder for the canons of the economist. A self-respecting anthropologist might refuse to have all the important questions asked by the economist and to be reduced to a handmaiden, supplying low-class empirical material for the high-class analytical structure of another discipline. Questions of status and precedence are, of course, not of concern to serious scholars; on the contrary, Keynes looked forward to the day when economists would have become like mechanics, when they "could get themselves thought of as humble, competent people, on a level of dentists . . ." (Keynes 1933).

But it may turn out that the whole notion of a production function is wrong or misleading. Perhaps there is no systematic relationship between inputs, whether of fertilized land (physical capital) or of educated farmers (human capital). It may be that output depends upon variables that have been constructed and analyzed by anthropologists: the relationship between majority and minority groups, religious beliefs (the Protestant ethic), or kinship systems. Or again, at a different level of discourse, it may be that large increases in output beyond a decent minimum are not a crucial component of development either at this stage or any other. The society may have opted for an alternative style of development, in which the ever-growing production of material goods is rejected. It prefers containment of wants and aspirations to increased production to satisfy ever-growing wants and infinite aspirations. Or, through a shift in valuations, unemployment may be converted into leisure. If this is the case, the crucial questions will have to be asked by the anthropologist or the sociologist. Which of these possibilities should be realized will depend, partly, upon empirical conditions, but, ultimately, upon our valuations and our choice of a style of life.

REFERENCES

HIRSCHMAN, ALBERT O.
   1970   *Exit, voice and loyalty*. Cambridge: Harvard University Press.
KEYNES, JOHN MAYNARD
   1933   "Economic possibilities for our grandchildren," in *Essays in persuasion*. London: Macmillan.

Conflict and Change as Aspects of Development

BOGUSLAW GALESKI

The nineteenth-century scholars (sociologists or social scientists in general) used the concept of "development" to explain human history. Spencer, for instance, and Marx as well, thought humanity was moving from one lower stage to another higher stage. This movement was uni-directional, followed some general laws (laws of history), and each society has passed, is passing, or will pass through similar stages. The problem was: (1) how to define the stages and the most important differences between them; (2) how to define the factors which determined the rapidity with which a given society passed through any given stage (or even jumped over a given stage); and (3) how to define the sources of this movement and the universal mechanisms governing it. In other words, they sought to discover the general laws of such development.

This holistic and universalistic approach was usually accompanied by an optimistic view of human history. Even when some scholars idealized the "first" stage of human history, a majority of them thought that movement from one stage to the other would enrich human life; that life would be more differentiated, richer in both material and cultural aspects, more rational, etc.[1] The ideological connotations or emotions involved with the term development gave it a meaning close

The paper was completed during the author's stay in the United States under the United States Department of State Exchange Programs. I wish to express my appreciation to American colleagues — particularly from the Department of Rural Sociology, University of Wisconsin, Madison and from the Department of Sociology, Louisiana State University, Baton Rouge — whose critical reading of an earlier draft of this paper was most helpful.

[1] The sociological concept of development usually included both the idea of growth and the idea of development (differentiation of functions).

to the term "progress," and both terms were frequently used synony-
mously.

In the twentieth century, the evolutionists' point of view was abandoned by the majority of social scientists, and gradually such terms as
progress or development disappeared from sociological language.[2] The
term "social change" replaced them. The term social change implied
no ideology associated with a past or future "golden age." It implied no
uni- or multi-directional history of human societies. It did not imply
the existence of universal laws of human history and did not regard
history as a logical sequence of rising or declining stages. As a term,
social change was much more neutral than development.

Unfortunately most social scientists did not only replace the term
development with the more neutral term social change, but they also
abandoned the problems which had been studied previously. The
majority of sociologists were interested now in studying the status quo
and not change, and even those who were interested in studying changes
focused their attention on short-range and recent changes. They did
not pretend to explain human history, but rather studied changes in
given phenomena (for example, social stratification) between time t_1
and t_2 to discover the factors that caused or just accompanied such
changes. Of course, to the social scientist who believes that each period
of human history should be regarded as part of long-range sequences,
and should be explained by general laws, the explanations or interpretations advanced by sociologists interested in such narrowly understood
and isolated changes were regarded as partial or marginal interpretations or half-truths and therefore wrong.

There are now two meanings of social change in social sciences: the
broader interpretation and the more narrow interpretation. The broader
interpretation of social change (common in the theory of cultural and
social anthropology) has the same meaning as the term development
had before but is shorn of its ideological implications and silent pre-
sumptions. Sociologists who interpret the term social change in this
manner try to distinguish different systems of social organization (or
different socioeconomic formations in Marxian language) in human
history and try to discover the sources and regularities involved in
transformation of one system into another. The second, more narrow
meaning (preferred by sociologists) refers not to human history but
rather to changes of given parts of social reality in a given society and
during a given time period. There is not a sharp distinction between

---

[2]   But it is still maintained in philosophical terminology (see, for instance, van
Doren 1967).

these two meanings, however (see Coser 1967: 27–29), and using Parsons's terminology we may say that very often the same changes are considered as changes IN society by one scholar and as changes OF society by another.

The term development has not disappeared completely, however. Once dropped from the language of theoretical sociology, it found a new home in economics (economic development) and social action. We now commonly use the terms: developed and underdeveloped (or developing) countries. These terms could mean that countries are ranked in a simple hierarchy according to a given index as, for example, income per capita. Countries with a higher value of a chosen variable (i.e. higher income per capita) are called developed and those countries with lower value are called underdeveloped.

It could hardly be expected, therefore that, future income per capita would be the same for every country; there will always be underdeveloped and developed countries. If the term underdeveloped means only a relative position on the hierarchical listing, it is not a very useful term. More often, however, an underdeveloped country is a country below a certain value of chosen variables (average income, level of education, percentage of nonrural population, etc.). It could, therefore, be expected that all countries would pass the line dividing underdeveloped from developed countries and all countries would be developed. Some social scientists (as for example Rostow) who apply this meaning to development distinguish different stages of development (take off, maturity, etc.) and speak about factors accelerating or impeding development. Consequently, the term development means just the increase in the value of a certain group of indices (or variables) and is almost interchangeable with such terms as industrialization, modernization, or economic growth. The connotation of development is broader, however, because it is possible to speak about preindustrial or postindustrial development (a broader concept than industrialization) and refers not only to economic development, but also to the development of education, medical services, public transportation, or social welfare in general (certainly broader than economic growth). The term development is very close to the narrow meaning of social change. But its connotation is more narrow. It covers only some changes (income and social welfare in the first place) and not others (like social stratification). The problem indicated by the title could be understood, therefore, as the problem of relationships between different social changes, and particularly between those in the areas of economies, educational level, and social welfare, and those in other social spheres such as stratification, social mobility, aspiration, cultural norms etc.

If we applied this latter interpretation, we could study the changes accompanying economic development, or, more ambitiously, we could study the causal relationships between development and social changes. If we used the term social change in its broader meaning, however, we would rather look for those relationships between development and other social changes which lead to the change of global socioeconomic systems (systems of social organization) or, in other words examine those changes IN societies which lead to changes OF societies.

The term development is now used with regard to social action. There is no doubt that each society, or, rather, governing body, is trying to improve economic and social conditions like income per capita etc. Each society has some governmental and nongovernmental plans to achieve such goals. Together with these goals, programs of action are formulated that may encompass such actions as land reform, organization of rural cooperatives, etc. There are programs or developmental plans on the national, regional, or local level. The recent use of the term development describes both increases of selected socioeconomic and cultural indices and plans of programs devoted to achieve such increases. Development is now regarded as a result of social action, but one of the most important goals of such action is usually not mentioned.

Social conflicts are usually not mentioned in the study of development goals. The goals of each program of development tacitly assume that it is possible to diminish existing social conflicts. More precisely, those who prepare the programs of development (government for example) are convinced that development plans can solve, or at least quiet, existing social conflicts. Of course, many governments are interested in fostering (or even implementing) social tensions and social conflicts between different social groups, according to the old Roman principle "divide and rule," but encourage only those conflicts which are not directed against government and which can be directly or indirectly controlled. The group in power regards uncontrolled social conflicts as a threat to the social order. Even if not formulated in official goals of programs of development, such programs are tacitly designed to solve social conflicts. If we assume that no government wants to fuel social conflicts (or uncontrolled social conflicts, to be more precise), but seeks to solve or quiet conflict through programs of development, then we should be surprised by the obvious failures of such action. No society has solved conflicts by means of programs of development. On the contrary, we suspect that the programs of development may even have sharpened existing conflicts by increasing inequality and may have introduced new social conflicts. Even in the societies where government has nearly absolute control over economic and political life, social conflicts do not disappear. It could be postulated that social tensions which accumulate for a longer time explode more violently in societies controlled by a strong government. Many of these tensions and conflicts could be regarded as direct but unexpected results of governmental programs of development, particularly of programs of industrialization. The fact that, contrary to expectation, development programs often result in sharpening (or even in creating) social conflicts, impels us to say that no society, not even one controlled by an absolute political power, fully controls its future. This means that the sources of social conflicts which play the most creative role in the change of social structure (which determines social consciousness and consequently the programs of development) are at least partly independent of material and social conditions changed in the course of programmed development.

Hence, the question is raised: what are the sources of social conflict and what is the relative importance of different kinds of social conflict?

The definition of social conflict by Dahrendorf (1962) seems quite satisfactory to me and I think his typology of conflicts is also useful. Of course, all types of conflicts could be studied in relation to development. Development certainly changes the situation of the family and the roles of the family members and this could generate new conflicts. The same could be said about conflicts arising from cultural patterns, professional and demographic composition, organizational work, etc. As all types of conflicts are interrelated, conflict or tension in one field will penetrate other fields. But some types of social conflict have more impact than others. The most important types of social conflict affecting general social change are, in my opinion, social conflicts which lead to changes in the macrosocial organization (or social order). Since the main tool for this type of change is political power, the most important conflicts are those which are oriented toward political power. I am, therefore, interested particularly in CLASS CONFLICTS.

Such class conflicts are rooted in the unequal access of different social groups to the universally desired but scarce benefits. Of course, each group is composed of individuals. But I refer to groups and not individuals because the position of an individual (position defined by access to mentioned benefits) is primarily determined by the position of the social group to which he belongs. Individuals are usually trying to improve their position and different socioeconomic systems offer them different chances for personal careers. If they fail, they could blame themselves for failing to exploit existing chances. Frustration and aggressiveness result, but this does not necessarily create hostility between social groups. Individual frustration is not a sufficient cause of social conflict. Only if an individual identifies himself as a member of a given social group, and believes he is underprivileged because he was born a black, a peasant, a proletarian, a Jew, etc., is his personal frustration translated into group efforts to change the situation of the whole group.

Such a change in the position of one group usually requires the change of the position of groups interested in maintaining the status quo; social conflict is inevitable. Social groups do not occupy a permanent place in history. Everyone is born into a society with a social structure, and his social position is primarily given to him by historical precedent. But all existing social groups have emerged once in history, and new groups are constantly emerging. Any collection of individuals can transform itself into a social group if they recognize their common inferior position. The factors creating social groups are, of course, numerous (and not limited only to a feeling of being underprivileged) and could operate for a shorter or longer time, could be associated with many or only a few aspects of life, and could be more or less important from a given point of view.

The categories used in schemes of social stratification are not social groups but rather social collections. I do not believe, therefore, that antagonisms or social conflicts arise between individuals earning from $300 to $799 a month and individuals earning from $800 to $1199 a month. But the stratification schemes are useful in describing the current social situation of existing social groups. Some collections (or categories) used in stratification schemes, as categories of owners and nonowners, occupational categories, etc., could be regarded as "potential" social groups and under certain conditions could transform themselves into acting social groups. The proletariat began as such a potential group or collection of individuals brought into the same underprivileged social situation. But very quickly (due to peculiar ties of industrial organization) members of this potential group recognized themselves as a social group and began to act as a social group first on the local and then on the national level. The Marxian distinction between CLASS IN ITSELF and CLASS FOR ITSELF could be very useful in the study of emerging social groups or groups in *statu nascendi*.

The access to desired benefits is unequal because such benefits are scarce. But there are two different reasons for such scarcity.

One is the scarcity of natural or material resources such as an insufficient level of production of given articles. For instance, if there is not food enough for all, some must starve. When there is enough food, everybody could receive a sufficient portion. It is obvious of course that inequality depends not only on level of production but on the system of distribution as well. But by this simple reasoning, any increase in production affects at least the potential to overcome scarcity of the product. Not all benefits can be increased by technological improvements and production increases. New needs are constantly emerging and since the means of meeting these new needs are usually scarce, new inequalities emerge. But material and natural scarcity is not the only reason for social inequality.

The other reason for unequal access can be found in the social organization. In the competitive, profit-oriented, economic systems, food, for instance, could not be distributed free without also stopping agricultural production. Consequently it may be true that in such systems of economic organization, inequality is the basic principle of functioning; it is necessary to keep some groups in underprivileged positions in order to secure a privileged position for other groups. Therefore, even for those benefits which could be increased with the help of improved technology, the main reason for inequality lies not in technical or productional limitations (or indeed natural limitations), but rather in social organization.

But there are other kinds of benefits which are purely social and their scarcity has much less to do with our technological or natural limitations or limitations of natural resources. Most important are such benefits as power and prestige. The level of technology is not without significance. It influences the structure of social prestige (especially prestige attached to different occupational roles and positions) and offers more material possibilities (military equipment, control of information, etc.) for exerting power in mass societies. But these inequalities are based solely on the social organization. Furthermore, they are peculiar in that even if access to them could be theoretically equal, their possession could not be equal. The access to power could be theoretically equal for everybody (I have not, however, seen such a society) but if equal possession of power existed, the power would not exist at all. In this sense the game of power, as of prestige, is a zero-sum game, and the distribution of power (prestige) is subordinated to the principle: "A in position p only and only when B in position non-p." As result of social conflict we could expect therefore either: (1) a change of distribution of power among social groups without changing the existing socioeconomic system; the changes within the existing socio-economic system are limited by the nature of the system and conflict will persist; or (2) a change in the socioeconomic system that results in a new social structure, new distribution of power, and consequently new patterns of inequality resulting in new social conflicts in the future (after formation of new social groups and transformation of them into groups "for themselves"). Two conclusions could be formulated now. First, the main sources of social conflicts are found not in technology but in social organization; and, therefore, any program of development which does not include the changes in social organization cannot solve any of the basic social conflicts (but certainly could change the sharp-ness of conflicts and the particular articulation of them). Second, all programs of development enter into existing social conflicts, and pro-grams should be regarded in the light of these conflicts.

We could say now that different continua of inequality are inter-related and have a tendency to cumulate. The underprivileged social group in the sense of income (or access to material benefits) also has inferior access to medical services, education, cultural benefits, etc., resulting from unequal access to power and prestige. If this observation is true, we can ask, "What kind of inequality is more important?" In the Marxian approach the most important inequality (the source of other inequalities) is (in societies with private ownership of means of production) unequal access to the means of production. The group (social class) which possesses the means of production also possesses power, higher prestige, better income, and better access to all material and cultural benefits. The access to power is, in this approach, of special importance because power is the key to all decisions regarding social organization. Those who possess power also possess the means to enforce any changes or to maintain the status quo. The relationship between ownership of means of production and political power requires more attention.

In Marx's time, the ownership of the means of production and political power were relatively separated; therefore, it was possible to speak about one factor determining the other. Of course, some political elites (presidents, secretaries of state, etc.) also owned large amounts of land or capital, but the government or state, as such, did not own significant amounts of the means of production, and even political power had little influence on the economy of the country. Since the time of Marx, however, the situation has changed. In some countries, the state is the exclusive owner of the means of production: land, financial capital, banks, transportation, industry, trade, etc. The political power or group in political power could be regarded, therefore, as the group that also controls the means of production. The owner is juridically "the state," (in some countries the given articulation is "the nation") but real control is wielded by the group that possesses political power. In other countries, the state is not the exclusive owner, but is still the major owner of the means of production (banks only or banks and transportation, sometimes the mining industry or heavy industry in general) and those who possess political power also control a significant segment of the means of production. In all countries, the state, and therefore the group in political power, controls the economic life via investments, credits, purchases (especially military purchases), taxes, and import duties. In all countries, therefore, the political power exerts a greater influence on the economic life now than during the time of Marx. That influence is steadily increasing.

It is not sufficient to speak about OWNERSHIP today, because ownership without control over the owned object has no material significance. In order to cover different socioeconomic systems it is necessary to replace the term ownership in the analysis of social inequalities and social conflicts by the more general term CONTROL over means of production and to regard ownership as only one form of control over means of production, a form whose significance is diminishing today in many socioeconomic systems. It is necessary to say also that the relationship between control of means of production and political power is now much more reciprocal. Not only is it true that those who control the means of production control people,[3] but it is true that those who control people control the means of production. The importance of the second relationship is increasing. In fact, this interrelationship is mutually reenforcing. Those who have political power (control of people) simultaneously manage the national economy (control over the means of production) and are therefore able to control people to a much greater extent. Of course, political power tends to maintain itself, and, therefore, to strengthen itself. Each political power has in consequence a "natural" dictatorial tendency. But the reenforcement described above gives new strength to this dictatorial tendency and creates new opportunities and incentives for the transformation of political power into dictatorial power.

Following the Marxian approach, we could say today that control over means of production and political power (or political power and control of the means of production) are increasingly inseparable and

---

[3] In some countries this determination is still the most important — for instance countries where political power is controlled by international capital.

this unity is the main source of all other social inequalities. The situation of each social group is not determined solely by its access to the control over means of production but by its access to political power as well. The notion of SOCIAL CLASS, if understood in economic terms only, is not today (and in fact never was) a sufficiently scientific tool for the study of social conflicts because social conflicts simultaneously emerge from the inequality of access to political power. The notion of social class should be defined more generally in Marxian terminology, or we should find other terms and notions to describe today's primary social inequalities and the main social conflicts.

I said before that all programs of development should be seen in the light of social conflicts: the struggle for political power. It is obvious that every group in power will judge any program of development from their perspective — will the program strengthen their power, enlarge the social basis or social support for the group in power or, on the contrary, would it be dangerous for the governing group? From the other side, the social groups who have no access to control of means of production and/or to power and, therefore, are underprivileged in all respects, will evaluate the program of development from the same point of view — to what extent could this program weaken the governing group, introduce new forces to the political fight, and allow them to gain power? The attitude of different social groups toward programs of development will, therefore, be determined, not so much by its abstract "economic" rationality, but rather by the existing conflicts between privileged and underprivileged groups.

However, many programs of development seem to be beneficial for all social groups even if they are implemented as governmental programs, and will certainly strengthen the existing political system. We might expect, for instance, that industrial investments, agricultural improvements, new seeds, the "green revolution" or more efficient machinery, better transportation, new education establishments and medical services are beneficial for everybody. Certainly the increase of material resources could diminish some particular inequality and change the objects of some social conflicts. A situation in which underprivileged social groups fight for better transportation, for instance, is preferred to conflicts where underprivileged social groups fight for goods necessary for bare subsistence, i.e. food, rudimentary shelter, etc. But without changes in the general system of social organization, the main conflicts will usually not diminish. Better technology can be adapted more quickly by groups in a better economic position (richer peasants for instance); and therefore, the social distances between groups will increase. Even if, as a result of development the underprivileged groups get more income than before, the income of privileged groups will usually grow much more rapidly, and the relative position of the under-privileged groups will be even worse than before. Better education and the improved access to information will increase the needs and desires of the underprivileged groups and their dissatisfaction with their social position will increase. We would expect, therefore, that development may heighten social conflicts. The international agencies supporting development in underdeveloped countries and international specialists working in this field should not delude themselves by thinking that their program is above social conflicts. It depends, of course, on whose program of development we are speaking about. Is it the old group in power that is in permanent conflict with underprivileged groups and constantly refuses (or is unable) to change the socioeconomic system? Or is it the program of the new group which emerged changing the socioeconomic system and creating conditions for a new social structure? In each case the social conditions for development are different and social results will be different.

Different typologies (or categorizations) are necessary, therefore, to study the relations between programs of development and social conflicts. First of all, the typology of socioeconomic structures and the political systems which determine the groups which are in conflict could help us establish the main social forces that participate in the struggle for power and give us a perspective on the most important social problems. This knowledge could help us formulate the needed changes in social organization. The typology of programs of development should then be constructed according to an evaluation of WHOSE program we are referring to, WHOSE interests are protected by this program and WHOSE interests are in danger. Since rural development programs are part of general programs of development, and most often the results of the programs of rural development depend on results of general programs (for example the results of rural programs differ according to their dependence on the extent and kind of industrialization occurring in the country, demographic increase, programs of education, and cultural patterns and norms), it is not possible to study them separately. Our present sociological knowledge does not permit formulation of such typologies, and we therefore concentrate on "case studies" which do not allow us to come to any general conclusion or "factor analysis" on a macrosocial level which gives us general knowledge about interdependences between chosen variables, but this knowledge is too general to apply to any given situation. Neither kind of study allows us to formulate any practical suggestions. The case studies are certainly interesting and important. Factor analysis is very important and promising too. But without typologies of existing structures we could not apply this knowledge. We should now encourage studies which would develop and test the necessary typologies. The lack of such typologies currently permits only very vague and imprecise statements. As we are primarily interested in studying so-called underdeveloped or developing countries, we could say, however, that these countries have some common features.

They are countries with predominantly rural or rather peasant populations, with a low level of industrialization, a high unemployment rate in the urban areas, hidden unemployment and poverty in rural areas, (cheap manpower, therefore), and low levels of education, especially a low level of technical know-how. They are primarily postcolonial countries and, therefore, lack national intelligensia and a national bureaucracy. They are very often countries characterized by sharp social conflicts between landowners or aristocracy on the one side and peasants on the other, with a relatively small middle class partly of foreign origin in urban areas.

In countries with such a social structure the main social conflicts arise between peasantry (including farm laborers, tenants, share-croppers, etc.) and land aristocracy who are, in our time, strongly assimilated with the bourgeoisie and solidly linked with international capital. In such countries, the level of industrialization is limited by the small market for industrial products because of the poverty of the majority of the population. Of course, some industry owned by international capital locates in the country because of cheap manpower, but the main industries locate there in order to exploit natural resources, i.e. petroleum. Political power in such a country is (or was), of course, influenced very strongly (or penetrated) by big landlords and international capital.

In such a situation, programs of development such as improved agricultural technology, new seeds, better transportation (partly for military purposes), education, medical help, etc. would rather sharpen the social conflicts. The majority of the peasants are too poor to benefit from any technological innovations in agriculture; their farms are too small; their potential for purchasing new equipment is very limited; their technical knowledge is also very limited.

New opportunities created by such purely technical programs of development will be fully utilized by higher and middle strata and by small groups of well-to-do peasants to foster their own interests. Unemployment will rise as those who can no longer survive in rural areas utilizing old production methods migrate *en masse* to urban areas. Differences in relative income increase and, therefore, the social conflicts will be sharpened. The best solution would be radical land reform and extensive industrialization which could allow large-scale migration of peasant families and therefore allow the creation of the kind of structure in agriculture which would provide the opportunities to implement a new agricultural technology. But political power as we described it before would not be able to include such goals in its program of development.

It is, of course, possible to improve the situation in a less radical way through migration to other, developed countries, relying on tourism to employ part of the remaining population. A gradual rise of the middle class and an increase in average income may foster slow industrialization, etc. In some European countries these factors were able to significantly improve the situation; still in these countries social conflicts have rather changed than diminished. But in most underdeveloped countries pressures do not permit slow changes or a gradual social and economic transformation. The majority of the population demands much more rapid and significant changes. In such a revolutionary situation on the verge of peasant rebellion the political changes must occur and are occurring despite strong military control.[4]

Such countries usually undergo violent transfers of political power. As conflicts rise and increase the governing group (or groups) must strengthen military control as a protection against revolution. The military group will gain, therefore, more and more power and very quickly attempt to gain absolute political power.

In the context of the existing international situation it is probable that young military groups will remove the old leaders and take full military and political power (the other possibility is power acquisition by social political parties). But even such groups ostensibly nationalistic and with an antisocialist ideology will tend to introduce some kind of socialist changes in the economic system, by nationalizing some part of the economy (industry owned by international capital, banks, etc.). Such groups will be pressed to introduce more radical land reform and start programs of extensive industrialization. At this stage, the programs of development have new potentialities. The possibilities for

---

[4] It could be said, however, that the new ways of exercising political and military control (mass media for instance, obligatory political training, etc.) stimulate the awareness by the underprivileged masses of their situation and give them new means of fighting against government.

change are open and formerly underprivileged social groups are actively engaged in an attempt to improve their position. The programs will be used by new political power groups to strengthen the nationalized economy and will simultaneously expand their political power and extend and strengthen social controls. The old social conflicts can be expected to gradually disappear and the development programs could be used with broad social support to create the economic (primarily industrial) basis for new social structure. But together with gradual disappearance of old social conflicts, new social conflicts will quickly emerge. Mass migration connected with industrialization will increase the demand for food. Probably, it will not be possible to import food or to rapidly increase the agricultural production, so a corresponding dissatisfaction among the new, urban population could result. In order to keep prices low, the government will be forced to impose controls on consumption. These controls will lead to further nationalization and to attempts to reorganize agriculture on the same basis as industry and to extract the means for development from agriculture. But such controls imply the loss of incentives and the bureaucratization of the state-owned or controlled economy. The work efficiency may decrease or negate potentials for increased consumption. Together with the erosion of revolutionary enthusiasm (which cannot be maintained indefinitely) the new underprivileged group, consisting of an industrial working class will become aware of its inferior status. New changes in socioeconomic systems will be needed, but all reasonable changes such as the reorientation of the economic system toward consumption, introduction of economic incentives, liberalization of political control, democratization of management, etc., are opposed by the government since these changes would diminish the basic privileges of the governing group. Now a new period of social conflicts opens with riots and changing of groups at the top. Again the degree of conflict, the relative strength of new social forces and the external situation of the country will determine the time and method of new changes in the socioeconomic system.

The general conclusion could be formulated as follows:

Programs of development cannot allay existing social conflicts if the general socioeconomic system remains unchanged. In such a situation, programs of development can stimulate rapid, general social change because they sharpen social conflicts and not because they stifle them. But this means that such development may lead to unanticipated results. Programs of development could be more effective if they were applied by a new political power which emerged during the process of change in the general socioeconomic system. In such a situation, the new power would be temporarily free of basic social conflicts, and programs of development could be more flexible in creating a new socioeconomic system and new social structure. Our knowledge about society does not allow us to predict the social consequences of development in a given country. The reasons for this lie more in the lack of an adequate theory of social change than in the lack of empirical data.

REFERENCES

COSER, L. A.
   1967   *Continuities in the study of social conflict.* New York: Free Press.
DAHRENDORF, R.
   1962   *Elemente einer Theorie des sozialen Konflikte, Gesellschaft und Freiheit.*
VAN DOREN, CHARLES
   1967   *The idea of progress.* New York, Washington and London: Institute for Philosophical Research.

The Efficiency of Traditional Agriculture, Phases of Development, and Induced Economic Change in the Waidina Valley, Fiji

HENRY J. RUTZ

INTRODUCTION

Recent studies in economic anthropology indicate a trend away from the self-conscious examination of conceptual problems in the formation of a subdiscipline[1] and toward an interest in the problems of micro-development. Microdevelopment may be defined as a comparatively long-run sequence of economic change in a locality within a nation-state.[2] The definition leaves unspecified the causal factors operating in

Field research was carried out in the Waidina Valley from December of 1968 to April of 1970 with the aid of a predoctoral fellowship from the Canada Council.

[1] The doctrine of "cultural relativism" applied to economic anthropology states that the economic categories and analytical tools developed for the economy of one culture cannot usefully be applied to the economy of another culture. This doctrine has created a controversy termed the "formal-substantive" controversy (e.g. Cook 1966). This stereotyping has largely dissolved into different focal points of interest in institutional characteristics which limit economic behavior and motivation, on the one hand, and, on the other, the performance of the economy no matter what its institutional arrangements. There has also been convergence through the recognition that constraints and incentives on performance vary from one culture to another, and that economic motivation is likely to vary according to one's culture no less than according to one's position within a culture (Cancian 1972; Berg 1961; Prattis 1973). Of course, the assumption that, GIVEN the ends, constraints, and incentives that limit alternatives, one will not choose an alternative that prevents achieving the desired end, seems to me to be a formal assumption that is universally sound, and relativistic in substance.

[2] "Economic change" is necessarily a broad concept that must include more than the economists' narrow definition of economic development as an average increase in real per capita income or an increase in net investment. In order to be useful for examining actual sequences of development, the concept must include some notion of structural transformation of the type described in Demas (1965). The concept of microdevelopment refers to geographical and political boundaries no smaller than

a given set of circumstances that limit the direction of change.[3] The conditions, causal factors, and direction are empirical problems to be investigated for particular cases with an analytical interest in and concern for possible generalization and comparison. There already exists in the literature a growing number of descriptions of actual[4] sequences of microdevelopment (Hill 1963; Salisbury 1962, 1970a; Pitt 1970; Epstein 1968) which reveal a variety of causal factors operating under varying sets of conditions, including an interest in cases which describe and analyze stationary development and underdevelopment (Geertz 1963; Johnson 1971). A number of models of microdevelopment have been suggested which attempt to isolate important dynamic relationships between factors at different phases of development (Fisk and Shand 1969; Lockwood 1971; Salisbury 1970b). Classification based on the relationships between differences and similarities in direction of change (development, stagnation, and underdevelopment), rate of change (gradual, rapid, and constant), and mechanisms of change (external, internal, or some combination), under varying conditions, (see Adelman and Dalton 1971) will allow these models to be tested for their general or limited applicability.

By looking at actual sequences of development while retaining a generalized interest, microdevelopment studies complement macrodevelopment models which abstract purely economic processes in order to prescribe the phases in which economic development, measured by

---

the village and not as large as the nation-state. It does not refer to the magnitude of change. "Local" is a term to be understood in this context, as are other terms such as "outside-inside," "external-internal," and "import-export." All have reference to a boundary between two units within a nation-state. The idea bears some resemblance to the economists' notion of the regional economy (Meyer 1968).

[3]   In order to compare and to generalize about directional development toward some defined economic progress, microdevelopment interests, therefore, extend to cases of economic backwardness, stationary economy, cyclical development, and underdevelopment. To facilitate the empirical investigation into sources of dynamism or its absence, the variety of causal factors can usefully be divided into those which are internal and those which are external. In most developing nations, external decision makers in the form of foreign experts, central planners, and administrators must be taken into account in any discussion of allocative decisions in microdevelopment. Even "ownership" of techniques, skills, sources of capital, and land is likely to be divided between external and internal decision makers, but the perspective of microdevelopment remains primarily local: external decisions and factors are important for the constraints and incentives they provide to decisions based on internal factors.

[4]   The use of the term "actual" is meant to refer to knowledge about historical experience gained from hindsight. The study of actual sequences complements the deductive approaches to stage sequences (e.g. Boserup 1965). The term "phase" is adopted in this paper to distinguish the description of a single sequence from the more abstract "stage" approaches.

a narrow quantitative indicator, ought to occur. Microdevelopment studies, therefore, have policy-making implications, because they show, albeit from hindsight, the possibilities of adapting *a priori* models of economic development, aimed at the achievement of national goals, to the development of particular localities within nation-states. These situations not only exhibit differences in resources and ecology; there is also partial retention of local control over allocative decisions. This becomes important when national "development" may have different and conflicting consequences from regional "development." This paper is a preliminary attempt at formulating microdevelopmental phases for the political economy of a single region in Fiji, the Waidina Valley,[5] from late precontact times to the present. It does so by distinguishing "within-phase" and "between-phase" changes in agriculture. "Within-phase" change is examined as increasingly efficient adaptation of agriculture to selected ecofeatures, with a more or less constant structure of demand and given technical possibilities. "Between-phase" change is marked by changing sociopolitical organization, viewed indirectly for its effects on changing demand and production organization. The argument is that agriculturalists in the Waidina Valley have developed an efficient system of "traditional agriculture." This argument is then used to discuss some aspects of a developers' model for inducing economic change in the valley from 1965 to 1970.[6]

THE EFFICIENCY OF "TRADITIONAL AGRICULTURE" AND EXTERNAL CHANGE

Since this paper is concerned with the possibilities of agricultural growth under a given set of circumstances and the factors leading to a change in those circumstances, the phases of development will be distinguished by those factors which limit increases in agricultural production and make further growth unlikely and those factors which result in new possibilities and begin a new round of adjustment. The

[5] The Fiji Islands consist of some 300 islands in the southwest Pacific at latitudes 15° and 22° south and longitude 180°. Viti Levu, the major island, has an area of approximately 4,000 square miles, with a mountainous volcanic interior; there are several major river valleys that extend to a short coastal plain, where the rivers empty into the ocean. The Waidina Valley contains the Waidina River in south-central Viti Levu. The discussion of agriculture refers to that part of the valley which is in Waimaro District, in the Province of Naitasiri.

[6] For a more detailed analysis of the precise nature of these discrepancies, see Rutz (1973b).

former I will call "within-phase" adjustments, and I will limit myself to a discussion of factors resulting in demand that might stimulate agricultural production. The latter I will term "between-phase" adjustments, and I will limit myself to a discussion of the consequences of colonial policies and practices on agriculture in the Waidina Valley.

I will assume that with a given set of technical possibilities and constant demand, production decisions involving the allocation of land and labor will be made in the most efficient[7] manner possible, i.e. in a way that maximizes physical product per unit of labor employed. In terms of "within-phase" development, growth is likely to occur under conditions of relative inefficiency, but is likely to become more stationary when a point is reached at which no reallocation can be made to improve the productivity of the labor factor. There can be no doubt that population growth will affect the degree of extensive or intensive use of land (Boserup 1965), but the tendency of agriculture to adjust to its environment in the most efficient manner is likely to be independent of population density.

Internal adjustments of given technical possibilities to ecofeatures therefore define one set of variables which place limits on agricultural growth where social and political processes result in near-constant demand. Following Schultz (1964: 3–4), I will use the term "traditional agriculture" for the tendency whereby producers practice "farming based wholly upon the kinds of factors of production that have been used by farmers for generations,"[8] and look for the limits to agricultural growth within phases in (1) limitation on demand for agricultural production determined by sociopolitical processes, and (2) the tendency toward increasing efficiency in adjusting technology to certain ecofeatures in the agricultural system.

---

[7]   In practice, the quantitative demonstration of the degree of efficiency is rather complex, because it involves a comparison of the same activities at different times, as well as a comparison of one activity with all other possible activities in terms of their productivities at the margin. But the point here is that, where land is abundant, the degree of intensity of agriculture might be affected, but efficiency in agriculture might correspond with intensive use of land even when population density is not great. This is true for the Waidina Valley.

[8]   The term "traditional agriculture" specifically avoids the confusion of associating notions of efficiency with a particular production organization, economic motivation, or technical apparatus. Whether or not production is for exchange or is consumed by the production unit itself, whether production organization is based on small-holding family units or large plantations, whether land is held under "absentee ownership" or "fee simple" — these features are not of immediate interest, though they may be of primary importance at some point in an explanation of differences in performance.

THE PHASES OF DEVELOPMENT IN THE POLITICAL ECONOMY OF THE WAIDINA VALLEY

The most obvious changes in demand and technical adjustment to environment in the Waidina Valley stem from the transition from precontact to postcontact political economy. This transition marks a much larger change in conditions for growth in agricultural production than commonly thought, because it marks both a change in the adjustment of agriculture to new ecofeatures resulting in intensive cultivation, and important changes in social and political organization that directly affected the structure of demand. Whereas there is little evidence for the label of "traditional agriculture" in the precontact phase, the postcontact phase is characterized by ever-increasing efficiency in "traditional agriculture" as it adjusted to a riverine ecology under the constraints of colonial policy.[9]

1. The Precontact Phase: An Unstable Political Economy

The rather meager evidence available[10] on precontact Waidina political economy leaves unanswered many important questions about the actual formation of groups, their relations with one another, and the amount of the flow of goods and services that marks these relations through various institutionalized exchanges, but it leaves little doubt that pacification and colonization had important consequences within a relatively short period of time. The evidence points to an unstable political economy — sociopolitical processes give no indication that a constant or near-constant level of demand for agricultural production had been reached by the middle of the last century. Nor had the agricultural system adjusted to known technical possibilities in any way

[9] Analytically, precontact efficiency might be visualized as a maximization of output for a given input, whereas postcontact efficiency might be viewed as the minimization of inputs for a given output.

[10] No accurate precontact population figures are available. There is a rich oral history which makes no distinction between myth and history. Part of this is preserved in the *Ai tukutuku raraba*, based on hearings before the Native Lands Commission in 1923. Records of the Fijian Affairs Board, *Ai Volai Kawa*, give some genealogical information. Old village sites can sometimes be located on Native Lands Commission maps. The Methodist Mission in Fiji has some old records, in the possession of the Fiji Archives. Old Naitasiri Provincial Council reports describe administrative problems. Brewster (1922) discusses some movements and skirmishes.

that was sufficient to discourage the reallocation of land and labor with a view to increasing agricultural efficiency.

The evidence indicates that the precontact political economy was based on two factors working in relationship to each other: (1) a large number of small, mobile, relatively autonomous, mutually hostile groups living in proximity to each other; (2) an adaptation of field-fallow methods for cultivating primarily taro and yams on thin hill soils[11] of the subtropical rain forest. Mutual hostilities seem to have resulted in settlement near hilltop fortifications rather than in villages or hamlets near the Waidina River on the valley floor. Settlement patterns, in turn, seem to have limited the exploitation of a whole range of ecozones in the valley to a primary adaptation of yams and taro on hill soils, utilizing methods of forest-fallow rotation. This, in turn, must have resulted in an extensive use of land, because yams are planted only once on a particular plot before it is left fallow for a minimum of six years.[12] Yams require much preparation of the soil by removal of surface brush and the burning of brush to form an ash cover. The soil is aerated and mounded, and a latticework is put in place for the vines. Yams also require sandy, well-drained hill soils, which occur in the Waidina hills only in limited amount. Taro requires less soil preparation and offers the possibility of more than one crop on the same plot, but informants in 1969 said that they experienced a rapid rate of diminishing physical productivity after the second successive crop of taro. The fallow period might be of the same length as that for yams. The most characteristic ecofeatures in this hillside adaptation are the knowledge of the location of sandy soils for yams and the presence of deeper colluvial soils at the base of slopes with steep gradients, where erosion worked to the cultivator's advantage. Forest products, such as wild tubers and green vegetables, as well as tree crops, were valuable additions to household diet and hence daily consumption, but these items are less important for the many exchange relations than products requiring the use of more labor.

[11]   Informants in 1969 recognized three HILL soils to be of primary economic importance for agriculture: (1) *gele damu*, or reddish-brown soils, used for yams and tapioca; (2) *gele dra kura*, or red clay soils, of limited economic value; (3) *gele loaloa*, or black soils, thought to be the most fertile, but found in relatively inaccessible locations. The *yagona* or *kava* plant, which requires this black soil, is the principal crop grown on these soils. For a more complete physical description of the Waidina Valley and the complete range of land-soil types, see Rutz (1973a).
[12]   This information is based on statements of informants in 1969, but with the exception of the loss of some of the associated ritual, the technique for preparation and planting has probably been similar over a long period of time. Several Lau Islanders have changed some of these methods in the last few years.

Demand for agricultural products came in response to several factors in the precontact political economy. First, there was the daily consumption by household units[13] of their own production. The expansion of agricultural production to meet demand by household units was limited by the slow increase in population and the apparent absence of demand for new consumption items in the daily diet that might have stimulated agricultural innovation.

Possibilities for stimulating agricultural production were two: (1) regional specialization and (2) exchanges of goods and services based on the political motive of seeking alliances and security against hostility within a political structure marked by the formation of loose and temporary coalitions. The organization of intergroup hostility in a centrifugal power structure generates group membership based on rather diverse principles of recruitment. Security in interior Fiji appears to be closely correlated with strength in numbers. In precontact times coalitions were — as they are still today — means for organizing even smaller groups and families for safety against encroachment by other similar but larger groups. However, this view of relative autonomy for a rather large number of groups implied the opposite of "isolation" defined as the absence of a number of kinds of relations. Specific alliance was probably impermanent, but not the fact of alliance itself. The available evidence indicates continual intergroup exchanges of women, goods, and services in a variety of institutionalized settings.[14] There appears to have been a strong tendency toward frequent migration of groups from one location to another (both within the valley and into the valley from outside of it), and few restrictions placed on the mobility of individuals and families and their ability to affiliate easily with other groups.[15] All these social and political processes facilitated and

[13] The basic production unit in precontact times is uncertain. Informants in 1969 insisted that "in the old days" there were men's houses, and they point to the location of their foundations in the village. It would appear that there were also single-family dwellings, or a combination thereof, and hence the household as the basic unit of production has remained the same over a long period of time during which technological changes and other sociopolitical changes took place.

[14] Today, affiliation is through patrilineal descent, putative or actual, and residence is overwhelmingly patrilocal. But under precontact conditions, it is likely that kin networks resulting from marriage were more important as sources for potential affiliation than at present, and mobility would probably have reduced the incidence of patrilocal residence.

[15] No group considers itself heir to lands held from "time immemorial." Present group identity is always given in terms of in-migration from another area, of struggles upon first arriving in the area, of protection offered by another larger group or security sought by a still smaller group. "Large descent groups" which use a patrilineal idiom quite often recognize that their solidarity stems from a history

encouraged agricultural production by creating a demand for agricultural products.[16]

Despite natural barriers on all sides of the valley, movements, migrations, and the retention of extensive kin networks through marriage reveal a whole range of "horizontal" links of small groups and even smaller production units within the valley, and between the valley and the outside. Old Native Lands Commission maps show a number of "Fijian roads" running in all directions out of the valley. Salt blocks were used in the Waidina Valley that came from the southwest coast of the main island of Viti Levu. Wooden bowls for mixing *kava* came from the distant islands of Lau, hundreds of miles to the east. Whales' teeth, valuable in all kinds of exchanges, came from coastal regions. The finest woven mats, prized by present-day villagers, came from some of the smaller islands and from Vanua Levu, as they do today. *Tapa* cloth, valued for exchanges in marriage ceremonies, came from one island to the south of Viti Levu and from the eastern Lau group. The only real exchange of goods and services which could have been provided by Waidina villagers would have been through the reexport of some of these items, in the role of middleman, or the marriage of women, or by supplying the demand for Waidina agricultural products, especially by people living on the coasts.

In sum, an outline of the precontact Waidina political economy reveals an economy based first and foremost on agriculture but stimulated by the particular existing political structure, characterized by tenuous chieftainship and temporary alliances of groups which retained relative autonomy. Demand in the short term seemed limited only by the ability to make new alliances, to develop part-time specializations in warfare[17] and related political activities, and to activate trade relations with regions of partial product specialization. Efficiency in agriculture may even have been encouraged by the alternative employment

---

of convergence and common residence. The cause of movement is most often political, and marriage is not infrequently discussed in an idiom of power.

[16] There is a vast array of exchanges of goods and services underlying social relations in Waimaro even today. These might be classed as continuous exchanges between individuals, cyclical exchanges between groups, or hierarchical exchanges over long periods of time. The *vasu* institution, for example, implies both interpersonal and intergroup exchanges extending beyond the lifetimes of particular individuals. The *tikotiko* is a presentation of goods upon entrance to a village for the purpose of residing in that village for any length of time. Birth, marriage, and death have associated sets of continuing exchanges.

[17] There is no present evidence indicating the prevalence of warfare. The organization of alliances, and political leadership in general, was probably more time-consuming.

of labor in political, military, and trade activities. An equilibrium does not appear to have been achieved between these various activities, for the employment of land and labor, and for the potential for changing demand inherent in multiple small-group autonomy. If this picture is accurate in outline, then a new phase of agricultural change began when pacification and colonization truncated this internal dynamic.

2. The Postcontact Phase: Development of an Agricultural Equilibrium

Pacification of hostile groups by missionaries in the decades prior to cession of the islands to Britain in 1874 and subsequent policies of the colonial administration had important consequences for the practice of agriculture in the Waidina Valley and its potential for growth from cession to the present time. The evidence for the direction of change in Waidina agriculture from the middle of the last century to the present is less hypothetical than that adduced for the period of pre-contact political economy. The trend can be documented from field research in 1969 and checked against a number of published and unpublished sources.[18] The trend in agriculture appears to be a process of adjustment to new ecofeatures in such a way that the only innovations adopted were those which could be incorporated into the existing methods of land use and cultivation. The consequence was an increasingly efficient "traditional agriculture" based on intensive exploitation of the riverine ecozones in the Waidina Valley. The demand for root crops stabilized at a low level, the cultivation of export bananas expanded up to a point, and there were few alternative opportunities for the employment of labor in agriculture. However, throughout this whole period there was a response to external political and internal ecological limits on agricultural growth. There were gradual shifts in demand and investment in both agricultural and nonagricultural activities which point to an internal dynamic that became important during the period of induced economic change after 1965. Waidina agriculture therefore only approximates the analytical requirements of the concept "traditional agriculture."

---

[18]   Fieldwork in the gardens and informants' garden histories are useful for checking other sources, such as the annual reports of the Department of Agriculture and Other official published and unpublished material.

With pacification,[19] small groups began to move down from the hillsides to settle in nucleated villages along the shores of the Waidina River. Colonial policies had further consequences for the adoption of new settlement patterns that began an adjustment of recurrent methods of cultivation to a new ecozone. First, early colonial policy encouraged the consolidation of villages, creating over time the present-day settlement pattern of villages strung every few miles along the river and ranging in size from 60 to 270 inhabitants. This practice, and the absence of hostilities that might have resulted in destruction of crops and villages, reduced the movements of groups into and out of an area. Pacification and resettlement into nucleated villages was followed by later colonial policies which had further indirect consequences for Waidina agriculture through their influence on the sociopolitical processes that determined the structure of demand for agricultural production. The establishment of an official native administration composed of hierarchical levels of administrative chiefs and councils replaced authority and leadership that had relied on the strength of warring alliances. Together with other policies, the appearance of a native officialdom marked the beginning of a trend away from "horizontal links" in the political economy and toward an inward idea of village self-sufficiency. A code of "Native Regulations" theoretically tied much of the labor of households to the service of constructing and maintaining administrative public works projects.

An important aspect of colonial policy was an evolving land law (France 1969) based on a belief in what native custom prescribed. The most important feature of the legislated land-tenure system in the Waidina Valley was not that it tied a producer to membership in a larger corporate lineage in order to secure tenure rights, as this aspect of the system appears to have been ignored in favor of a local system of regulation (Rutz 1973a). Rather, the importance of legislated tenure in the Waidina Valley was that it was another step in the isolation of villages one from another. For purposes of land ownership, two segments of the same lineage in two different villages were determined to be separate corporate kin groups. It is the "localization" of land rights by tying kin groups to residence that was important in Waidina, because it set every village off from every other as the permanent center of lands marked by the outer boundaries of its resident lineages. No shift in these boundaries could take place, nor could any individual

---

[19]   There was an increase rather than an immediate reduction of hostilities, as *lotu* groups (converts) fought against heathen neighbors (see Brewster 1922).

migrate from one village to another and formally own rights in land. Accompanying these changes from the open society, based on "horizontal" links, to the nucleated "communal" village as the end point of a hierarchical political structure, was the adaptation of recurrent agriculture to new ecozones in response to a new and gradually shifting structure of demand.

The change in settlement pattern from hillside to river's edge allowed the exploitation of new ecofeatures through the adjustment (without any real alteration) of recurrent methods of cultivation practiced on the hillside to the alluvial soils formed by the action of the Waidina River. The Waidina River floods during the rainy season from December through March, carrying silts from upriver and depositing them in pockets along meanders and cutoffs. The action of the river has created a series of terraces and pockets of alluvial soils. Taro can be grown on the pockets of alluvial soil[20] almost continuously and on the river terraces with only a three- to six-month fallow period between crops. In addition, the labor requirements on these soils are much less for a single crop than on hill soils, because the vegetation is a tall grass that is cut with a cane knife. It requires no burning and no complete removal in order to use the dibble stick.[21] Present-day informants say that it would require a larger area on the hillside to produce the same physical product for a given area of the flatland soil types. It appears that the shift away from the hill soils was in the direction of increasing efficiency, with two ecozones being exploited — yams on hill-soil plots and taro on pockets of alluvial soils, with some degree of labor saving. Because the alluvial soil types could also be cultivated in a much shorter cycle, the shift from the hills to the valley was also a shift from less intensive to more intensive agriculture.

The early adaptation was neither simple nor automatic. In early records of the Naitasiri Provincial Council there are requests from Waidina villagers to the new government for food relief. Periodic scarcity resulted every few years from heavy flooding that washed away taro crops and damaged scattered tree crops. In fact, it was the early

---

[20] Informants in 1969 recognized two VALLEY soils to be of primary importance for agriculture: (1) *gele nukunuku*, sandy soils deposited by the river and prized for taro cultivation; and (2) *gele dina*, or river terrace soils of gray or gray-brown color, prized for banana cultivation. See Note 11.

[21] The mean labor input (MLI) in man hours per acre per annum for taro on alluvial soils was 3662 in 1969, compared with an MLI for tapioca on hill soils of 4402. But when the cultivation cycle was taken into account, it was approximately 2209 against approximately 500. Therefore, use of outer soils required a higher labor input for a single crop, but over time the land was used much less intensively.

struggles with adapting recurrent methods to the riverine ecology that led the Department of Agriculture to introduce and encourage the cultivation of tapioca.

Yams require dry, sandy, well-drained soils and sufficient sunlight to dry the bush for burning in order to have an ash cover. The pockets of sandy hill soil are limited, and the daily average number of hours of sunlight in some years is only around four. In 1969, it rained almost continuously from the end of May through mid-July, necessitating a late start in preparing yam gardens or, in several cases, the abandonment of a yam garden altogether for that year. Tapioca has none of these problems. It grows in most poor soils, requires no burning to prepare gardens, is less labor-intensive than yams, and produces an equal or better yield. Tapioca can be planted in Waidina hill soils in four or five successive crops before a fallow period of from five to fifteen years. It is not surprising that tapioca experienced steady and increasing approval in the early part of this century, to the point where, in 1969, yams had only an insignificant part in Waidina agriculture. Tapioca grown on the alluvial soils requires more labor than taro, though less than yams, the crop with which it competes in the same ecozone. Because of the length of the cultivation cycle, it is less intensively cultivated than taro. In sum, by the late 1920's, Waidina agriculture was adapting to the riverine ecology in a pattern of increasing intensity as one moved from the perimeter of settlement to the center, and it appeared to be adjusting to different ecozones in an overall efficient manner. Before discussing the demand for agricultural production and the limitations on agricultural growth with this adaptation, it is necessary to mention one more innovation that was introduced and easily adopted at about the same time as tapioca.

Beginning in the second decade of this century, bananas were introduced into recurrent cultivation as an export crop. Bananas fit easily into the evolving pattern of ecozonation and into recurrent methods of cultivation. The fruit matured in nine to twelve months. After initial planting, the labor requirements were minimal. The flower of the banana had to be powdered, but little care was required in thinning, pruning, or mulching. Most important, bananas could be grown on the river terraces adjoining the pockets of alluvial soils. Although in danger of periodic flooding, banana cultivation in this ecozone was practically semipermanent, lasting from ten up to twenty years before fallow periods. The fact that the terraces were near the river facilitated transportation down river by bamboo raft to packing points. In fact, logistical tasks were much more labor-time consuming than production tasks.[22] For very little labor and almost no labor expenditure on improvements, bananas gave a comparatively high yield.

The pattern that emerged in Waidina agriculture by the 1960's was one of recurrent methods of cultivation applied to a pattern of ecozonation in the subtropical riverine forest ecology that resulted in an intensive pattern of agriculture and an efficient allocation of labor and land. Taro was grown overwhelmingly on the inner-zone pockets of alluvial soil, where the use of land was maximized and labor use highly efficient. Bananas for export were grown in the next ecozone, the river terraces, where labor on logistical tasks was minimized and land was maximized through its semipermanent use. Tapioca was raised on less valued land on the perimeter of the river terraces, where land was sufficient to meet the requirements of a longer cultivation cycle. Despite the fact that production decisions in the Waidina Valley are made not through cooperative or communal village decision but by individual household units, the aggregate pattern was one of distinct ecozonation which, on the aggregate village level, maximized the intensive use of land and the efficient use of labor under recurrent methods.

However, there were also definite limitations implied in rationalized recurrent agriculture. The area of pockets of alluvial soil is miniscule as a proportion of the total lands of any single village.[23] River terraces probably amount to less than 3 percent of total available lands. Even the most desirable hill soils within easy distance of residence in the village amount to less than 6 percent of the total lands available. Also, population has increased in the latter part of the postcontact period, but the rate of increase has accelerated in the last two decades.[24] Further adjustments must occur, either in the direction of putting more land of less desirable quality under cultivation, requiring an increased labor investment for what may initially be a lower return, or toward

---

[22] Bananas cultivated with recurrent methods required about 118 man hours per acre in 1969. Plantation bananas required about twice as much labor. However, with the introduction of the road and changes in logistic tasks, labor requirements for plantation bananas were actually about half of what they had been previously. These figures do not include the initial investment required to prepare and plant new areas.

[23] To illustrate, I have good figures for the village of Wainawaga. Out of a total 2420 acres available, there were 3 acres of *gele nukunuku*, 70.5 acres of *gele dina*, 80 acres of *gele damu* and *gele dra kura* soils, and perhaps 20 acres of *gele loaloa* soils. The remaining 2261.5 acres were unknown bush.

[24] The average rate of annual increase for all of Waimaro District from 1946 to 1966 was 3.28 percent.

more intensive use of the most desirable lands, with a possible drop in productivity.

Demand for agricultural production closely parallels the increasing efficiency of "traditional agriculture" in the Waidina Valley. With few exceptions,[25] demand for root crops has come primarily from within the valley itself. Taro is the most highly-valued food staple in household consumption and is a requirement in ceremonial exchanges. Tapioca, by contrast, can be substituted for taro in household consumption but not in ceremonial exchanges. But there is little evidence that demand for taro or other agriculural products has increased in the postcontact period as a consequence of either increased frequency of ceremonial use or increased volume. The evidence is rather the opposite: the ceremonial events I actually observed in 1969 were nowhere near the ideal number, and if the argument is accepted that colonial policy had the effect of reducing still further the extensive "horizontal links" indicated above for the precontact period, then there may even have been a reduced demand for agricultural products over this period.[26] The slow increase in population probably did not make up for these other processes. As for household consumption, the evidence for changing demand is not in the direction of increased consumption of Waidina agricultural products but rather the opposite: increasing consumption of imported food items substituted for root crops and other local products.[27] Until the 1950's, inaccessibility to urban centers and other regions did not

[25]   There are really only two exceptions of which I am aware: (1) Waidina cultivators supplied root crops for large numbers of troops stationed in Fiji during World War II; and (2) during the 1950's cultivators made periodic sales of root crops to a middleman who supplied the Vatukoula Gold Mines. Neither of these activities has had any lasting effect.

[26]   Decreasing demand for root crops in ceremonial activities may have been offset partially by the increasing demand by officials of the native administration and the support of labor services on administration projects. Complaints of "absenteeism" and "laziness" suggest that villagers themselves met only minimal obligations, if even these, and, of course, the small remuneration for labor services was a disincentive for stimulating agricultural production.

[27]   Tea, sugar, and biscuits seem to have been introduced into daily diets rather early, though just when is uncertain. Flour, lard, and tinned fish are now important items. Steel tools, clothes, cash building materials, and furniture are other cash expenditures met by household income. Secondary education is increasing, and costs may rise over $100 per annum. Taxes are $11 per adult male per annum, and the village levies additional amounts of cash savings for meeting social overhead projects such as electricity, water pipes, lawnmowers, and water-seal latrines. Finally, in ceremonial exchanges, all manner of household items, from matches and soap to mosquito nets and dinnerware, are given, and often there is an exchange of cash.

offer good marketing possibilities and thereby precluded the stimulus to agricultural production offered by outside demand.

However, bananas offered the first and only possibility of a PERMANENT stream of cash income, and this demand was external, primarily from New Zealand. But the number of bananas that could be supplied was restricted by the limitations imposed on "traditional agriculture." Records of annual banana exports over the last forty years give evidence for the argument that producers expanded their banana acreage only up to the limits of available river-terrace land. As banana acreage went out of production, this land was slowly replanted, resulting in cycles of high and then low productivity. The number of bananas available for export was also limited by the heavy labor demands in moving bananas from garden to wharf, most of the labor being supplied by the producers themselves. A third factor that limited the supply of bananas to meet overseas demand was the mode of transportation; bananas came down the Waidina River by bamboo rafts which could carry at a maximum some fifteen cases, or about fifty bunches of bananas.

Banana income has itself been a stimulus for gradual shifts in demand. Cash goods have been substituted for local items in the daily household diet, for locally-available building materials, and for goods exchanged in ceremonial activities. But, most important for the Waidina economy, savings from banana income have been invested by local individuals, groups, and whole villages in such a way that a growing labor force, with few opportunities for alternative employment,[28] has been partially absorbed in a way that has generally benefited the whole population.[29] The role of partial autonomy for investment through various organizational arrangements is important for understanding the total response of producer-cultivators to induced economic change in 1965, but the remainder of this paper will touch briefly on the implications of the developers' model in the context of efficient "traditional

[28]   There really is no history of alternative job opportunities for any but a very few individuals in Waimaro. Colonial policies restricting mobility into the towns, few real job opportunities, and the disadvantages of a "hillbilly" socioeconomic status are factors inhibiting wage or salary alternative forms of employment. In years when banana production is down, men have gone to western Viti Levu to cut cane in the harvest season or they have taken "work holidays" in New Zealand for three months. Usually, life histories include a brief sojourn out of the valley in one's youth, to work on a boat, on the Suva wharf, or at some manual labor in and around the towns. Still fewer individuals have become schoolteachers, and one or two hold decent bureaucratic posts in Suva.
[29]   See Rutz (1973a) for the entrepreneurial role and alternative organizational possibilities for savings and investment in Waimaro.

agriculture" and possibilities for further agricultural growth under conditions obtaining in the valley in 1965.

3. The Phase of Induced Economic Change

In order to understand the model which developers used to increase the production of the banana export industry, it is useful to understand briefly the Waidina Valley in the context of the Fijian economy, and especially the developers' understanding of the place of Fijians in that economy. The economy of Fiji has depended upon agriculture in the past and will continue to do so into the indefinite future. Sixty-five percent of the country's total population in 1966 were classified as rural dwellers (*Census of the population* 1966). But Fiji is a plural society and has a dual economy. Only 14 percent of the Europeans (who comprise only 1 percent of the population) live in rural areas. Sixty-one percent of the Indians (who comprise 50 percent of the population) and 76 percent of the Fijians (who comprise 42 percent of the population) live in rural areas. Europeans own the towns — their commercial, banking, and large business sections. But the ethnic division between the rural Indians and Fijians is also a geographical and economic one. The Indians live largely along the coasts of the two main islands, in sugar-producing areas. They live in scattered hamlets and on smallholdings, as either tenants or leaseholders. In 1963, the contribution of sugar to export receipts was 58 percent. In contrast, the Fijians live in villages in the outer islands and in the interior of the main islands. Their major export crops are copra and bananas, both of which make up a small share of total export receipts. The Indians sell their product and purchase their consumption, while the Fijians largely consume what they produce. The Indians cultivate land efficiently and intensively, the Fijians use extensive methods and are inefficient. Yet the Fijians own 84 percent of the lands of Fiji as the result of a legislated system of tenure (France 1969).

The picture that emerges is one of 42 percent of the population cultivating 84 percent of the land extensively and inefficiently without contributing their share to the growth of the national economy through agricultural production. Most observers, experts, and developers see the causes of this situation in one of two factors: (1) the system of land tenure, which provides security of tenure without having to meet an economic rent, and which encourages extensive use of the land through a favorable population-to-land ratio; or (2) "communal" village social organization, which discourages efficiency through some notion of co-operative sharing, and which encourages limited aspirations similar to a target income.[30] Individual initiative is truncated either because food is "so easy to obtain that one need not work much," or because "if a man works to get ahead, his relatives will take from him."

The Waidina Valley would appear to be a classic example of this thesis. In the district of Waimaro there are few Indians, the Fijian population lives in nucleated villages, and the amount of land per capita in 1966 varied between 23 and 100 acres.[31] Land is nominally in the hands of patrilineages [*mataqali*], and land use follows an apparently extensive system of field-fallow agriculture on various scattered plots that result in a "fragmented pattern" that can easily be construed as casual or haphazard use of land under conditions of relative abundance.

During the decade from 1959 to 1969, imminent independence for Fiji increased interest in more rapid economic development, and a number of economic development projects were begun in the country-side. One such project was begun in the Waidina Valley after a hurricane in 1964 that destroyed many banana stands. The government took his occasion to reorganize the banana export industry in the valley along "more rational" and "efficient" lines. Their model called for moving banana areas from the river terraces to the hillsides, and using plantation methods of cultivation, including fertilizers, even rows, sprays, pruning and thinning, and periodic and regular weeding. Along with the notion that "traditional agriculture" was inefficient and extensive (and hence low in productivity), there was the idea that "traditional agriculture" could be equated with village "communal" social organization. This somehow tied the notion of extensive cultivation and agricultural efficiency to the production organization, and the prevailing belief was that village cooperative social organization and its associated institutions were somehow nonproductive and discouraged productivity in agriculture. Against this model of village agriculture there were two "more rationalized" alternatives: plantation management, where village labor was essentially applied to allocative decisions con-

---

[30] "Extensive" and "inefficient" are developers' terms which apply to the PRODUCTIVE UNIT, and "tradition" is the term most often applied to social organization based on residence in the village and membership in a corporate kin group. This paper adopts a formal rather than a substantive definition.

[31] I have not averaged population against total land available in Waimaro, but the village of Wainawaga, which is the most land-short village of its size, had 53 acres per capita in 1911 and 23 acres per capita in 1966; Nadakuni, the most land-rich village, had 288 acres per capita in 1911 and 128 acres per capita in 1966.

trolled by outside administrators; or rural smallholding [*galala*], where the individual lived outside of his village on his land and could devote full time to a family-type farm.

The Waidina Scheme Project was an attempt by developers to apply the plantation model of agricultural growth to a particular industry. Producers were not involved in the initial plan, which established village plantations on hill soils, the use of fertilizers, and the indebtedness of whole villages by being incorporated as legal cooperative organizations. When the scheme was implemented, it was discovered that even with fertilizers there were rapidly diminishing returns after only two years, reducing incomes and increasing the cost of plantation methods. Outside management was predicated on the goal of achieving average increases in production per acre over the whole scheme, but it soon became apparent that variability in individual skills and in ecological conditions from one section of a plantation to another and between plantations was so great that some producers experienced rising incomes while others were falling into debt. Fertilizer indebtedness based on village liability merely encouraged misapplication by individual producers with impunity. Labor requirements on plantations increased, as fertilizer had to be carried up hills on the backs of producers and banana bunches downhill to the river the same way. When the high costs of hill-site plantations and their impermanency became evident, indebtedness proved a disincentive to regular weeding and maintenance. Next to the efficient use of labor and the intensive use of land described for "traditional agriculture," plantation methods proved to be both extensive and inefficient. Producers began to react almost immediately by moving bananas back to the river terraces, and by 1969 nearly every village had abandoned its scheme plantation at great sacrifice in initial labor costs. In early 1970 the developers abandoned the scheme by writing off the indebtedness at great capital cost and additional costs in recurrent expenditures, including the salaries of a rather large bureaucracy.

CONCLUSION

The confusion between a "traditional" or "modern" production organization and its relation to efficient and intensive cultivation can be seen in the case of the Waidina Valley. In 1969, developers were proposing the subdivision of Waidina into smallholder plots that producer-cultivators would lease from their owners. The idea was that the smallholder would be more efficient than his village counterpart, thereby raising productivity and achieving agricultural growth, while at the same time he would use land more intensively, thereby creating additional acreage for cultivation by an expanding rural population prevented from migration to urban areas by limited employment opportunities.

But if the first experiment in plantation management in the valley had failed,[32] the alternative form of smallholder production organization appears also to offer only limited possibilities for further agricultural growth. As a consequence of the new road into the valley during the Waidina Scheme years, a number of villagers had independently taken the option of moving out of the village and onto lands near to the road. An examination of these cases does not support the contention that smallholding is a more efficient or intensive form of agriculture than the ecozone adjustment described above as "traditional agriculture." Because of the hill soils exploited, much more labor investment must be made in clearing and preparation. There is a lower yield per unit area when compared to yields from valley soils, and the cultivation cycle is considerably longer. Also, cultivation of gardens occurs in a spiral rotation around the residence site, which suggests that distance between gardens and house is likely to increase over time. It appears that to replace village "traditional agriculture" with smallholder agriculture might require capital improvements beyond the immediate means of the cultivators, as well as high labor costs in the shift from valley to hill exploitation. Unless new methods were applied in

---

[32]   The most important induced change from the standpoint of further possibilities for agricultural growth was the introduction of the road. By lowering transportation costs to the villages, the road affected demand for imported items. It also opened up the growing urban demand for agricultural production to Waidina producers and led to new alternative PERMANENT income streams by giving cash yields for root crops. Although labor and capital were being invested in the expansion of banana acreage throughout the Waidina Scheme years, a class of producer-cultivators invested labor-time in competing economic opportunities such as stores, cattle, trucks, taro land, boats and outboard motors for hire as river transportation (for both the export and the internal market), housing, education, and a variety of village public works projects. When I left the field in 1970, these activities were already reorganizing production decisions by reallocating the use of land and labor. Most of this activity was the result of local entrepreneurial leadership, internal savings from cash income, and membership in a variety of existing organizations which had taken on economic functions. These new sources of investment and demand, as unintended consequences of the developers' attempts to rationalize export agriculture in the valley, suggested several alternative directions for continued growth, including all the forms of production organization suggested as homogenous alternatives in developers' conceptions of economic change in the valley.

the shift, the shift would result in MORE extensive cultivation and LOWER efficiency. With recurrent methods, there would be less land per capita and increased labor requirements.

The amount of physical product is often pointed to by developers as an indication of the superiority of smallholder agriculture and the positive incentives to agricultural growth that this implies. But it is doubtful that a shift from more efficient to less efficient agriculture would be welcomed by the majority of producer-cultivators in the Waidina Valley. Those individuals who have moved out onto lands near to the road did so because of the special economic advantages of a short-term nature that accrued to this choice. It remains to be seen whether this choice will have long-term positive net effects for agricultural growth, such as investment of capital and labor for permanent improvements on hill soils by adopting different methods. At the moment, reduced efficiency has been offset by an increase in the number of hours worked per day, and it is true that total production is greater, even if productivity of land and labor is not. This option seems to be a limited one, since those few who have moved out of the village did so because they had access to soils acknowledged to be the best in the area. Other hill soils are thought to be less productive, raising the question about the high costs to the majority of villagers who would, as smallholders, have to raise productivity with a lower resource endowment.[33] A development decision that would invoke a uniform smallholder organization for the entire population might result in a pattern of vacant farms next to fairly successful enterprises.

REFERENCES

ADELMAN, IRMA, GEORGE DALTON
   1971   "Developing village India: a statistical analysis," in *Studies* 7. Edited by G. Dalton. Washington, D.C.: American Anthropological Association.
Ai tukutuku raraba ni Veiyavusa ni Tikina ko Waidina
   n.d.   Informants' statements before the Native Lands Commission hearings held in Waimaro, 1923. Suva: Fijian Affairs Board.

[33]   The lands of economic value under current conditions of labor costs and available capital are extremely limited, perhaps less than 15 percent of the total available acreage. These facts give a very different picture of the practice of "traditional agriculture" in the Waidina Valley than the stereotyped view of developers imbued with the idea of rapid agricultural growth predicated on smallholder agriculture.

Ai Volai Kawa
  n.d.   Registration of Fijian births and deaths according to lineage
          [*mataqali*] membership. Suva: Fijian Affairs Board.

BERG, E. J.
  1961   "Backward-sloping labor supply functions in dual economies —
          the Africa case (1961)," in *Social change: the colonial situation*.
          Edited by I. Wallerstein. New York: John Wiley and Sons.

BOSERUP, ESTER
  1965   *The conditions of agricultural growth*. Chicago: Aldine.

BREWSTER, A. B.
  1922   *The hill tribes of Fiji*. London: Seeley, Service.

CANCIAN, FRANK
  1972   *Change and uncertainty in a peasant economy*. Stanford: Stanford
          University Press.

Census of the population 1966
  1968   Legislative Council Paper 9. Suva: Government Printer.

COOK, SCOTT
  1966   The obsolete anti-market mentality: a critique of the substantive
          approach to economic anthropology. *American Anthropologist*
          68:323–345.

DEMAS, WILLIAM G.
  1965   *The economics of development in small countries: with special
          reference to the Caribbean*. Centre for Developing Area Studies.
          Montreal: McGill University Press.

EPSTEIN, T. S.
  1968   *Capitalism, primitive and modern: some aspects of Tolai economic
          growth*. Canberra: Australian National University Press.

FISK, E. K., R. T. SHAND
  1969   "Early stages of development in a primitive economy: the evolu-
          tion from subsistence to trade and specialization," in *Subsistence
          agriculture and economic development*. Edited by C. Wharton.
          Chicago: Aldine.

FRANCE, PETER
  1969   *The charter of the land*. Melbourne: Oxford University Press.

GEERTZ, CLIFFORD
  1963   *Agricultural involution*. Berkeley: University of California Press.

HILL, POLLY
  1963   *The migrant cocoa-farmers of southern Ghana*. Cambridge: Cam-
          bridge University Press.

JOHNSON, ALLEN W.
  1971   *Sharecroppers of the Sertao: economics and dependence on a
          Brazilian plantation*. Stanford: Stanford University Press.

LOCKWOOD, BRIAN
  1971   *Samoan village economy*. London: Oxford University Press.

MEYER, J. R.
  1968   "Regional economics: a survey," in *Regional analysis*. Edited by
          L. Needham. Harmondsworth: Penguin Books.

PITT, DAVID
  1970   *Tradition and economic progress in Samoa.* Melbourne: Oxford University Press.
PRATTIS, IAIN
  1973   Strategizing man. *Man* 8(1):46–58.
RUTZ, HENRY J.
  1973a "Local-level responses to induced economic change in the Waidina Valley, Fiji: a case study in anthropological economics." Unpublished doctoral dissertation, McGill University, Montreal.
  1973b Uncertainty and the outcome of a development process. *The Canadian Review of Sociology and Anthropology* 10(3):231–251.
SALISBURY, RICHARD F.
  1962   *From stone to steel.* Melbourne: Cambridge University Press.
  1970a *Vunamami.* Berkeley: University of California Press.
  1970b "Development through the service industries." Paper read at the Conference on Formal Methods in Economic Anthropology, Center for International Studies, University of Missouri, St. Louis.
SCHULTZ, THEODORE W.
  1964   *Transforming traditional agriculture.* New Haven: Yale University Press.

Reciprocity, Redistribution, and Prestige Among the Polynesians of the Society Islands

CLAUDE ROBINEAU

In a society so complex and so acculturated as Tahiti, the study of social phenomena, particularly the people's behavior and the motivations behind what they do, does not work well without appealing to history, notably the history prior to the arrival of Europeans. Whatever upheavals Tahitian society may have experienced for almost two centuries, it is unthinkable that the institutions, the conduct, the old ways of thinking have not left some traces today and that recourse to the past cannot serve to explain present characteristics. That is most true of the Tahitian economy and of the search for an explanation of present behavior. We have experimented with this method in studying ostentation phenomena in the present economy (Robineau 1968).

On the practical level, this course of action brings up the problem of the Tahitian economy's capacity for transformation in the face of industrial societies in relationship to which eastern Polynesia is peripherally located. On the theoretical level, it raises the question of evaluating the validity of history as an explanatory factor for the transformation of societies. In other words, does the present state of the Tahitian economy depend upon historical conditions that have been remodeling it for 170 years or upon some intangible cultural datum other than history? We think that this latter explanation, which we shall call "culturistic," cannot give an adequate picture of Tahitian reality and that the cultural state of reality, no matter how well set

The present text owes much to the exchanges of views I have had with the archaeologist, Bertrand Gérard, both as to the state of the economy in the district of reference and the function of ostentation and the role played by the chief's headquarters in this district.

forth, must be integrated into a dynamic structuring that is inherent in human societies and that our historical perspectives attempt to explain.

I.   Tahiti is known to harbor a markedly pluralistic culture. As a result of the processes of acculturation and colonization that marked the end of the nineteenth century, one could observe the establishment and peopling of European and Chinese colonies and a widespread racial admixture in the population, more so than in the other islands of central Polynesia. Aside from foreigners, described as *popa'a* and as *tinito*,[1] the population is made up of two distinct groups: the *ta'ata tahiti*, or *ta'ata ma'ohi* whom we will call "Polynesians,"[2] and the *ta'ata 'afa popa'a* who are generally called *demis* [half-breed, half-caste].[3] This distinction, theoretically based on cross-breeding, is more cultural than biological, on which point all of the authors agree (Finney 1965; Moench 1963; Ottino 1965, 1972). We will leave aside the phenomenon of class that some have tried to read into it (Panoff 1964: 126–133) as being irrelevant for the rest of the exposition.

What is of interest for us to observe here is that the *demis* are located on the borderline between two cultures, assuming traits from both cultures at once and utilizing the potentials of both. They consider themselves as being Tahitians and are considered by everyone as belonging to Tahiti because of their attachment to certain specific values, notably competition and prestige (Robineau 1968). However, they are distinguished from "natives" [*indigènes*] (a French term still used currently in Tahiti) by their mastery of the workings of modern economy, their avidity for work for profit, their business sense, and their desire to accumulate. Confronting a Polynesian community, a dynamic *demi* installed in a village plays the role of animator. This is very clear-cut on the economic level, so much so that a notable Tahitian of this sort from the neighboring island of Moorea, who is Polynesian of blood, language, and culture is so attached to these values that, from the economic point of view, he is a *demi* because, on this level, he behaves just like a *popa'a*.[4]

---

[1]   *Popa'a* [white man, European, or of European family origin (Caucasoid); North American, Australian]; *tinito* [Chinese].
[2]   *Ta'ata tahiti* [literally "person of Tahiti"]; *ma'ohi* [native].
[3]   *Ta'ata 'afa popa'a* [person half-Tahitian, half-breed]. In Tahiti, speakers of French use the neologism *demi* [half] to designate a half-caste Polynesian and European.
[4]   In the economic order, the overall economic success of the half-caste cannot be denied, but the differences in economic status are no less great between the big, wealthy *demis* of the capital and the small, country *demis* in the rural districts.

Field studies were made in a rural district of Tahiti where we analyzed the internal economic relationships. A few years ago, a study of fishing, one of the main activities of this district, was conducted there (Ottino 1965). Besides this, the community was noteworthy as having been the location of the exploits of the Spanish Catholic Mission that, nearly two hundred years ago, came to evangelize the Tahitians. Thanks to it there is the *Journal de Maximo Rodriguez* (Rodriguez 1930) that describes the functioning of a fragment of this society in minute detail. To start with, then, we propose to analyze the *Journal*, in order to explain the relationships prevailing in Tahitian society at that time, and afterwards to carry out an analysis of the present relationships in the district chosen.

Tahiti is said to be divided into DISTRICTS, a term used in both English and French to translate the Tahitian term *mata'ina'a*. These districts, which group together one thousand or more inhabitants, correspond to historical divisions of the island; their present boundaries were set some hundred years ago. Thus, what is called in Tahiti the Taiarapu Peninsula (La Presqu'île) or Tahiti-iti [Lesser Tahiti] and which, at the time Maximo Rodriguez wrote the *Journal*, was Teva-i-tai brings together five districts, each with an elected council and chief (*tavana*). These districts correspond to five parishes of the Evangelical Church, each with representative institutions (assemblies of believers and deacons).[5] It is one of these districts that we shall take as an example.

II. The *Journal de Maximo Rodriguez* (Rodriguez 1930) relates the stay in Tahiti, during ten months in 1775, of a Mission of Spanish priests who had been sent out by the Catholic Church and the vice-royalty of Lima to evangelize the Polynesians. Maximo Rodriguez was an officer in this Mission, an interpreter who took care of relationships with the local authorities and who was given the task of observing what went on in the indigenous society and the customs prevailing there. Rodriguez made daily notes of his relationships with the inhabitants, visits that he paid or received, the trips that he undertook, and the

[5] The Evangelical Church of Polynesia is made up in each village or village sector of a congregation of faithful followers, *'amuira'a*, who elect their deacon. A parish is made up of several *'amuira'a* and directed by a pastor. The parishes are grouped into wards (or synods) represented by councils, the delegates to which constitute the Superior Council in Papeete, the highest body. The Superior Council designates the president of the Church, cansecrates and appoints pastors, and heads the whole religious community. On the economic level, the Church serves, through its *'amuira'a*, as a model for structuring work groups and keeps up a lively ceremonial communion among its members (Robineau 1968).

incidents that did not fail to arise within the population while the Spanish vessels were present or, after their departure, with the Mission and its members.

The *Journal*'s value lies in the fact that its author, who seems to have been a good observer, to have had a balanced and open character, and to have been capable of adapting easily to a foreign world, very quickly became a friend of the *ari'i* or Tahitian [great chiefs] who had parcelled out the governing of the island among themselves. For them he became a highly appreciated mediator and spokesman concerning incidents that occurred during this ten-month stay on Polynesian soil. While the ships were present, there were numerous minor incidents, largely sailors' escapades, and when the Spaniards' numbers were re-duced to the members of the Mission, the climate tended to deteriorate because of the narrow-mindedness, blindness, and unawareness of the fathers who made up the Mission itself. They limited themselves to praying and cultivating the garden which had been set aside for them and had the briefest and most infrequent contacts possible with the neighboring Tahitians. Materially speaking, they were "hangers-on" in the Tahitian society, while they disdained its institutions, its beliefs, and even those Tahitians who did not share their Catholic faith, which included everyone by the end of the Mission. There was no propagation of the faith; rather one might speak of propagation in reverse because they were to lose the few converted souls who had come back to their land with them. This explains why the fathers decamped upon the arrival of the frigate which was sent out either to replenish their stores or to take them back.

It is known that social and political stratification in ancient Tahiti revolved around a few categories — chiefs (*ari'i*) and, below them, deputies or subchiefs, landowners (landed proprietors), commoners, and various categories of public and private servants. Because the authors vary both as to terminology and function, we shall not try to be more exact here, being satisfied with referring back to the sources (de Bovis 1855; Henry 1962; Morrison 1966; Tekau Pomare 1971) and to the bibliography about the subject (Williamson 1924; Handy 1930; Sahlins 1958; Newbury 1967). For it matters little to us, as Maximo was not very clear. Aside from the *ari'i*, his *Journal* distin-guished only their men of trust, called by the author "intendants," "captains," and "chiefs of guard" (of the valley); below these was the general population. This lack of detail was the result of the fact that he was mainly in contact with the *ari'i*, and with two of them in par-ticular, Vehiatua and Tu, whom he often accompanied when they moved about and thanks to whom he was introduced into Tahiti's *ari'i* society.

These *ari'i*, chiefs of the districts (*mata'ina'a*) and the political units into which Tahiti was divided before the unification introduced at the instigation of Europeans, were related among themselves. Outside of political struggles that might temporarily separate them, the *ari'i* visited each other, exchanged presents, and participated in the same ceremonies on certain of the most celebrated cult sites (*marae*). Vehiatua, who was, according to the *Journal*, the *ari'i* of the district where Maximo resided,[6] had authority over all of the chiefs of the peninsula,[7] a listing of whose respective districts and subdistricts we can reconstruct (Anuhi, Aiurua, Vaiaotea, Vaiuru, Taiarapu, Mataoae, Toahotu, and Afaahiti. All of these districts together made up, as we know, Teva-i-tai, one of the two units of the Teva domain, the other being Teva-i-uta, made up of three districts: Papara, Mataiea, and Vaiari (Papeari) in Tahiti-nui. Tu (or Otu as he was called by Maximo), the second *ari'i* with whom he was familiar and the companion of Vehiatua, was the chief of Pare and of the northern districts of the island: Arue, Matavai, Papenoo, and Tiarei. Papenoo and Tiarei, for example, had Tu's brothers as *ari'i*; Tu or Vairaatoa or yet again Pomare Eirst was on top and also *ari'i rahi* of Tahiti, a title which he had just taken away from the *ari'is* of Papara; in Maximo Rodriguez' time, the *ari'i* of Papara was Amo, whom Maximo saw when he went through the district and who was the chief of the Teva group and therefore superior in a certain way to Vehiatua.[8]

Concerning Tahiti's peninsula and the rights that could be exercised there, the *ari'is'* world had four levels: that of the districts, that of the whole peninsula (Vehiatua for Teva-i-tai), that of the Tevas, and finally the level of the *ari'i rahi*, then held by Tu.[9] In reading the *Journal*, we see that Vehiatua, in his capacity of superior *ari'i* of Teva-i-tai, paid constant visits in his domain and that numerous exchanges of presents were made on such occasions. Tu, with whom Vehiatua was allied after having been his adversary, shared his time between his own domain and Vehiatua's, and his stay in the peninsula was marked by

[6] Maximo Rodriguez does not tell us whether the divisions he calls "district" here and there in his *Journal* are all on the same level.
[7] "Vehiatua, proprietor and chief of the district of Ohatitura" (Rodriguez 1930: 14).
[8] One hesitates to write that Amo was paramount to Vehiatua, as it seems wrong to interpret, *ipso facto*, the political relationships within Tahiti as feudal tenureships.
[9] We know that Tu was the operating name that Vairaatoa bore as his Tahitian title before the supreme title passed along to his son, who was Pomare II; thus, we use here the only name that Maximo seems to have known.

large transfers. Maximo's *Journal* thus allows a study of the exchanges and the economic behavior of Tahitians on the level of the *ari'is* and of the relationships that the chiefs maintained with the people. We see here two aspects: (1) that of the relationships that the Tahitian society, the *ari'is* and the people, kept with the officers of the Spanish vessels, with the Mission, and most particularly with Rodriguez; and (2) that of the internal relationships of Tahitian society, between the people and its chiefs.

As in the case of the arrival of Wallis (Wallis 1774) or other navigators putting in at the oceanic archipelagoes, the first contacts between Tahitians and Spaniards were marked by exchanges of gifts. The Tahitians brought bananas, breadfruit, and coconuts and also offered pigs, mats or *tapas* [cloth of beaten bark]. In exchange, the Spaniards gave metal objects, axes, knives, nails, fishhooks, glass trinkets, and European cloth. In Maximo's account, these exchanges of presents were concomitant with an offering by the chiefs present of a banana shoot as a pledge of peace; this indicates that these exchanges were more social than economic, intended to some extent to seal friendly relationships. When these relationships had been established, exchanges of an economic sort were organized to correspond to the respective needs of both parties: the Europeans needed drinking water, firewood, and fresh produce; the Tahitians demanded alcohol, arms, and manufactured products, such as European clothing and cloth, hardware, and iron tools.

This satisfaction of the respective needs of both parties would seem to be the basic purpose of these exchanges. However looking at them more closely, one can see that the transactions became very personalized after the first exchanges when the parties hardly knew each other. They concerned the *ari'is*, Maximo, the commander of the Spanish vessel, and the missionaries. It is necessary to take into account this personal quality in order to catch the significance of these exchanges. According to the *Journal* (Rodriguez 1930: 6), Maximo was adopted by Tu as his brother ("son of his own mother and father") and considered to be an *ari'i*; hence the transactions in which Maximo was involved were exchanges of presents between *ari'is*, whether they were between Tu and Maximo, between Vehiatua and Maximo, or between Maximo and the various other *ari'is* of the island upon visits that he made during the ten months of his stay.

In their peninsular establishment, Maximo and the Mission subsisted thanks to the supplies brought to them by the inhabitants. These were provided systematically by the people of a valley "earmarked" by

Vehiatua. More or less assimilated by the *ari'is*, Maximo and the Mission members were treated as *ari'is*, and therefore the inhabitants of a specific locality were charged with bringing them the items they needed to subsist. It was a tribute for which the fathers gave a few metal gifts (knives, fishhooks) or glass trinkets in exchange. However, unlike the true *ari'i*, they did not assure the security that the people might expect from any chief; the real basis of this tribute was in fact the protection and benefit that Vehiatua hoped to draw from business with the Spanish vessels and from the technology of which they were bearers — hence the numerous exchanges of gifts whose function was to maintain the alliance between the chiefs and the whites.

The practice of exchanging products is deeply embedded in Tahitian society; the indications given by the *Journal* are revealing in this regard. In the *Journal* may be found the main traits or features of a system that assure the cohesion of a social pyramid: tribute from the people to their chief; tribute from *ari'is* to other *ari'is* to honor visits made to them; and large quantities of subsistence goods when an *ari'i* (with his family) goes to stay at the home of one of his peers. Relationships within Tahitian society are introduced or sealed by exchanges that show their reciprocal nature (between *ari'is*) or their asymmetry (tribute). Tribute, however, is made only as one aspect of a larger exchange between the *ari'is* and their people, in which the people in return enjoy the protection of the chiefs.

III.   In proceeding to the present-day analysis of the district we have chosen, we set ourselves the task of showing that the present-day relationships expressing the functioning of the Tahitian economy of this area form, under a superficial modernity, a structure which reminds one of that prevailing two hundred years ago upon the arrival of the Europeans.

Located at the extremity of Tahiti's peninsula, the district presents, economically and objectively, both the advantages and disadvantages inherent in such a location. Compared to the other districts, it has a much more extensive lagoon, and therefore a greater potential wealth of fish. The main valley, occupied by coconut plantations, pastures, and coffee groves, has resources analogous to those of the other districts, but the length of the shore allows for an outlet from other large valleys which, at the time of Maximo Rodriguez, seem to have been separate, autonomous districts.

The population is grouped together in a compact village at the mouth of the main valley, while the fishermen's households are scattered about at the edge of the lagoon on the beach, which extends to the south of the village. Perhaps one can see in the district in this predominant presence of the ocean one of the reasons for the important role of activities connected with the ocean, whether it is a matter of fishing, for which the village owns large nets — though other districts own such nets, too — or outrigger canoe races, for which the district has a solid tradition of virtuosity and for which they are recompensed each year by winning the first prizes at the Tiurai.[10]

In this district, as elsewhere, Tahitian land holdings are small, cut up into parcels, often encumbered by joint rights of ownership resulting from the succession of generations and the crossing of family rights through the interaction of matrimonial alliances. These small holdings contrast with the large, single-tenanted properties belonging to the wealthy half-caste or *popa'a* families from Papeete who particularly monopolize the valley districts of which Maximo Rodriguez speaks. Aside from the district chief's public works and transport enterprise, of which we will speak again and which employs a certain number of workers, salaried employment outside of the district, especially in greater Papeete, is, along with big net fishing, the sole source of moneyed income for the population. For any one of these activities, the location of the district "at the end of the island" is a disadvantage in terms of transporting fresh products to the market, and also in terms of the daily commuting to Papeete. This isolation of the district, still more noticeable a decade ago when the village was connected with the rest of Tahiti only by a poor trail, explains why employment offered by the chief seems like a windfall in the eyes of the population, and thus underlines the eminent functions of the *tavana* in the village.

Actually, these functions are executed not by the nominal chief, but by his adoptive son, who is connected by blood with one of the most illustrious half-caste families of Tahiti, of which the Polynesian side descends through the women of the Tevas of Papara, and therefore from the *ari'i rahi* of Tahiti before the title fell to the Pomares. The young chief — his adoptive father, though nominal chief of the district is obliged because of the weight of his years to rely on his son for the administration of the district — performs at the same time the official functions of *tavana*, the burden of his enterprises, and to some extent the village's social arbitration. Protestant, he belongs to the predominant church; his wife is the principal schoolmistress in the district's public school. Because of the new municipal institutions es-

---

[10]   *Tiurai* [the month of July] designates the festival that takes place in Tahiti beginning with July 14th, the French national holiday.

tablished in 1972, the young chief has become mayor of the commune or town (*'oire*) regrouping four districts of the peninsula and of Tahiti-nui (Pueu, Tautira, Afaahiti, Faare) and the councilor in the Territorial Assembly, the lower legislative house.

In addition to all of these activities, the young chief owns a big net (*'upe'a rahi*) for fishing *ature* [scad: *Selar crumenophthalmus*], which abound in the lagoon in the first months of the year. These fish are greatly appreciated by Tahitians, and they sometimes make sensational catches whose sale brings in considerable income (Ottino 1965). In 1963-64, the chief busied himself with the matter, organizing teams, or staff, launching the net, presiding over the catches and shipping them quickly to Papeete, keeping a watch over the sale, and dividing up the income. Our interest in this enterprise comes from the fact that it entailed the participation, in the name of kinship or through ties with clientele, of a very large majority of the population of the village. It associated participation with the results, not through salary, but through the sharing of the product and the profits. It realized, between the majority of the village and its chief, a model of relationships based on reciprocity in the means of production — the chief providing the capital represented by the net and the means of transporting the product to the market, with the village, for their part, providing the work. A corresponding reciprocity occurred in the division of the profits, half of the sale going to the chief (the owner of the net, transporter of the product, and organizer of the operation) and the other half going to the workers. According to the ethnologist, Ottino, the sellers of the product at the Papeete market are called *'opere* [apportioner] by the owners of the net, while the buyers generally use the term *ta'ata ho'o* (Ottino 1965: 59) to designate the sellers at the market place; that also underlines the redistributing role the chief holds as a corollary of his powers of organization.

After 1964, the adoptive son of the district's *tavana* expanded his activities by setting up an enterprise for public works and heavy trans-port and, while his wife continued in her occupation as village school-mistress, he split up his time between the district, where his net was, and Papeete, where he had his new business. This made for more em-ployment in the village. Afterwards, his relatives took back the big net, and while two other big nets appeared later on the young chief concentrated his activities on the public works business.

Through the economic role that he plays in the district, this chief is, for everyone — and in everyone's eyes — the protector of, and spokes-man for, the people. Therefore, he is credited with a capital of prestige that he must show and illustrate if he does not want to fall in the esteem of his compatriots. In exchange for this credit, recognized and "reimbursed "to some extent by the chief's eminent action, the district grants him its confidence. In the political elections, not only does the district vote for the chief but also for the men or parties that he recommends. This prestige function of the chief is complex. He has prestige in his district because he is the defender of its interests. He is the village's biggest entrepreneur. He furnishes employment, giving the village the possibility of acquiring cash income. The inhabitants also are aware that he is well known as an entrepreneur throughout Tahiti and displays tact and cleverness in his dealings with the political powers — it is a flattering thing to have as *tavana* a well-known, even famous man. Finally, by his prowess (at the Tiurai races, for example), he makes it possible for the district to be winner in competitions among the different districts of the island. Thus, the chief's prestige in the eyes of his people is the result of many factors; if one of them turns out to be in his disfavor it cannot compromise him all at once — the fall of the chief's prestige would result only from a general and appreciable crumbling of the positions that this prestige has assured him thus far, a disintegration implying a slow one-way process over several years.

The prestige that the *tavana* enjoys in this instance in the eyes of those he administers is not a static phenomenon: the economic and social positions deteriorate, and even without that, habit dims their attraction in people's eyes. In the same way, a benefit or service is rendered only once and the prestige with which the people credit their chief in exchange for objective or subjective services that he renders requires that these latter be numerous and constantly renewed. Thus the chief is caught up in a PRESTIGE DYNAMICS that he must master if he wants to maintain his status. In other words, between the people and their chief, there is a DIALECTIC OF RECIPROCITY through which the chief provides services — material in the form of subsistence or money, moral owing to the district's renown — and the people provide their allegiance. The chief keeps his position through the prestige he enjoys in regard to his people, and he enjoys the benefits that having the people on his side confers. Much of this may be explained by describing an event that happened in 1971: the marriage of the chief's daughter.

The *tavana's* attitude of active collaboration with the political powers made the district appear to the observer to be like a government fief whose orientation in representative actions is bent in his direction, as in the Territorial Assembly, legislative elections, referenda, and, very recently, the township of East Taiarapu; this attitude was possible because of the authority that the chief had over his people, an authority founded on the prestige that he enjoyed due to services rendered. It permitted the installation of a resting and exercising base for the Army in the village. This livens things up a bit there and brings in some cash income, but it also brings forth the bad humor that builds up in every Tahitian when foreigners lack discretion and take up too much of the human landscape.

This base has been advantageous for the powers that be because it is installed in a locality where the chief is favorable to it. It was also advantageous to the chief because of the base's help in organizing his daughter's wedding celebration. Actually, aside from the village, this celebration brought together two to three thousand guests who came from Papeete, the governor of French Polynesia (then a minister), a secretary of state, and a former governor who had come from France on an official visit and who was invited to the event. The village, left to its own resources, could not have served as host to so many people. So the chief did not appeal to it for the usual preparation of such a *tama'ara'a* [Tahitian feast], and the village felt left out of things. It sulked, it seems, at the church ceremony, but not at the feast. The chief was criticized for having had the celebration organized by strangers instead of having solicited help from the village, which was ready to reply to his appeal. But the people were secretly flattered at having hosted and greeted so many important persons and consequently the chief's prestige was bolstered.

Upon this occasion, the chief's position appeared in all its complexity. The *tavana* enjoys a reciprocity of exchanges with his people (services exchanged for support), but he is also in a similar position in relation to the government. He brings political support from his district in exchange for official services, which extend from the use of public equipment to the supplying of service and work for the benefit of the district. Thus, he is an agent for the redistribution of goods and services obtained in exchange for his collaboration and the flattering self-image those in power can derive from his district.

IV.   Tahitian society in a district like the one we have just studied is based, on the economic level, on a complementary twofold system of reciprocity and redistribution, involving a people and a chief and recognized by the people in a dialectic of exchange. This legitimate dialectic, the power of the chief over his people in exchange for honor and prestige for the people in comparison to those of rival districts, constitutes the essence of the Tahitian community.

This structure of reciprocity and redistribution based on the chief's prestige seems analogous to that which prevailed in the former society with which Maximo Rodriguez was familiar at the dawn of the arrival of Europeans two hundred years ago. This analogy permits us to illuminate, with the light of the present institutions, the past about which the notes available to us seem but poor and fragmentary. Inversely, it also suggests that the changes to which Tahitian society has been subject for two centuries have not altered the deeper principles of organization, and we may be led to believe that it will always be so.

Would it be reasonable to do so? Might one not think that the situation just described arises essentially from subjective factors, for instance, from the exceptional personality of the chief? Might one not also think that a more profound change than that which has occurred in Tahiti might modify that structure? We need to refer briefly to the Tahitian evolution and the conditions under which it took place. The political and social organization of ancient Tahiti foundered in 1815 with the defeat of the traditionalist chiefs by the innovating Pomares and the foreigners at the battle of the *fe'i pi*; the *ari'i rahi* became a Biblical king, the ONLY *ari'i* of Tahiti, and the chiefs became *tavanas* or governors. The society, deprived of its political heads who were also the heads of great lineages, was reduced to a collection of minor lineages and more or less extended families. These crystallized into households that seemed like some sort of Biblical families and gave the missionaries the illusion of creating a Christian universe.

Anyway, the economy changed little; colonial exploitation, in this case copra production, did not get going right away and the depopulation (which occurred right after the coming of the Europeans) diminished to quite an extent the pressure of the population on the resources and freed lands where coconut groves for copra could be planted. The economy, at the lowest levels, remained a village economy, based on self-subsistence, while surpluses went into the ceremonial economy circuits — the *pure*, for example — reinvented by the missionaries as a substitute for manifestations connected with the former politico-religious structure or reimposed on the new structure by the faithful of the new church as a relic of the past. Besides this, one might advance the hypothesis that when the colonial economy of copra was put into operation, the work carried out on the owners' plantations followed tradition again, by simply transposing tolls formerly due to various categories of the chiefs of ancient Tahiti by the commoners. In this economy, the processes of intra- and interfamily cooperation and intra- and intervillage cooperation continued to occur and, as a corollary, so did the manifestations of reciprocity in exchanges of redistribution and prestige on the part of the chiefs.

For a decade now, Tahiti has functioned fully as a moneyed economy which already has had the effect here and there of stretching family ties, of giving economic autonomy to the reduced families consisting only of couples and their children, and of creating new consumer needs. The big family reunions have not stopped, nor have the ceremonial manifestations, but it is well known that the time required for social transformations is greater than that for economic innovations. Moreover, our district has remained on face-to-face speaking terms with its chief, but it is known that it is poor and isolated, and that he has prestige and has mastered the mechanics of modern economy, is dynamic, and has relationships with the most powerful *popa'a* known in Tahiti. But the village may lose its chief; he may be introduced into more active economic circuits, and money may slowly accomplish its job of erosion. Is it not conceivable that the present manifestations of this ancient Tahitian structure based on reciprocity and redistribution will ultimately disappear? Even if the answer is not clear, this deeply-rooted social system is one factor that must be taken into account in considering the future evolution of Tahiti.

REFERENCES

DE BOVIS
    1855 *État de la société tahitienne à l'arrivée des Européens.* Paris: Éditions maritimes et coloniales.

FINNEY, BEN
    1965 *Polynesian peasants and proletarians. Socio-economic changes among the Tahitians of French Polynesia.* Polynesian Society Reprints series 9. Wellington.

HANDY, E. S. C.
    1930 *History and culture in the Society Islands.* Bernice P. Bishop Museum Bulletin 79. Honolulu.

HENRY, TEUIRA
    1962 *Tahiti aux temps anciens.* Publications de la Société des Océanistes 1. Paris: Musée de l'Homme.

MOENCH, RICHARD U.
    1963 *Economic relations of the Chinese in the Society Islands.* Cambridge: Cambridge University Press.

MORRISON, JAMES
    1966 *Journal de James Morrison, second maître à bord de la Bounty.* Papeete: Société des Études Océaniennes.

NEWBURY, COLIN
1967   Aspects of cultural change in French Polynesia: the decline of the Ari'i. *Journal of the Polynesian Society* 76:7–26.

OTTINO, PAUL
1965   La pêche au grand filet. *Cahiers ORSTOM Série Sciences Humaines* 2(2).
1972   *Rangiroa. Parenté étendue, résidence et terres dans un atoll polynésien.* Paris: Cujas.

PANOFF, MICHEL
1964   *Les structures agraires en Polynésie française. Rapport d'une mission effectuée dans le cadre de l'ORSTOM 1961–1963.* Paris: E.P.H.E. et Centre Documentaire pour l'Océanie.

ROBINEAU, CLAUDE
1968   Economie ostentatoire chez les Polynésiens: l'exemple des Iles de la Société. *Économies et Sociétes. Cahiers de l'I.S.E.A.* 2(4): 819–832.

RODRIGUEZ, MAXIMO
1930   *Journal de Maximo Rodriguez premier Européen ayant habité Tahiti (Tautira). 1774–1775.* Papeete: Imprimerie du Gouvernement.

SAHLINS, MARSHALL D.
1958   *Social stratification in Polynesia.* Seattle: University of Washington Press.

TEKAU POMARE (PRINCESSE)
1971   *Mémoires de Marau Taaroa reine de Tahiti.* Paris: Société des Océanistes.

WALLIS, SAMUEL
1774   "Relation d'un voyage fait autour du monde dans les années 1766, 1767 et 1768," in *Relation des voyages entreprsi par ordre de S.M. Britannique.* Edited by J. Hawkesworth. Paris: Saillant et Nyon.

WILLIAMSON, ROBERT W.
1924   *The social and political systems of central Polynesia.* Cambridge: Cambridge University Press.

Interdisciplinary Research on Uncontrolled Urban Growth as a Contribution to National Development: The Pakistan Case

J. H. DE GOEDE

INTRODUCTION

This paper will discuss some aspects of the interdisciplinary research project on slum improvement and urban development that is being carried out in Karachi by the Free University of Amsterdam and the Karachi University. I will focus primarily on three elements of the project design which have proved especially effective in ensuring the value and utilization of the project findings:

1. The built-in continuous interaction between the project and the regional and national planning agencies.
2. The development of conceptual and operational definitions that view the slum both as a problem in itself (as a living environment, hazardous to health) and as a symptom of wider problems, (inadequate income).
3. The selection of the objectives and the way they are formulated.

We start with a short overview of the urbanization process in Pakistan and then turn our attention to one of the negative effects of the rapidity with which the urbanization process took place — the development of slums in the main urban centers of Pakistan. Next we deal with the low-cost housing policy in national planning, focusing on the development of strategies in which problem-oriented research in urban centers came to be more and more a felt need and indicating the possibilities for such research to contribute to national development. The next section gives a short account of the objectives of the project, its interdisciplinary character, and the different project activities which were initially formulated in order to realize the objectives. Finally, we present some conclusions and recommendations.

We do not claim to present a comprehensive analysis of the value of the interdisciplinary research project on slum improvement and urban development to overall national development in Pakistan. The primary purpose is to give impetus to further discussion of research-oriented areas of mutual concern and to further sharing of insights into their problems.

The views and opinions expressed in this paper are those of the author and not necessarily those of the Joint Research Project IV — Slum Improvement and Urban Development.

URBANIZATION IN PAKISTAN

Pakistan has a long urban history. According to Sir Mortimer Wheeler (1968), the first cities developed about 2350 B.C., when the Indus civilization was at its height. The main cities during that period were Mohenjo-Daro and Harappa, located on the banks of the Indus River.

Many other cities developed in the Indus Delta near the Arabian Sea (e.g. Bambhore) but eventually disappeared because of environmental changes.[1] Although the decline and fall of the Indus civilization is often related to the consequences of environmental abuses such as excessive tree felling and unrestrained grazing by goats and sheep, which are recognized as desert-producing agents,Wheeler has serious doubts about this view: "Let it be stressed that the causative factor in deterioration has little or nothing to do with climate. . . . This problem of environmental change has long been under suspicion" (1968 : 8). Based on various excavations in the Indus Valley, one can add that the decline and fall of the earliest cities in the Indus Valley seem to have been related also to the invasions of Aryan-speaking peoples and hill tribes (1968 : 126). In the long urban history of Pakistan one fact, however, is clear: the Indus River remained and remains the most important factor in the location of cities. The land near the river is fertile, providing the possibility of a food surplus to feed the urban population. The river also provides the access needed for a settlement to function as a marketplace. It follows that the main cities of Pakistan, Karachi, and Lahore are located in the valley of the Indus: Lahore, in the neighborhood of the remains of Mohenjo-Daro and Harappa and Karachi in the Indus delta on the coast of the Arabian Sea near the remains of Bambhore and Debal.

[1] For a detailed study of the rise and fall of cities in the Indus Delta, see Herbert (1968: 256).

Today, cities do not decline and fall so easily. Technology has advanced; the environment is subject to greater control. At the same time, national and international realities serve to hinder invasions from neighboring regions or countries. This state of affairs need not continue, however, as recent developments in Indo-China, the Indian subcontinent, and the Middle East attest. Nevertheless, the urban population in Pakistan is growing at a high rate, with Karachi and Lahore serving as the main poles of urban growth. Table 1 gives an impression of the growth of the urban population in Pakistan.

Table 1. Total urban population 1901–1970 (Husain and Shibli 1967: 43)

Year	Number of urbanites
1901	1,619,000
1950	6,000,000
1960	9,830,000
1965	12,880,000
1970	17,100,000

Although the absolute figures presented above give an impression of the magnitude of the urbanization process in Pakistan, especially since independence in 1947, the urban population still represents only a small proportion of the total population. In 1951 the urban population represented 16.7 percent of the total population, and this percentage rose from 21.9 in 1961 to 25.1 in 1965 (Jedraszko 1966 : 16). An impression of the annual percentage increase in the urban population of Pakistan can be grasped from Table 2 representing the growth of the main cities of Pakistan.

Table 2. The growth of towns in Pakistan 1941–1961 (Aziz 1969: 25)

Town	Population			Percent annual increase	
	1941	1951	1961	1941–1951	1951–1961
Karachi	435,887	1,137,937	2,044,044	10.1	6.0
Lahore	671,659	849,476	1,296,477	2.4	4.3
Lyallpur	69,930	179,144	425,248	9.8	9.0
Hyderabad	134,693	241,801	434,537	6.0	6.0
Multan	142,768	190,122	358,201	2.9	6.5
Rawalpindi	185,042	237,219	340,175	2.5	3.7
Peshawar	173,420	151,776	218,691	1.2	3.7

In general, the annual rate of urbanization was approximately 5.5 percent. The rate of increase for the total population was approximately 3 percent, indicating a rate of increase for the urban population nearly two times greater than that of the total population.

There were several reasons for the increase in urban population in Pakistan. In the first place, there was the influx of refugees from India after the partition of the Indian subcontinent in 1947. This large-scale movement of migrants, resulting from tensions and conflicts between Muslims and Hindus, covered a period of four years up to 1951. Of the estimated ten million refugees, 10 percent settled in Karachi, 10 percent in the other urban centers, and the remaining 80 percent in the rural areas of Pakistan (Hasan 1956). It is possible that the arrival of the refugees in the rural areas influenced migration of individuals already residing there, and in this way contributed indirectly to migration of the rural population, although no empirical data on this subject are available.

The second important reason for the fast growth of cities was migration from the rural areas to the urban centers. Of the push-pull factors that account for migration to the urban centers, it is the push factors that are dominant in Pakistan. To be more specific, these include the economic push forces that generally result in massive migration — the forces of poverty, because of land fragmentation and unemployment or underemployment, aggravated by the introduction of advanced agricultural production techniques without alternative employment opportunities in the secondary or tertiary sector in the same rural region.

Because the rural economic situation is the main reason for migration, many urban newcomers are reluctant to become integrated into city life. This reluctance is evidenced by their regular visits to their place of origin, not only to meet family or friends, but also to participate in various ceremonies related, for example, to birth, marriage, and death. One might say that many migrants live in the cities without being urbanized. They are rural at home and are urbanized only in their place of work; or, according to Pahl (1969 : 28), "Urban by day and rural by night." This notion — that the city is regarded first as an environment for earning, and only secondarily as a living environment — has its consequences, not only for the migrants themselves (in terms, for example, of isolation and deviation), but also for policy-oriented activities that are to guide the urbanization process in the future.

The third primary cause that fostered urban growth was, of course, the natural increase of the urban population. In 1970 the annual increase in the population of Karachi due to excess of births over deaths was 2.8 percent, as compared to a migration excess of 3.2 percent. It is Kingsley Davis (1966) who points out that the biological increase of the city population is becoming more and more important in the urbanization process, contrary to the popular opinion that rural-urban migration is the main factor.

A somewhat less important factor in the growth of cities in Pakistan is what one could refer to as the "passive urbanization" of villages that have come into the urban context due to the fast horizontal growth of cities like Karachi and Lahore. As a general survey of slums in the Karachi metropolitan region has revealed (*General survey of slums* 1970–1971; see also Siddiqui 1971), a considerable number of "Goths" have become part of the city. A study by Agha Sajjad Haider (1960) in Lahore revealed the effects of "passive urbanization" on the behavior of the villagers. Inasmuch as former villages or "Goths" are at present integral parts of cities like Lahore and Karachi, more empirical research is needed to achieve insight into the effects of passive urbanization on the social life of the inhabitants. Such research might result in a valuable contribution to guiding principles for the future growth of urban regions.

THE PROBLEM OF SLUMS

It will be evident that the fast urbanization process in Pakistan (due mainly to the influx of refugees, rural-urban migration, and the natural increase of urban populations) has resulted in an uncontrolled urban growth, visible in the development of slums and shantytowns in the urban centers of Pakistan. In comparison with other regions of the world, Pakistan had the additional burden of accommodating the refugees from India, which (especially in Karachi) created an immediate backlog in low-cost housing. Table 3 gives an indication of the extent of the problem in major towns in Pakistan. According to a report of the United Nations (1971), 600,000 persons, representing 27 percent of the

Table 3. Number of shelterless families in major towns in 1965 (Town Planning and Housing 1969: 2)

Town	Number of shelterless[a] families
Karachi	75,000
Lahore	33,000
Lyallpur	32,000
Hyderabad	35,000
Multan	22,000
Rawalpindi	4,000
Peshawar	5,000
Total	206,000

[a] Shelterless is defined as living in *jhuggis* and impoverished shelters under slum or near-slum conditions. The average size of a family is five persons.

total population of Karachi, resided in slums or uncontrolled settlements in 1968. The definition of slums in the context of the Pakistani society has long been discussed, and the discussion is still continuing, reflecting the discussions on a broader level of the formulation of an operational, interdisciplinary definition suitable for cross-cultural comparison.

In Pakistan the following definitions have been developed:

1.   An area where general housing and living conditions are so dilapidated, unhealthy, and dangerous that the conduct and growth of safe, healthy, and normal life becomes difficult (Shibli and Ullah, et al. 1965).

2.   An urban settlement, generally unplanned, legally or illegally inhabited by underprivileged people or people of low socioeconomic class, and characterized by insanitary conditions; overcrowding; and makeshift, deteriorated, or deteriorating dwellings, either completely lacking facilities and amenities, or serviced with facilities and amenities far below the minimum acceptable standards of the city, thus predisposing the area to be hazardous to the physical and social well-being of its inhabitants (Samdani 1972).

3.   A residential area of which the majority of dwellings are *juggis*, *kucha*, or semi-*pucca* built close together in an unplanned way, with insufficient public facilities or amenities, sometimes located in danger spots (such as river beds), often overcrowded and congested, with a population of which the majority belongs to the lowest socioeconomic class of the society (de Goede 1971 : 8).

4.   A residential area where housing conditions, in the broader sense, are substandard to such an extent that it is clear that for one or more explicit reasons the physical health of the inhabitants is endangered by these conditions (van der Linden 1972 : 10).

Although it is beyond the scope of this paper to discuss these different definitions in detail, some remarks can nevertheless be made about them.

In these and other definitions developed elsewhere, we can distinguish three broad categories in the terminology which is used: (1) terms related to the physical aspects, such as "dilapidated," "old," "unplanned"; (2) terms referring to the socioeconomic position of the population, such as "poor," "isolated"; and (3) terms referring to the negative consequences of the aspects mentioned under (1) and (2), such as "dangerous," "unsafe," "unhealthy." Sometimes the third category is subdivided into negative consequences for the inhabitants of (a) the slums, and (b) the city as a whole.

In general, there is a tendency to concentrate on aspects of slums that can be observed. As a consequence of this approach, the slums may become isolated from the broader local, regional, and national levels of the society of which they are an integral part and thus isolated from redress of the underlying causes when solutions for slum problems are formulated. In Pakistan, this approach is often referred to as the "public works approach." Improving physical conditions in order to avoid danger (e.g. to health) does not solve the problem of slums and can be a useful target only in short-term planning for *ad hoc* solutions.

Short-term planning for *ad hoc* improvements can be of strategic importance only when it is embedded in long-term planning which involves the broader levels of society, including important variables such as the difference in income between rural and urban regions that causes migration. It is for this reason that in Pakistan low-cost housing is included in the overall five-year planning, some of the socioeconomic objectives of which are: (a) to reduce interregional and intraregional disparity in per capita income and (b) to direct the forces of economic and social change toward the establishment of a just society (Pakistan 1968 : 3).

A second consequence of an approach to slums in terms of aspects that can be observed is that attention may be given only to the large and clearly visible slum areas of the city, overlooking the numerous small clusters of substandard dwellings located more toward the center of the city in the vicinity of residential areas for middle- and higher-income groups. It would not be an exaggeration to say that these "mini-slums," taken together, represent a very substantial proportion of the total substandard slum dwellings in Karachi. Based on my own observations in Karachi, the development of "mini-slums" is related in part to a long distance between home and work and to a shortage of public transport. Many laborers, especially among those working in the tertiary sector of the economy, who live with their families on the fringe of the city, build (whether alone or in collaboration with colleagues) "a second *juggi*" close to their place of work, where they live except during the weekends.

LOW-COST HOUSING POLICY AS PART OF THE NATIONAL PLANNING

Since independence, the Pakistan government has given due attention to the provision of low-cost housing for urban newcomers. The massive arrival of refugees in the urban centers of Pakistan, especially, created problems in housing. Many refugees settled illegally on vacant land, having no means of finding decent accommodation. During and after the arrival of the refugees, migration from the rural areas added substantially to the shortage of housing facilities in the urban centers.

In the revised first five-year plan (1955–1960), one of the objectives was "to create 250,000 building plots and to provide nucleus houses or material for 'self-built houses' on half the "plots" (Mahbub Ul Haq 1966 : 135). This target, however, was not achieved, mainly because "a lot of investments went into the housing sector but private luxury buildings and government offices took precedence over the essential program of low-cost housing" (1966 : 171–172). In the second five-year plan, the objective was to provide 300,000 low-cost dwelling units. In the first two years of the plan period only 42,000 units had been provided (1966 : 190), while after completion of the second five-year plan the actual performance was reported to be half of the initial target (Masadul 1966). The third plan initially started with a target of 350,000 housing units, embedded in "a modest comprehensive programme for physical planning and housing both on a curative and preventive basis" (Pakistan 1970a : 247). In the revised plan, however, the target was reduced by 34 percent, while the comprehensive approach had to be abondoned (1970a). Finally, it was expected that only 50 percent of the revised allocation would be realized after completion of the third five-year-plan period (Town Planning and Housing 1969 : 8). It will be no surprise that in spite of the fact that low-cost housing was a part of the overall planning, the backlog increased from 600,000 in 1960 to 1,200,000 in 1970 (Shibli 1966 : 49).

During the execution of the five-year plans certain strategies were developed to contribute to the solution of the low-cost housing shortage. Toward the end of the first five-year-plan period a start was made on a scheme of slum clearance and subsequent resettlement of the slum population. An example often referred to is the Korangi resettlement scheme in north Karachi. The results of the scheme turned out to be not according to the initial expectations. The financial investments were comparatively high, and moreover the resettlement caused a number of negative side effects for the resettled slum population, such as a sharp rise in cost of shelter (often too high in comparison with the average income) and a long distance between home and place of work, with consequent relatively high transportation costs.[2] A similar

---

[2]   For comments on the Korangi Scheme, see Shibli, Ullah, et al. (1965).

situation is described by Peter Marris (1966), who studied a rehousing project in Lagos.

Because of the considerable financial costs of resettlement projects, as well as the socioeconomic problems for the resettled population, in the third five-year-plan period (1965–1970) the Karachi Development Authority (KDA) more or less revised the concept of low-cost housing and subsequently launched the idea of "plot townships" as an additional solution to the low-cost housing shortage in Karachi. This revision was stimulated by one of the objectives formulated in the chapter on physical planning and housing of the third five-year plan:

In order to cater for the incoming poor rural immigrants, consideration is to be given to provide each urban centre with a special reception area, consisting of developed land with immediate essential services and facilities provided it is proved feasible to regulate the inflow in line with the facilities provided. The immigrants will be encouraged to build their own temporary or permanent houses on developed plots in this area provided free of cost under government technical supervision (Pakistan 1965: 375).

The main idea behind the development of plot townships is "that small size plots, with modest scale of development, should be given to the squatters who should be encouraged to build houses on a self-help basis" (KDA 1969 : 1). The Karachi Development Authority started to develop three plot townships (Aurangi, Qasba, and Baldia), with a planned capacity of approximately 600,000 inhabitants after completion. At present there has been no evaluation of the final results, but it would be advisable to study the outcome in the near future, especially because of the recent attention to "sites and services" projects as primarily preventive solutions to accommodate urban newcomers.

Sites and services projects defined as projects to provide urbanized land on which the occupants can build their own dwellings, using self-help methods (World Bank 1972: 64), have been initiated also in Africa and Latin America. The difference between "plot townships" and "sites and services" projects, as far as we can see, is that in "sites and services" more explicit attention is given to the development of community services such as welfare centers, health clinics, and educational institutions. However, when sites and services projects are not an integral part of comprehensive planning in which socioeconomic aspects are given due attention, there will be the same negative side effects as in the case of resettlement projects. In that case, the sites and services will deteriorate to a substandard level and become the slums of the future.

Besides slum-clearance resettlement, "plot townships," and "sites and services" projects, the idea of slum improvement was also introduced as a possible strategy for the solution of the shortage in low-cost housing. The idea was proposed for the first time in the third five-year plan (1965–1970), as part of the housing program (Pakistan 1965 : 381–382). In the fourth five-year plan the idea of slum improvement was presented in a more elaborated way as part of an "environmental approach to low-income housing." The approach was partly as follows:

a.   existing housing stock even in slums will be preserved wherever possible;
b.   major and rapid improvements in the living conditions of slum dwellers will be achieved through well-organized programmes of environmental improvement (Pakistan 1970b: 474).[3]

At present no data are available concerning the results of the proposed environmental approach, although various slum improvement projects have been initiated or are under preparation. It is somewhat surprising that, despite the efforts of the government (in terms of finance, as well as in terms of discovering new strategies), the housing shortage has not decreased, and that, on the contrary, the housing situation has gradually detoriated. Although it is beyond the scope of this paper to analyze in detail why the housing situation did not improve in spite of the various government efforts, we will summarize a number of somewhat interrelated reasons.

On the macrolevel several factors contributed, among which were:
1.   the influx of refugees after partition in 1947 and a massive rural-urban migration, which resulted in "over-urbanization" in Pakistan[4];
2.   the rapidity of population growth, rural as well as urban;
3.   a condition of underdevelopment in terms of national income;
4.   political instability on the national level; and
5.   international tension and conflicts with India.

On the mesolevel we find:
1.   an absence of a developed conceptual awareness of comprehensive regional and urban planning (Pakistan 1966b : 22);
2.   an absence of a systematic administrative machinery for implementation of such an approach (Pakistan 1966b: 22);
3.   the presence of an excessive number of administrative bodies with partial and overlapping jurisdiction, and a lack of coordination among

[3]   The idea of slum improvement is further elaborated in Pakistan (1966a).
[4]   Overurbanization is defined as "a situation in which larger proportions of [a country's] population live in urban places than their degree of development justifies" (Hauser 1963: 203).

the various policy-making and executive authorities dealing with urban problems (Pakistan 1964 : 4); and

4. a low priority of operational research and analysis, lack of any process of evaluation and feedback, and lack of trained manpower (Pakistan 1970b : 472).

On the microlevel contributing factors were:

1. the poverty of slum dwellers and squatters;
2. lack of security of slum dwellers and squatters, discouraging private investment in housing;
3. isolation and consequent lack of participation of slum dwellers and squatters in decision-making processes on the urban level;
4. perception of the city by slum dwellers and squatters as a place for earning rather than as a place for living;
5. a spending pattern of household income in which the immediate living environment generally does not have priority; and
6. poverty of family members in the rural place of origin which leads many migrants to send part of their earnings back home.

JOINT RESEARCH PROJECT IV: SLUM IMPROVEMENT AND URBAN DEVELOPMENT

One of the reasons mentioned above for the critical housing situation on the mesolevel was the low priority of operational research, lack of evaluation and feedback, and lack of trained manpower. As a logical development, therefore, the National Planning Commission, being a mesolevel institution of the Pakistan society, started to promote activities to remove this bottleneck (Pakistan 1970b: 475). One result was the initiation of Joint Research Project IV, as a part of the overall Regional and Urban Development Project of the Pakistan Government.[5] Dutch participation in Joint Research Project IV was mainly as a result of a report by two Dutch researchers of the Free University of Amsterdam, framing suggestions for modest improvements in a particular slum area in Karachi, based on a socioeconomic survey (de Goede and Segaar 1970). On the Pakistan side, the project was subcontracted to Karachi University by the Planning Commission.

---

[5] The Regional and Urban Development (RUD) Project is an overall framework for national pilot projects and joint research projects initially carried out under the supervision of the National Planning Commission and later on by the Ministry of Presidential Affairs, Town Planning and Agrovilles.

The general objective of the project, which started functioning in August 1970, was "to undertake action-oriented research in the slum areas of Karachi in order to provide information on the ways and means of improving slums with minimum investment of resources." More explicitly, among our objectives were:

1. to provide the central government with empirical data and policy-oriented suggestions based on empirical data, to be incorporated in the development of short-term and long-term strategies for slum improvement and urban development;

2. to provide the local urban government with empirical data and policy-oriented suggestions based on empirical data to be of use for *ad hoc* solutions in urgent housing problems, thematic as well as geographic, in the Karachi metropolitan region; and

3. to create the opportunity for training in policy-oriented research on problems of slums and shantytowns and urban development in general.

To achieve these objectives the project staff initially formulated several project activities, among which were:

1. a general survey of slums in the Karachi metropolitan region, to collect basic data about the nature and extent of the problem of slums, thereby providing empirical data to formulate an operational typology of slums;

2. in-depth studies of different types of slums in order to deepen the insights into the nature and underlying causes of slums and subsequently to develop policy-oriented suggestions for slum improvement, to be initially tested for validity as pilot projects in improvement experiments;

3. the execution of improvement experiments in cooperation with the local urban government authorities, such as the Karachi Development Authority and the Karachi Municipal Corporation; and

4. evaluation of the improvement activities and feedback.

At a later stage of the project, more attention was given to the initiation of thematically-oriented research, in addition to the in-depth geographically-oriented studies of different types of slums.

Based on the different aspects related to the problems of slums and the proposed action-oriented research for slum improvement, the following disciplines were initially represented among the staff of the project: sociology, physical planning, economy, social geography, and public administration. To date, the project has completed the general survey of slums, together with a limited number of in-depth studies and a number of thematically-oriented studies. The present project staff is engaged in formulating policy-oriented suggestions to be presented to the central government, as well as to the local government, as a possible contribution to a further development of short-term and long-term planning strategies for the solution of the critical low-cost housing situation.[6]

SOME CONCLUSIONS AND RECOMMENDATIONS

1.   In view of the numerous and varied bottlenecks in Pakistani society on the macro-, meso-, and microlevel, causing a gradual deterioration in the low-cost housing situation, an interdisciplinary research project on slum improvement and urban development, having as its field of inquiry only the microlevel, can contribute toward a solution only on a very modest scale.

2.   An interdisciplinary research project on slum improvement and urban development should be an integral part of a more broad-scale approach, including activities directed toward removing bottlenecks that are not within the scope of a research project on slum improvement and urban development restricted to the microlevel.

3.   Interdisciplinary research on uncontrolled urban growth as it has been carried out in Pakistan to date has focused mainly on problems related to the microlevel and has tried only to discover barriers to a solution for low-cost housing inherent in the socioecological environment of uncontrolled urban settlements.

4.   An important potential for contributing to national development has been created by a functional connection of the research project with government institutions on the mesolevel: the Planning Commission; the Ministry for Presidential Affairs, Town Planning and Agro-villes; and the government of Sindh. Through this connection, elements related to the situation at the microlevel of the national society can be incorporated into overall short-term as well as long-term planning.
5.   At the same time, the project can serve as a channel through which

---

[6]   Although it would be possible to frame a number of policy-oriented suggestions based on the research findings of the project, these are not presented here because the final version of the recommendations has not as yet been completed by the present project staff.

the poor and often illiterate slum population can bring their problems and grievances to the notice of government levels to which they did not have direct access earlier.

6.   In discovering and analyzing the underlying causes of the development of slums and shantytowns, which is of crucial importance in framing suggestions for slum improvement, the project can contribute by giving more empirical weight to the arguments for realizing the general objectives in development planning in Pakistan, which are:
a.   to maintain the tempo of development in the country, through a determined effort to secure the greatest and most efficient utilization of our material assets and human resources;
b.   to reduce interregional and intraregional disparity in per capita income;
c.   to move toward a viable synthesis between the claims of economic growth and social justice through the pursuit of pragmatic policies; and
d.   to direct forces of ecoonmic and social change toward the establishment of a just society. (Pakistan 1968.)

7.   The research project on slum improvement and urban development should give due attention to the many villages which are in process of "passive urbanization"; this because of a possibly different reaction pattern of the villagers in "becoming urban." At the same time, research is needed to analyze the nature and extent of small clusters of semi-permanent dwellings representing a very substantial proportion of the total substandard housing environment in the Karachi metropolis.

8.   In view of the importance of a constant flow to governmental planning agencies on the mesolevel of information concerning micro-level aspects of uncontrolled urban growth, it is advisable to add "institutionalization" as one of the major objectives of action-oriented inter-disciplinary research projects on urban problems.

9.   Because the underlying causes of excessive uncontrolled urban growth are not related to the urban situation alone, and because strategies in finding solutions will have to include variables on the regional and national level, the region, at least, should be included in the activity field of applied problem-oriented urban research. In this respect, one of the conclusions of McGee about the Third World city is of importance:

... the city must be seen as a symptom of processes operating at a societal level. Thus, to diagnose accurately the characteristics and roles of these cities one must investigate the conditions of underdevelopment which characterize these countries, of which cities are only part (McGee 1971: 31).

REFERENCES

AZIZ, SARTAJ
  1969 *Industrial location in Pakistan*. Karachi: National Publishing House.
DAVIS, KINGSLEY
  1966 "The urbanization of the human population," in *Cities*. Edited by Dennis Flanagan, 3–25, New York: Alfred A. Knopf.
DE GOEDE, J. H.
  1971 "On a definition typology of slums in Karachi metropolis." Joint Research Project IV. Karachi.
DE GOEDE, J. H., T. J. SEGAAR
  1970 *Azam Basti: a sociological inquiry and recommendations for development work*. Amsterdam: Institute of Social Sciences, Free University.
General survey of slums
  1970–1971 *General survey of slums in Karachi metropolis*. Joint Research Project IV. National Planning Commission of Pakistan, Karachi University, and the Free University of Amsterdam.
HAIDER, AGHA SAJJAD
  1960 *Village in an urban orbit: (Shah-di-Khini), a village in Lahore urban area*. Lahore: University of the Punjab.
HASAN, R. S.
  1956 Refugee population and prospects of its resettlement in urban and suburban areas of Karachi. *Pakistan Geographical Review* 11: 33–47.
HAUSER, P. M.
  1963 "The social, economic, and technological problems of rapid urbanization," in *Industrialization and society*. Edited by Bert F. Hoselitz and Wilbert E. Moore, 199–208. Paris and The Hague: UNESCO-Mouton.
HERBERT, WILHELMY
  1968 Verschollene Städte in Indus Delta. *Geographische Zeitschrift* 56: 256–294.
HUSAIN, A. F. A., KHALID SHIBLI
  1967 "Urbanization and urban development policy in Pakistan," in *Problems of urbanization in Pakistan*. Edited by Shafik H. Hashmi, Garth N. Jones, et al., 36–69. Karachi: National Institute of Public Administration.
JEDRASZKO, A. B.
  1966 "Introduction," in *The problem of shelterless people and squatters in Pakistani cities*. Edited by M. Ahmed Ali, Shafik H. Hashmi

and Andrzej B. Jedraszko, 15–25. Karachi: National Institute of Public Administration.

KARACHI DEVELOPMENT AUTHORITY (KDA)

1969   *A note on KDA's plot townships at Aurangi, Qasba, and Baldia.* KDA Document Number A (d) – 6.

MAHBUB UL HAQ

1966   *The strategy of economic planning: a case study of Pakistan.* Karachi, Lahore, and Dacca: Oxford University Press.

MARRIS, PETER

1966   *Family and social change in an African city: a study of rehousing in Lagos.* London: Routledge and Kegan Paul.

MASADUL, HASAN

1966   "The problem of shelterless people and squatters, a survey," in *The problem of shelterless people and squatters in Pakistani cities.* Edited by M. Ahmed Ali, Shafik H. Hashmi, and Andrzej B. Jedraszko, 59–65. Karachi: National Institute of Public Administration.

MC GEE, T. G.

1971   *The urbanization process in the Third World: explorations in search of a theory.* London: Bece.

PAHL, R. E.

1969   "A perspective on urban sociology," in *Readings in urban sociology.* Edited by R. E. Pahl, 3–40. Oxford: Pergamon Press.

PAKISTAN, GOVERNMENT OF

1964   *Urbanization in Pakistan.* Karachi: National Planning Commission, Physical Planning and Housing Section.

1965   *The third five-year plan (1965–1970).* Karachi: National Planning Commission.

1966a   *Urban improvements — a strategy for urban works: observations of Sir Patrick Geddes with special reference to old Lahore.* Karachi: National Planning Commission, Physical Planning and Housing Section.

1966b   *National and regional physical planning — a new conceptual approach to development planning in Pakistan.* Karachi: National Planning Commission, Physical Planning and Housing Section.

1968   *Socio-economic objectives of the fourth five-year plan (1970–1975).* Karachi: National Planning Commission.

1970a   *Outline of the fourth five-year plan (1970–1975).* Karachi: National Planning Commission.

1970b   *The fourth five-year plan (1970–1975).* Karachi National Planning Commission.

SAMDANI, G.

1972   Cyclostyled paper of Joint Research Project IV, cited in *Some remarks and suggestions towards a better definition and a better typology of slums.* Edited by J. J. van der Linden. Joint Research Project IV. Karachi.

SHIBLI, KHALID

1966   "Low-income housing policy for urban areas," in *The problem of shelterless people and squatters in Pakistani cities.* Edited by M.

Ahmed Ali, Shafik H. Hashmi, and Andrzej B. Jedraszko, 49–55. Karachi: National Institute of Public Administration.

SHIBLI, KHALID, SALIM ULLAH, *et al.*

1965 "Housing: short-range tactics and long-range strategy." Karachi: National Planning Commission, Physical Planning and Housing Section.

SIDDIQUI, ISLAMUDDIN

1971 *Goths at a glance.* Joint Research Project IV, Report 23. Karachi.

TOWN PLANNING AND HOUSING

1969 *Low income housing, problems and prospects: with special refer-* National Planning Commission, Physical Planning and Housing Communications and Works Department.

UNITED NATIONS

1971 *Improvement of slums and uncontrolled settlements.* New York: U.N. Department of Economic and Social Affairs.

VAN DER LINDEN, J. J.

1972 *Some remarks and suggestions towards a better definition and a better typology of slums.* Joint Research Project IV. Karachi.

WHEELER, SIR MORTIMER

1968 *The Indus civilization.* Supplementary volume to the *Cambridge history of India.* Cambridge: Cambridge University Press.

WORLD BANK

1972 "Urbanization." Section working paper. June.

The Strategy of Peasant Mobilization: Some Cases from Latin America and Southeast Asia

GERRIT HUIZER

INTRODUCTION

It is surprising that among development workers, as well as scholars concerned with rural societies, the image of peasants as apathetic, fatalistic, and "resistant to change" continues to prevail. This is in spite of the fact that during the last few decades the peasants in several countries have paticipated actively in such revolutionary or liberation struggles of worldwide import as the Russian and Chinese revolutions and the anticolonial wars in Algeria and Indochina (Wolf 1969).

Even politically aware persons of Marxist orientation in many countries seem — in spite of the obvious — to be hesitant or reluctant to see, in an effort to organize patiently and mobilize the peasant masses, a means of gaining power and transforming their society.[1] Up to the end of the last century, however, practically all peasant rebellions failed dismally, and proof that peasants can be organized effectively for radical social transformation is, historically, relatively recent.

In practically all cases, the growth of such peasant movements was a reaction to the introduction or extension of some form of colonialism. The large majority of rural dwellers came to be economically exploited by a relatively small elite, either local or foreign, generally concentrated in the cities or the smaller provincial capitals. In Latin America, the Spanish conquerors established the system of *haciendas* (large estates) from the sixteenth century onward. Lands which were formerly mainly

---

[1] Probably this is partly due to the doubts expressed by Marx about the revolutionary potential, based on experience with small landholding peasants supporting Louis Bonaparte in France in 1848.

communal property of *comunidades* (indigenous communities) were taken away and given to the members of the colonial elite. After the liberation from Spain at the beginning of the nineteenth century, this process of usurpation of indigenous community land was accelarated. While under Spanish colonial rule there was some protection of the remaining *comunidades*, in the second half of the nineteenth century the new elites, descendants of the colonial rulers, introduced private property as the only possible system of landholding that enabled them to take over community lands in an aggressive way.

Protest movements against these activities by the Indian population were bloodily repressed, but resistance flared up time and again. Some movements became so well organized and large scale that they had nation-wide impact and brought the land reform issue — redistribution of large estates — strongly to the fore. Among such movements were the unsuccessful revolt by Zarate Willka and a great part of the Bolivian peasantry in 1899, and the peasant guerrillas revolt led by Emiliano Zapata in Mexico (1910–1919), which will be described below.

In most rural areas in Latin America, where peasants vainly tried to defend their traditional rights and possessions, a permanent state of potential violence resulted. The anthropologist Holmberg, who studied a typical area in Peru, called this situation the "culture of repression." It appears that the peasants' proverbial apathy, laziness, and unwillingness to change is not an inherent characteristic, but clearly a result of the "culture of repression" under which they live. Whenever there is a real chance to alter fundamentally the repressive conditions imposed upon them, they will do so with all the energy they have.

When speaking of repression, it should be noted that in several Asian countries the contrast between wealthy landlords and peasants is much less obvious than in Latin America. Except for the Philippines, in most of Asia there are few typically large landholders, but there are many small landlords who may own plots of five to twenty hectares and let that considerable land be cultivated by a number of tenants or sharecroppers. Furthermore, there is a large number of middle-income farmers who work part of their plots (a few hectares mostly) and lease the rest to tenants or sharecroppers. In addition to the large percentage of small owner-farmers, there are in most Southeast Asian countries many peasants whose plot is too small to maintain their families, and who, for that reason, either have to rent additional land from others or work part-time as agricultural laborers. Then there are those tenants who own no land at all, but have a certain security through rented land. At the bottom of the hierarchy are the landless agricultural laborers.

Looking at the prevailing rural social structure in Asia from the bottom up, reveals that it is not too different from that in Latin America: being exploited by a large, wealthy landowner or by a rich or middle-income farmer is basically the same. Sometimes exploitation by small landowners is worse than by mighty and powerful ones. This makes it understandable that peasant rebellion has been as endemic — at times — in Asia as it has in Latin America.

The most striking precondition for the occurrence of peasant movements is the change in the rural status quo in ways that create acute frustration among the peasantry. The development of peasant organizations has, without exception, been a reaction to inequalities, either in land tenure or the social structure, and particularly to the growth of such inequalities. It was generally a deterioration of a more or less stable, not too unbearable situation, for the peasants that initiated some kind of protest movement — either spontaneous and violent, or well organized and channeled.

In both continents certain, generally economic, developments have taken place within the traditional system which have undermined its stability and brought some awareness of the need for change to the peasants. In many instances, landlords have themselves broken the status quo by altering the prevailing system. They have tried to extend their estates or plots at the expense of small landholders, and they have tried to evict tenants in order to start cultivating new cash crops for expanding world markets — actions that introduced or extended the plantation system in some countries.

Particularly if such changes were brought about in a rapid way and without consideration for the rights (traditonal or legal) of the peasants involved, the need for protest and revolt could easily arise. Several of the peasant revolts that took place in Bantam, Java, in the nineteenth century, and the communist-led rebellion in Sumatra in 1926, were directly related to such changes — changes introduced by the elite. In the Philippines, peasants had experienced deteriorating living conditions, particularly after the Spanish colonial regime was replaced by the American system following a largely agrarian revolt in 1898. Not only did the American regime maintain the *caciques* (local landlords and chiefs), but the spread of democratic ideals and, subsequently, some degree of education, made the peasants recognize that their living conditions were intolerable. The introduction of commercial plantation agriculture, particularly in central Luzon (Pampanga and Nueva Ecija), was accompanied by a concentration of land into increasingly larger holdings. Rents went up from 38 to 60 percent between 1903 and 1946. Land grabbing by large owners from adjacent small owners added to the discontent and led to protest movements in several areas, such as the Colorum movement in 1923 in Mindanao; the Tangulan movement in 1931 in central Luzon; and the Sakdal movement in 1935. The latter became a political organization which was dispersed after a violent uprising.

In order to gain a deeper insight into the conditions under which peasant organizations arise, develop, and, in some cases, become more or less effective revolutionary movements, a number of concrete examples in various parts of the world must be described and analyzed. Some outstanding peasant movements, which caused more or less radical changes in the areas where they took place, were the peasant-guerrilla movement headed by Emiliano Zapata in the state of Morelos in Mexico (1910–1919); the peasant syndicates in the area of Ucureña, Cochabamba Valley, Bolivia (1936–1953); the peasant federation headed by Hugo Blanco in the Convención valley, Peru (1955–1963); the peasant leagues headed by Juliao in northeastern Brazil (1955–1969); the Huk movement in central Luzon, Philippines, headed by Luis Taruc (1938–1952); the tenant unions in Japan (1919–1938); and the Indonesian Peasant Front (*Barisan Tani Indonesia*, BTI), which developed in Java between 1953 and 1956. Because they are less well known, the three movements in Asia will be described in more detail than the Latin American ones.[2]

THE PEASANT GUERRILLAS IN MEXICO (1910–1919)

In the Mexican Revolution, which started in 1910, the peasantry played a crucial role. This should be seen as a reaction to the usurpations of communal lands by large *haciendas*. This took place in the second half of the nineteenth century. Many indigenous communities tried in vain to retain or recover the communal lands from which they had been displaced under new legislation favorable to private property. The *haciendas* had expanded considerably, at the expense of the communities. As a result, in 1910 the peasantry was ready to answer the call to armed revolution.

One of the most outstanding peasant leaders was Emiliano Zapata, the son of a small farmer who had lost his land because of despoliation by the local *hacienda*. It has been said that Emiliano Zapata, when still a child, tried to console his weeping father, saying: "I will take it back when I grow up." At the age of thirty he was elected president of the com-

[2]   For ample descriptions of peasant movements in Latin America, see Huizer 1972a; Bandsberger 1969; and Stavenhagen 1970.

mittee of his village, Anenequilco in the state of Morelos, which was attempting recovery of the lost lands. This took place shortly after Zapata had returned from a period of forced military service and work with a *hacendado* in Mexico, work imposed on him as a kind of punishment for his rebellious attitude. During this period, Zapata gained experience and insight that served him later as a peasant leader.

Because of his able leadership, three other villages with similar problems formed a committee. These villages, led by Zapata, hired a lawyer to defend their rights in the court against the claims of the large *haciendas*. After legal means proved ineffective, the peasants took the law into their own hands and joined the revolutionary guerrilla movement begun in 1910.

The insurrection was supported in the hope that the revolutionary forces, once they were in power, would do justice to the peasant cause as had been promised. But when the new president gave only lip service to the agrarian reform question, Zapata formulated his own *Plan de Ayala* in November, 1911. This plan demanded radical land reform measures. In accordance with this program, Zapata distributed land to the peasants in the areas that fell under the control of his guerrilla troops. In 1915, President Carranza, to weaken the cause of the peasant guerrilla forces that practically controlled Mexico City, published a decree (January 6, 1915) incorporating the main points of Zapata's program. This is generally considered to be the formal starting point of the Mexican land reform movement. No effective execution was given to the new decree, so the guerrilla groups led by Zapata withdrew from the capital, but kept military control of large areas in and around the state of Morelos. In those regions, a land distribution program was executed. Help was given by a group of agricultural engineering students from the National Agricultural University.

Thanks partly to this continuous organized peasant pressure in various parts of the country, the ideas of the *Plan de Ayala* were integrated into the Mexican Constitution (Article 27) in 1917. In spite of this official acceptance, however, effective distribution of lands took place only in those areas where the peasants were well organized or armed. Arms were needed because the opposition of the landlords to agrarian reform took violent forms. The landowners in many areas formed the so-called "white guards," bands of gunmen who defended the landowners' interests. They did this by intimidating or terrorizing the peasants who had organized the agrarian committees to petition for land. In the meantime, Zapata resisted many attempts to frighten or to bribe him. In 1919, he was assassinated by a man who had pretended to be his ally, but who was actually in league with the government and the landlords.

BOLIVIA: THE PEASANT SYNDICATES IN COCHABAMBA

In Bolivia, scattered peasant revolts had occurred as a reaction to the abuses of the prevailing system of servitude. The Chaco War against Paraguay (1933–1935) accelerated the disintegration of the traditional system. Thousands of Indian soldiers for the first time left the *haciendas* and entered the outside world. Bolivia's defeat left many frustrations and much political bitterness.

In the aftermath of the war, peasant unrest increased in many areas of Bolivia. In 1936, a rural syndicate was formed in Ucureña, in the temper‐ ate, fertile Cochabamba Valley, one of the most prosperous agricultural regions in Bolivia. In this area, the Santa Clara monastery had leased some of its land to large local landholders, and the lease included the right to the labor of the resident peasants. The peasants, in turn, decided to organize a union to rent the land themselves from the Santa Clara monastery, and thus avoid the onerous obligation of working for the landholders. Their efforts met with strong opposition from various local landowners who saw in them a direct threat to their traditional rule. It was ultimately the landholders who bought the land from the monastery and evicted the peasant families who had been living and working there for years, destroying their homes and forcing them to leave the area or to revert to serfdom. A young radical peasant leader, José Rojas, whose father had been dispossessed in this fashion, had to escape to Argentina, where he worked as a laborer and acquired a political education. He re‐ turned secretly to Bolivia a few years later and became the undisputed leader of the revived peasant movement in Ucureña.

In the 1952 revolution, a middle-class government, which depended partly on peasant support, came to power in Bolivia. This government, headed by Paz Estenssoro, had to speed up the promulgation of radical land reform legislation when the peasant syndicates in the Cochabamba area, headed by José Rojas, began taking over the estates by force and creating a movement that threatened to spread all over the country.

In the years following the revolution of 1952, and the radical peasant actions of that period, most of the large estates in Bolivia were taken over by the peasant syndicates in a legal, orderly way as part of the official land reform program. The peasants took or received arms to defend the new situation against the landed elites' efforts to turn the clock back. The fact that the majority of the Bolivian peasants now work their own land and that the *hacienda* system has been abolished explains why movements, such as the one created by Ernesto Guevara, found little response among the Bolivian peasantry.

PERU: THE PEASANT FEDERATION OF LA CONVENCIÓN

In Peru, one of the most important peasant organizations was the federation of peasant unions headed by Hugo Blanco in the Convención valley in the Cuzco area. The *arrendires* (peasants of the valley) had to render services and a certain number of days of unpaid agricultural work for the landlord in return for a plot of virgin land. When the virgin land was cleared and started to give the *arrendires* a reasonable yield, the landlords increased their demands. The local federation of unions of *arrendires* and their *allegados* (subtenants) was soon strong enough to respond to the challenge of the landlords. The intransigence, and at times abusiveness, of the latter made it easy for radical leadership to propagate, through the federation, action in favor of land reform.

The most effective method was the strike, consisting of a refusal by the *arrendiras* to do any work for the landowners while continuing to cultivate their own plots. Their idea was that they had paid for their plots during the years they had worked without pay for the landowners. The peasants also organized local self-defense groups, in order to be able to prevent the landowners or the police force (generally known to work with the landowners) from dislodging them from the plots they were working. Various acts of violence from both sides occurred. When the movement became so strong that many landowners left the area, the government promulgated a land reform decree (Decree Number 14444 of March 28, 1963). This decree was especially designed to bring the conflict in the area to an end. The producers' cooperatives which were later formed in the area, with the assistance of the land reform agency, appeared to enjoy a good start because of the organizing experience obtained by the peasants in the unions of the prereform period.

BRAZIL: THE PEASANT LEAGUES OF THE NORTHEAST

In Brazil, the *Ligas Camponesas* (Peasant Leagues) were created in the northeast from 1955 on. This movement was started by local peasants in the Galileia estate. They formed an association to raise money to enable them to buy from the landlord the estate on which they worked. This was considered undesirable and the landlord tried to throw the peasants off the land. They called upon a lawyer, Francisco Juliao, who sympathized with them and was willing to defend them in the courts.

It was Juliao's idea to extend this local initiative to the state of Pernambuco and the whole northeast of Brazil. The Peasant Leagues were thus created. Once the movement had gained strength and become more radical, as a reaction to the opposition of the landlords, other groups were created. Some were established by the Church to counterbalance the influence of the leagues. The peasants of the area — both the leagues and other groups — became increasingly convinced of the need for radical reform. A program of *concientizacao* (making people aware of their needs) by encouraging them in literacy, a method used by Paolo Freire, helped in this. It was probably the growing strength of the whole movement, in which the leagues, the Church, and other groups participated, that caused such fear among the ruling class that the army intervened and organized the *coup d'état* of April, 1964. After that the leagues, as well as the other groups, were repressed.

PHILIPPINES: THE HUK MOVEMENT

In one of the most troubled agricultural regions of Central Luzon, Pampanga, not far from Manila, the foundations for the Huk movement were laid by Pedro Abad Santos, a Socialist Party leader and lawyer who was also a wealthy landlord in the area. In 1930, he created *Aguman Ding Maldong Talapagobra* (AMT) (The League of the Poor Laborers), which gained strength in the Pampanga area by organizing strikes and protest demonstrations. One of the important collaborators, who helped Abad Santos to spread his movement, was Luis Taruc, son of a peasant who had had some education. Such collaborators visited the villages, organized meetings, and explained the purpose of the organization. Taruc (1953: 37–38) described his own trial-and-error approach as follows:

... I first sounded out the people about their problems and grievances, and then spoke to them in their own terms. Instead of carrying out a frontal assault on the ramparts of capital, I attacked a case of usury here, an eviction there, the low crop rate elsewhere. These were things which our organization could fight, and around which the people could win small, but enormously encouraging victories.

I had to prove to the people that our organization and its leaders were of them and close to them. I sat down with them in their homes, shared their simple food, helped with the household chores. I walked in the mud with them, helped them catch fish, crabs and shell fish, worked with them in the fields. It was not hard for me, nor was it new to me. I was merely rejoining my own people. In their turn, the people would go out of their way to feed and to accommodate the AMT leader.

Within three months I had organized my whole area.

The peasant organizations generally used nonviolent methods — demonstrations, sit-down strikes — to let everyone be arrested and go together to jail. Dramatic stage presentations and similar cultural activities were used to teach the peasants about the labor struggle, and to turn the strikes into public manifestations. By 1938, the AMT had 70,000 members who participated to some extent in the organization (Taruc 1953: 38–45).

In 1938, the AMT joined with the illegally existing communist peasant movement, KPMP. As a reaction to the Japanese occupation, the combined peasant organizations created on March 29, 1942, the Hukbalahap (*Hukbo ng Bayan Laban sa Hapon*) (Peoples' Army against the Japanese). The aims of the Hukbalahap movement were expulsion of the Japanese, cooperation with the allied armies, apprehension and punishment of traitors and collaborators with the Japanese, complete independence for the Philippines, and the establishment of a democratic government with land reform, national industrialization, and guarantees for a minimum standard of living.

From 1942, when the armed struggle against the Japanese was initiated, many peasants carried arms and formed squadrons of approximately a hundred men each. The armed units operated in the areas around the homes of their members.

The Huk movement rallied many people and became so strong that it controlled whole areas of central Luzon where the Japanese could not enter. In those areas, *de facto* political control and local government was in the hands of the resistance forces which had their base in the peasantry. The property of many collaborationist landlords was taken over by the Huks, in areas controlled by them, and harvests were no longer handed over. Landlords who supported the Huk movement could remain on their land, but had to be content with a fixed rent. In some provinces, Huk leaders were elected as governors in December, 1944.

Although the efforts of the Huks considerably facilitated the American Army's liberation of the Philippines, relations between the Huks and the Americans were never good. There was fear that the Huks would radically change the social order in the Phiippines if they got the chance.

A popular front formed between Huks and other groups could not win the 1946 presidential elections, but elected representatives were not even allowed to ocuupy their seats in the National Chamber. The new president, Roxas, a protégé of the United States Army, started a campaign to persecute the Huks. This was done so cruelly that in many areas, as a reaction to the repression, the Huks won increasing support from the peasant population, and gained effective control of large parts of central Luzon. When this became threatening, a new policy, with the advice of United States' technicians, was initiated by the Magsaysay government, i.e.

to win over the peasants by reformist measures while using military force in a sophisticated way. It was particularly through inner divisions that the Huk movement finally became so weakened that the government campaign became more or less succesful. Luis Taruc surrendered and was imprisoned in 1954. Constant flare-ups of Huk or related movements have, however, continued until the present time.

JAPAN: THE TENANT-UNIONS BETWEEN TWO WORLD WARS

In Japan the first World War brought about many changes, mainly favorable to the landlords. Land prices went up and landowners had many opportunities for profitable speculation, while small farmers lost their lands through indebtedness, partly as a result of inflationary tendencies. Absentee landlordism increased, and tenant farmers were forced to pay higher rents in kind. This reached such extremes that tenants had insufficient rice for their own survival. The result was the last and largest spontaneous peasant revolt, the Rice Riots of 1918, that spread to more than thirty prefectures and lasted forty-two days.

On the other hand, rapidly increasing industrialization during these years gave greater employment opportunities, causing an influx of the rural population to industrial areas. The bargaining position of urban labor and of the peasantry improved somewhat through the formation of labor unions and the occurrence of strikes. Thus, one effect of industrialization was an improvement in the tenants' bargaining position. Because of the relative labor shortage, they were able to threaten the landlords with noncultivation of the land if they did not get a reduction in rent.

The influence of people who had worked in industry was strongly felt after the war when industry passed through a severe crisis. Many workers were dismissed and returned to their already overcrowded villages. Tension increased rapidly because the backward conditions in which tenants generally lived were more acutely felt by those who returned. The organizing experience they had gained in industry was soon applied to bargaining for better conditions.

The first formally organized tenant unions grew up in the areas around the new industrial centers, particularly Nagoya. The first local tenant organizations were reported around 1916 in the prefectures of Aichi, Gifu, and Mie, soon to be followed by those of Osaka, Hyogo, and Okayama, and a few years later in several prefectures of Kyushu, where there were many former industrial workers from the city of Fukuoka

(Totten 1960: 194; 204; Dore 1959: 69).[3] Local unions grew more or less spontaneously around rent disputes, and generally at the *buraka* (hamlet) level. Workers who had been dismissed because of union activities, and who had to return to their villages, were particularly influential in these activities. Several of them became effective peasant organization leaders.

The need for an organization at the national and prefectural levels was increasingly felt, but did not materialize until 1922. The increasing acceptance of Christian, democratic, and socialist ideas by Japanese intellectuals, and the spread of these ideas in many circles, helped to prepare the ground. Thus a group of intellectuals, pressmen, a missionary, and a labor leader took the initiative in creating the *Nihon Nomin Kumiai* (abbreviated: *Nichinō*) (Japanese Peasant Union).

By 1926 the *Nichinō* claimed a dues-paying membership of about 68,000 peasants. Its principal aim was still to reduce rents, but it also had such political aims as legislation protecting the tenants and the rather vague objective of "socialization of the land." After universal suffrage was introduced in Japan in 1925, and the number of voters rose from three million to fourteen million, *Nichinō* became politically more influential. *Nichinō* leaders circulated a request to the twenty-eight labor federations, with more than 1,000 members, to unite in a Workers' and Peasants' Party. Increasing involvement in political and ideological issues caused many consecutive splits and mergers among peasant organizations and political parties, difficult to unravel. One divisive point was whether to include all peasants and small landowners, or only tenants. Another was between those who saw the tenants' struggle against the landlords as a class struggle directed at overall social change and those who were more in favor of compromise and the achievement of concrete benefits.

It was observed that:

These differences were primarily differences between leaders. Which national organization any particular local tenant union was federated with depended more on personal connections with particular leaders than on ideological attachment to one doctrine rather than another. And, indeed, in their practical activities the various federations differed little from each other. Their chief function was to assist tenants engaged in disputes, to encourage the formation of local tenant unions in districts hitherto unorganized, and to direct and coordinate the formulation of tenants' demands (Dore 1959: 77).

Whatever occurred at the national level, the main function of tenant unions was at the local level, in rent disputes with landlords. Many of these disputes had been taken up by *buraku* unions before the national

---

[3] Information supplied by K. Aoki, a former peasant organization leader.

organization existed, but the struggle at the local level was made more effective through the national union and its officials.

In the campaign to spread the movement, those *burakus* were chosen in which the most severe and acute problems existed. Great obstacles had to be overcome. Very large landowners were helped by police repression; smaller landowners used their traditional paternalistic control to exert pressure on tenants against joining a union. Kin relationships, refreshments, favors, and threats to force people to pay their debts were also brought to bear. These obstacles could only be overcome by the immediate organization of a union. In the *burakus*, *org* (potential activists) had to be sought, and a meeting organized with their help. Once a meeting was held, it was essential to continue it until a union had been effectively created by the election of a president, vice-president, and treasurer, and the payment of dues. Some such meetings lasted a day and a night, or even two days.

As peasant unions spread throughout the country and became better organized, the character of their demands changed. Initially, demands were mostly for postponement or reduction of rent payments in cases of a bad harvest and an emergency; later, demands for a permanent rent reduction of 30 percent were increasingly heard.

Landlords more often tried to evict peasants when they began to organize unions. The fact that more and more disputes were brought to the courts (rather than solved through negotiation), which generally ruled in favor of the landlords, made the peasant organizations more aware of the need for political action at the national level. Radical views on the need for drastic social structural change in order to improve the life of the peasants found increasingly positive response. The (leftist) Workers' and Peasants' Party, on the whole supported by the *Nichinó* (both undergoing parallel splits and mergers), won considerable influence during the 1928 elections for the Diet.

The government, alarmed by the rising tide of radicalism in the peasant and labor movement, ordered nationwide arrests of movement leaders in the so-called 3–15 event (March 15, 1928). Most of the top leaders at national and some prefectural levels were imprisoned, a serious blow to the *Nichinó*. Some, such as national leader Tokuda, remained in jail until after World War II.

Despite mounting difficulties, local action continued, showing how strongly the needs and demands of the tenants were felt. In September, 1931, the Manchuria incident took place: an explosion engineered by the army near Mukden was used as a pretext for the occupation of Manchuria. This action considerably augmented the authoritarian tendency of the

Japanese government and the influence of the army. A period of serious repression had begun.

This shows how serious the land tenure situation was, and makes it understandable that the efforts to propose reform legislation were on many occasions undertaken by the more enlightened politicians, albeit in vain. It prepared the way before and during World War II for the land reform, somewhat reduced as a result of revived elitist pressure, finally carried out in 1946 (Dore 1959: 69).

THE INDONESIAN PEASANT FRONT: BTI

One of the most spectacular peasant organizations in Asia was the *Barisan Tani Indonesia* (BTI) (Indonesian Peasant Front), created and directed by the Communist Party. In 1953, Aidit became secretary-general of the PKI (Indonesian Communist Party). From that time on, the communists tried to come to a "united front" policy and to build up a mass organization, particularly among the peasants.

The strategy followed by the Communist Party workers and the BTI activists was developed by Aidit. In the first place, survivals of "feudalism" in Indonesia were denounced. The need to organize peasants, taking as a point of departure their most strongly felt demands and grievances, was emphasized. It was suggested that local organizations be created around such demands, varying for each particular village or area (Hindley 1951: 63, 161). In each area or community, party cadres were instructed to identify their most acute problems in meetings with the peasants. In order to achieve an appropriate relationship between the cadres and the village population, the policy of "Three Togethers" was followed. Activists were to "live together, eat together, and work together" with the peasants. They were also to help them in the solution of all kinds of practical day-to-day problems regarding rent payment, legalization of titles, etc.

"Small but successful" actions were seen by the PKI and BTI cadres as the best way to mobilize the peasantry. It was emphasized, however, that these "small but successful" actions should be accompanied by stimulating among the peasants an awareness that the basic solution to their problems would come only with the end of landlord exploitation, and that this could be achieved through organized struggle. Actions that would directly affect the relationship with the landowners were not to be undertaken, however, until the organization at the local level had gained enough strength. Then the demands for joined land-rent agreements, or for lowered interest rates on loans, or lowered land rents, could be brought up.

The surprising thing about the spread and development of BTI and its activities in Java was that it came about in a society still dominated by tradition and respect for established leadership. However, the first signs of a decline could be noted. To undermine systematically the hold of the traditional wealthy leaders over their villages, and bring the people to the point where they would oppose that leadership on such crucial issues as land tenure, was a big step in a tradition-bound society.

It would be an exaggeration to say that there was a clear-cut introduction of class struggle, but there were certain elements of application of the conflict model. Taking up examples of existing, but hidden, grievances against those in power, people were made aware that the harmony in their villages was disappearing or did not exist. Various abuses, such as usury, became more obvious under the modernization process. An awareness of exploitation was bound to increase and the BTI took up these issues as a means of organizing the peasants as an interest group.

In addition to the existence of strongly felt grievances, mainly related to a deteriorating land-tenure situation, strong new leadership was needed to rally the people against the traditional elite. Identification with the fate of the poor peasants was the initial step in gaining the loyalty and admiration of the people.

Loyalty to charismatic and particularly able or courageous leaders became, in many cases, a factor which rallied the Javanese peasants to a struggle for improvement and change. Such leaders could then also take over the "father" role that landlords and wealthy farmers traditionally played among the peasants in their villages.

Once traditional patronage was undermined and new leaders enjoyed enough prestige, it was possible to compete successfully with old leaders in elections for *lurahs* (village heads), and for even higher positions in local government. In several areas, particularly in central Java, BTI or PKI leaders were thus gradually taking over official positions from the established elite.

In spite of many difficulties characteristic of organizational efforts in the highly traditional rural areas, the BTI was the most impressive of all the communist-oriented mass organizations in the country. At the end of 1953 it had a membership of several hundred thousand; by September, 1964, it claimed 8.5 million members. The growing strength of the communist and communist-oriented mass organizations provoked a strong response from the army. A PKI Party Congress to be held in 1959 was first forbidden by the army, but was later allowed, thanks to the support of President Sukarno.

The 1959 elections, which could have given the Communist Party a majority, or the most influential position among other parties, were not held. Presidential rule, "guided democracy," was initiated, and President Sukarno tried to keep a balance between the army, the Communist Party, and other forces, checking one force with the other. The BTI bargaining position and mass organization was, however, strong enough to be able to successfully take up the land reform issue at the national level, and to obtain the promulgation of a land reform law in 1960.

However, as a reaction to the slow and defective implementation of this land reform, and the determination of which surplus lands were to be expropriated, the BTI and PKI (Communist Party) stepped up their activities and became more militant, endangering the more or less harmonious collaboration which had existed at the national level between them and the various other political currents.

In order to exert pressure for the speed-up of the reform program, Aidit endorsed and encouraged in his 1963 report the so-called *Gerakan Aksi Sefihak* (unilateral action movement) of the peasants. It is difficult to assess whether the "unilateral action movement" was instigated by the BTI or PKI leadership, or was a spontaneous reaction of the peasants themselves to such doubtful practices as eviction by landowners.

While the landowners tried through "unilateral actions" to avoid the land distribution, or the peasants' claim to their new rights, the "unilateral actions" of the peasants were directed towards the initiation and acceleration of the land distribution process. The primary tactic used by the peasants was occupation of the lands to which landless peasants were entitled by law. By occupying certain plots of land, the peasants involved tried to indicate which lands were to be distributed.

The frequency and impact of the "unilateral actions" are difficult to estimate. The fact that President Sukarno in August, 1964, more or less endorsed the movement, and that during the second half of 1964 measures were taken to accelerate drastically the stagnant land-reform program, may indicate that the "unilateral action movement" took on considerable import. This would indicate how effectively the BTI and PKI had organized the peasants. Militancy is generally not considered a characteristic of the Javanese peasants, and the traditional approach at the village level has always been the search for compromise and harmony.

The fact that in a good many instances this pattern was abolished, seems to show how far the process of "de-traditionalization" had gone in Java. On the whole, it seems that local people took the new course of events for granted, and about half-a-million peasants could benefit from land reform in a relatively short time (the second half of 1964). It seems that during the rapid land distribution in the second half of 1964, little violence occurred. A ferociously violent reaction came after October, 1965, when, following an abortive coup by leftist officers, a military regime came to power. Sectors of the army, together with the youth of the mainly Islamic rural elite, assassinated over half-a-million peasants and peasant leaders. After this massacre, the BTI virtually ceased to exist (Wertheim 1966: 7).

OVERALL CONDITIONS FAVORABLE TO THE RISE OF PEASANT MOVEMENTS

In comparing the different agricultural areas where important regional or nationwide movements began, it appears that they were not the poorest, most "marginal" agricultural areas. This was true of the sugar plantation area in the state of Morelos where the Zapata movement started and of the department of Cochabamba, one of the richest agricultural areas of Bolivia. Also, La Convención valley in Peru; the sugarcane area in northeast Brazil; Pampanga in central Luzon; Java in Indonesia; and other regions, where at one time or another important peasant organizations came into being, have this in common. Another characteristic that these areas appear to share is that they are not isolated — most of them having easy access to major cities — and that they are less rigidly traditional and feudal than other areas. They are also densely populated.

In such areas, it seems to be the weakening, generally through economic developments, of the status quo that causes the peasants to organize. The situations where organizations have sprung up tend to have in common what could be called an "erosion of the status quo," which may occur in many ways. A CHANGE FOR THE WORSE in the peasants' living conditions can awaken them to defend the little they have. This happened, for instance, in the area where the *Ligas Camponesas* were started in Pernambuco, Brazil. The desire of the landowner to introduce sugarcane production on lands which for years had been cultivated on a tenancy basis for subsistence and commercial crops, and the efforts to effect this change through violent means, provoked the peasants to organize and defend their interests.

In Java the process of "agricultural involution"[4] implied slowly worsening conditions for the rural population. In Japan, the economic diffi-

---

[4]   For a definition of "agricultural involution," see Geertz 1963.

culties that occurred in industry and agriculture at the end of World War I caused rural tension. In central Luzon, the concentration of land in the hands of a few owners, and the "proletarization" of peasants, transforming small farmers into wage laborers, set the stage for agrarian unrest. Also in Morelos in Mexico at the beginning of this century, it was not the balance between *latifundios* and indigenous communities, but the usurpation of those communities by the land-hungry, sugar-estate owners and despoliation of indigenous peasants which set off what may have been one of the bloodiest revolutions in modern history.

The increasing demands of the *hacendados* versus their *arrendires* set off the peasant movement in La Convención, Cuzco. The wish to turn back the clock in land-tenure conditions in Ucureña, Bolivia, provoked a small peasant organization to become a radical, large-scale movement. It thus appears to be either the increasing exigency of economic power-holders or the "resistance to change" of the traditional landed elite against the "revolution of rising expectations" of peasants which finally creates the ideal conditions for the rise of militant movements.

A highly important side effect of the trend toward concentration of land in the hands of a few, mainly absentee, landowners, was that the traditional bond between landlords and peasants underwent a change. The exploitative aspects of the traditional system became more clearly visible.

THE PATRONAGE SYSTEM AND OTHER OBSTACLES

One of the results of increasing absentee landownership, or other modern economic forces, was a decline in the paternalistic type of control (often called PATRONAGE) that the landlords traditionally had over the peasantry. Patronage is based to a large extent on continuous personal contact and mutual obligations sanctioned by tradition and by social control of the village society as a whole. The relationship of landowners not living in the villages with their tenants could more easily become blatantly exploitative. This enhanced the chance of class conflict in the rural areas. Originally, the patronage system may have had some benevolent implications for the peasants, but these were limited. Peasants were born into this system and more or less doomed to live under it all their lives, unless they were willing to take considerable risks. The patronage system and the resultant psychological coercion on the peasant to conform, appeared to be a main obstacle to the organization of peasant-interest and pressure groups.

In countries where landlords themselves lived in the villages, and had only a small number of tenants with whom they were in almost daily contact, the patron-client relationship was particularly strong, and the tenants hesitated to be disloyal to their "patron" by joining a union or organization dedicated to the defense of their rights. The "patron" could indulge in illegal practices, e.g. asking a sixty-forty share of the harvest while the law allowed fifty-fifty, forty-sixty, or even a twenty-five-seventy-five division. But for emotional reasons, as well as to insure minimum economic security, peasants often did not take steps to demand that their legal rights be respected. Economic changes that caused deterioration of the status quo could rouse the peasants to action, especially when the "patron" clearly showed his true face.

In addition to mere absentee ownership, other modernizing influences, particularly among the younger generation of the elite, contributed to a loosening of the emotional, paternalistic ties by which the poor peasants were bound to the upper classes. In some cases, the change in attitude was merely a more businesslike approach and neglect by the wealthy of feudalistic patronage obligations.

In some cases, it was under emergency conditions that the patrons showed that they were "protective" towards the peasants only as long as it was highly beneficial. Thus a great deal of more or less organized peasant protest in Japan occurred during the periods of bad harvests, when landlords refused to reduce either the rents or their share in the harvest, in order to give the tenants a chance to survive. Such occurrences enhanced, at least temporarily, the peasants' awareness of merciless exploitation at the hands of their patrons.

One of the factors, however, which in some countries complicated the picture, was the entrance of party politics and election campaigns. Traditionally, the rural elite was divided among itself, and in most villages there were factions. It often happened that party affiliations among the electorate followed the factional divisions of the elite, rather than class interest lines. Particularly in the Philippines, but also to some extent in Indonesia, the parties tended to make possible a strengthening of the patronage system. Political functions for which the election campaigns were held generally implied that the local elite influenced or directly controlled certain government resources such as funds for roads, schools, medical, and health services. These modern resources could be utilized in addition to the more traditional ones of land and power to keep the peasants in a state of dependency. Promises of official help were used to make the peasants conform.

Because the large landowners in most developing countries had almost absolute control of economic, social, and political life in the rural areas, there were many ways in which they could prevent peasant organizations from arising. The most common means used to effect this were economic and other sanctions against the founders of peasant associations. Agricultural wage workers who began such activities were easily thrown out of their jobs, unless they found ways to organize a group of colleagues in secrecy or in a simulated way under the cover of a literacy club or mutual aid society. Tenants could, for the same reason, easily be evicted from their land. Generally by agreement among the landowners in a certain area, peasants who had been discharged or evicted found it very difficult to get a job or a parcel of land elsewhere in the same region. It was also found that because most agricultural workers and tenants had incomes at a mere subsistence level, there was little chance that they would take the risk of losing their jobs or plots, as this would practically mean starvation. The severe underemployment and indebtedness that existed in the rural areas made the risk of losing their means of survival even greater.

When economic sanctions were not enough to block the emergence of a peasant organization, other means were tried. One was to buy off a leader of a strong organization by offering him money, land, or access to higher social status. This was tried several times with Emiliano Zapata and many other leaders.

Frequently, when all other means failed to undermine a growing movement, its leader was assassinated. Countless cases of assassination of peasant leaders have taken place in Latin America, as well as in Southeast Asia. Violence in the rural areas under discussion was not introduced there recently by insurgents or revolutionaries, but has existed for many decades. With few exceptions, the formation of organizations that attempted a legal defense of the rights of the peasants was blocked by the traditional holders of power.

GROWTH OF "CLASS-CONSCIOUSNESS"

No matter where conditions for the creation of a peasant movement exist, little will occur if there is not among the peasants themselves an awareness of their conditions, including a belief that something can be done about them. In cases where peasants have an ideologically clear understanding of their conditions, one could speak of "class-consciousness." A clear consciousness of being a class, in the Marxian sense, is rarely present among peasants. This does not mean, however, that there is necessarily complete confusion about such issues.

In Marxian terms, the key issue was how certain categories of peasants could turn from being a "class-in-themselves" to becoming a "class-for-themselves." It was in this process of "becoming conscious," "conscientization," or "politicization," that a number of sociopsychological factors played an important role, often neglected by those interested in mass or class organizations. In some way or other, most of the peasant organizations described have utilized, more or less purposely, these sociopsychological factors concerned with:

1. Stimulating in the peasants an awareness of being exploited.
2. The role of strong or even charismatic leadership and a vanguard to counteract the residual influence of traditional patronage, which kept the peasant in psychological dependency.
3. The utilization of the "conflict model" to bring peasants together in cohesive and militant groups.

Stimulating Awareness of Being Exploited: Use of "Counterpoints"

A better understanding of exploitative conditions, and the possibilities of changing them, could be stimulated among the peasants. This happened partly through the influence of outsiders, such as the fieldworkers of the Brazilian program of *concientizacao* (according to the method of Paolo Freire), or the Communist Party cadres, as in Indonesia. Such outsiders generally utilized certain elements in the peasants' lives and culture considered to be "counterpoints" to the prevailing "culture of repression" in which the peasants lived.[5]

It was crucial to find "counterpoint" elements in the peasants' submissive attitudes and value system, in order to be able to show them that they were already involved in some kind of resistance against the repressive system, and that the fatherly authority of the landlord was basically fiction. Such elements could be found in folktales and in the history of the village, particularly in the means through which the elite — by taking over more and more land — came to power. Thus, explaining to the peasants that their distrust was justified was a means of bringing greater awareness and some amount of self-confidence to them. The BTI activists in Indonesia did this in a more or less systematic way. The campaigns of the Communist Party leader, Aidit, to study local folklore and culture (which always contain a great deal of "resistance" elements and "counterpoints"), as well as the present and past land-tenure situation, were highly

---

[5] The "counterpoint" concept is elaborated in Wertheim (unpublished manuscript). For the situation in Indonesia, see Huizer 1971: 104 ff.

important. Knowing the background of the peasants' grievances, and the forms of expression of those grievances tolerated by the establishment as a safety valve (jokes and tales, for example), could help the organizers to rally the peasantry, in a more conscious way, to the defense of their interests. This approach had certain similarities to the campaign of "conscientization" initiated by the basic education movement toward radical social change in northeastern Brazil from 1963 to 1964, and the use of rebel folk songs by the peasant league organizers there.

Some additional factors that made the trend toward "conscientization" in the rural areas feasible were:

1. The increasingly important role of primary education, and other forms of contact, and acquaintance with the world that differed considerably from the traditional peasant frame of reference.

2. Better communications with urban areas through roads and modern means of transportation. In particular, such densely populated areas as Pernambuco in northeastern Brazil; Cochabamba, Bolivia; Java; central Luzon; and, in Japan, the prefectures close to the big cities, showed the influence of this trend. Also, in some cases, the introduction of transistor radios had an impact.

3. The process of industrialization in some countries, particularly in Japan during World War I, gave many peasants a chance to participate in urban life and in new forms of organization. After a recess in the industrialization process, these persons had to go back to their villages, and, as a result, the potential for new forms of organization and solidarity there increased. Some combination of the three above-mentioned factors, or their separate appearance, became more and more frequent. These are the reasons why, in Japan, the first large-scale, union-oriented peasant organizations were created exactly in those areas where urban influences were strong and growing — such as the regions around the industrial cities of Nagoya and Osaka, and later, Fukuoka and Tokyo. The urban experience factor played a particularly important role in the case of Zapata, and of the peasant syndicates in Bolivia, which came up after peasants returned from the Chaco War. In other cases, the presence of a mining industry was a catalyst to the growth of a peasant movement.

Community development and similar programs can have a stimulating effect on the growth of peasants' critical awareness and readiness for action and organization, but the contrary may also be true. When community development was channeled merely through established traditional leadership, such as most of the *lurahs* in Indonesia, or the *barrio* notables in the Philippines, it could well strenghten the hold of these traditional leaders over the poor peasantry. Existing patronage relationships, which were an impediment to the creation of peasant protest against the traditionally dominant powers, were reinforced, and peasants were made more dependent. Such programs existed in most countries, but were generally rather ineffective.

In evaluating the reasons why community development programs in so many countries have stagnated, the United Nations has emphasized the difficulty of bringing change to rural societies controlled by a traditional elite. In a document regarding the future evolution of community development, it was noted that in such cases "... conflict and disagreement rather than cohesiveness is a more true and realistic measure of development of communities, and in that way of the success of community development programs" (United Nations 1971: 6ff.). The United Nations document recommended that efforts be undertaken to stimulate new and more dynamic leadership representing the interests of the majority, rather than working through the traditional leaders who generally belonged to a small elite. A confrontation of the new with the old leadership was seen as unavoidable, and to be introduced gradually.

The Role of Leadership and Vanguard

It seems that the availability of charismatic, or at least solidarity-inspiring, leadership among the peasants is highly important in getting an organization to the point where it may confront the elite. A principal characteristic of such a leader is that he is able to express clearly what his peasant-followers feel more or less vaguely about their repressed condition. On the one hand, this capacity of the leader helps the peasants in their process of "conscientization." On the other hand, it facilitates a strong identification with the leader. This identification has to grow in such a way that the peasants feel through it a kind of horizontal solidarity among themselves.

Initially, vertical ties of admiration with the leader may be important. The leader has, to some extent, to replace in his followers the sense of security that was formerly inspired by the landlords, i.e. the PATRON, who played the role of a kind of father figure to the peasants. When the father image cannot be maintained any longer and takes on the characteristics of a tyrant, the possibility for replacement arises. Strong personalities among the peasants may take on this role. Sometimes they inspired respect for their skill and experience — a result of working for some time in the towns. They helped the peasants to break through the traditional patronage system and the hold the landlord had over them, not only economically, but psychologically. Thus, several peasant organizations that occurred locally were the result of the almost accidental presence of such a special leader among the peasants themselves. Taruc, Zapata, and José Rojas are cases in point. It seems, however, that it is not necessary "to wait" until such a leader happens to appear.

Under certain conditions, other figures could fulfill the same function. Both the Japanese and the Indonesian peasant movements were built up mainly by organizers who came from an urban background and "went down to the villages." At the beginning, such organizers generally encountered resistance and distrust, but if they managed to overcome this distrust through their personal qualities and the methods they employed, they could, relatively easily, become respected leaders. Villagers often (and with considerable justification), passively rejected an outsider. Once he had proved himself trustworthy, however, his nonpeasant background and dedication to the peasant cause could command for him more respect than if he had been a peasant. This explains the considerable success of persons like Hugo Blanco in Peru, Aoki in Japan, and the organizers of the BTI in Indonesia — many of whom were former students who gave themselves to the peasant struggle and won the peoples' hearts by going "down" to the villages under something like the rule of the three "togethers." But simply identifying himself with the peasants was not enough. For an organizer to become a leader, he had also to prove himself in ability to deal with and stand up against the powerholders to whom the grievances or demands of the peasants were directed. The leaders could not be easily intimidated, and at times had to take the risk of going to jail or facing threats from the landlords or local authorities.

When the leader of a peasant organization, because of his personal qualities, took over the landlords' "father" role, the danger existed that the strength of the organization might remain too long dependent on that specific leader. It has happened frequently with large-scale or small-scale organizations that, when a strong and dynamic leader disappeared or was eliminated, the organization, as such, collapsed, largely because there was no person or group of persons to replace him. This happened to Zapata's movement after his assassination in 1919. In some ways this was also true of the Huk movement in the Philippines when, in 1954, Luis Taruc surrendered. The continuation of an organization in the face of "decapitation," imprisonment, or elimination of its main leaders can be guaranteed only when a core of replacement leaders is available.

In the process of creating a peasant organization, it is, therefore, an essential strategy that initial leaders stimulate leadership qualities in potential successors. It is also essential to stimulate in the membership enough self-confidence to replace that confidence in charismatic leadership, so crucial to the initial process.

To guarantee the continuity of the organization in Japan, as well as Indonesia, one of the first activities of the initiators was to look for aides and give them a kind of in-service training. Once acquainted with the local situation, and with the confidence of the people, it was generally not too difficult to find peasants with special qualities who could fulfill leadership functions in a militant organization. Especially after demands for action or protests about grievances had been made, potential leaders could make themselves known and go through a process of winning respect and adherence, similar to that of the original leader.

From almost all the cases known, it seems that the peasants who were relatively better off were most apt to participate as leaders or vanguard in the initiation of a movement. They were a little less dependent on the landlords or rich farmers, and could thus afford to take more risks. For this reason, the Peasant Leagues in Brazil purposely bet on the relatively independent small landholders, only attempting to attract the mass of landless peasants after a start had been made and some strength gained. Alavi noted a similar trend in China from the twenties onward and in some of the peasant movements in India (1965: 241-277; Wolf 1969). The leadership of the newly created organizations generally came from a group of peasants who were somewhat better off.

It should be noted, however, that it was probably not the "middle class" peasant, as such, who was in the vanguard of peasant protest movements, but rather those among the "middle class," who for some reason felt their relative security threatened or who were clearly frustrated by the power of the economic and political elite or by other forces.

The fact that leaders of peasant organizations have to fulfill a certain type of patronage role in order to compete effectively and replace the traditional "patron," explains why, not infrequently, leaders came from dissident sections of the traditional elite itself. Even in the communist-oriented BTI, a number of local leaders were landlords. This was the situation in the Philippines, most outstandingly, in the case of the founder of the socialist peasant organization, Pedro Abad Santos. Similar situations obtained in Japan, in northeastern Brazil, where Juliao was originally a landlord, and in Peru, where Hugo Blanco came from a well-to-do family. One of the dangers of this situation was that leaders who had all the capacity to compete with the traditional patronage system were not consistently dissident in their own class, but became themselves a traditional type of "patron." They then had a moderating, rather than a militarizing, influence on their followers. Some of the leaders of the BTI may have been examples of elitist revolutionaries, and certainly many of the local leaders of the Petani (Nationalist Party Peasant Organization) and Islamic peasant organizations in Indonesia were from this class.

Alternatively, peasant organizations are sometimes formed by members of the rural elite in order to compete with the more radical leftist organizations. The Federation of Free Farmers created in the Philippines during the 1950's was such an organization; its leaders were moderate dissidents of the rural elite. In northeastern Brazil, the Church created such an alternative movement that was radicalized and integrated with the Leagues at a later stage.

The Role of the Conflict Model: Utilizing Concrete Grievances

Once new leadership was solidly established, a confrontation with the old order might be initiated more openly by utilizing the CONFLICT MODEL as opposed to the HARMONY MODEL, frequently used in rural and community organization. The harmony model took as a point of departure the belief that basically all different interests at the community or regional level could be developed simultaneously and harmoniously. But because many concrete cases where this approach was tried were failures, the conviction grew that conflict, instead, might prove to be a rallying force in creating effective groups.[6]

After the peasants had been made aware of being exploited, and while their organization was still in the process of creation and growth, it could benefit from the existence of an "enemy," or a "negative reference group." Having an "enemy" helped to foster cohesiveness in the group (Coser 1956) because the peasants' great resentment toward the traditional landlords made of this class a natural enemy. Through the formation of representative interest groups of their own, the peasants brought into the open their resentment and channeled it in an effective way. Counterforces, provoked by utilizing the conflict-model, could awaken the peasants even more strongly to their best interests.

Efforts by the landed elite to halt the rise of the new peasant interest groups had a double effect. On the one hand, it could hinder considerably the process of forming the representative peasant organizations. On the other hand, however, it could accelerate the process through which the traditional form of dominance through patronage loosens its hold. As a

---

[6] For a case study where the conflict model was applied in a community development project in Chile, see Huizer 1972a.

result of repressive measures, peasants were brought to see increasingly that the traditional system was basically not benevolent and did not give the kind of "protection" and security they needed. The "true face" of the landlord was seen to be not that of a father, but of a tyrant.

It was particularly when clearer forms of repression entered the scene that such concepts as "village devils" (a term applied in Indonesia to landlords, merchants, and money lenders during the land reform campaign) began to express what the peasants felt about their "patrons." It was essential that great care be taken to distinguish between the "devils" and those landlords and merchants who fulfilled their traditional role without great excesses or abuses.

Going too far in this approach could easily lead to a reaction on the part of those rural people who were not directly involved in the conflict, such as small landholders and artisans, who feared that an unjust struggle on the part of the peasants might disrupt all their values. It may well be that the massacre of members of the BTI in Indonesia in 1965 was, in places such as Bali, a reaction to overzealousness on the part of the BTI in not taking traditional factors sufficiently into account and disrupting village harmony beyond the limits felt to be just and bearable by those not directly involved. Through the years, similar factors have played a role in the serious setbacks suffered by the Huk movement in the Philippines. The overly doctrinaire approach of some of the leaders alienated them from important sectors of their followers, and when one of the more charismatic leaders, Luis Taruc, surrendered, partly for this reason, the movement lost strength very rapidly.

From almost all experiences cited, it can be seen that peasant movements generally develop only when there is a concrete event or acute conflict about which people become excited. It seems that, even if conditions are bad and growing worse, peasants will be mobilized only when there is some kind of clear-cut conflict. Moderate demands, however, can sometimes lead to such a conflict because of the intransigence of the elite. Peasant organizers generally look for sensitive points in the local setup if a clear, rallying issue is not too readily available. In Java, particularly, this strategy was utilized consistently, thus successfully introducing the conflict-model in a society in which *rukun* (harmony) was highly appreciated.

In applying the conflict-model, it was important to determine the kind of peasants on which the organization would base its strength. In countries where there existed a clear polarization between rich landlords and poor tenants, organizations simply represented the tenants' interests. They rallied the peasants in the villages or on the *haciendas* around such issues as security of tenancy, better tenancy legislation, share-cropping arrangements more favorable to tenants (e.g. forty-sixty instead of fifty-fifty), or even land reform, as a final or principal demand. The latter possibility came up particularly when landlords insistently rejected the other demands or indulged in illegal practices.

Where the land-tenure pattern was more complicated, it was more difficult to determine what kind of organization to create. There were often share-croppers who tilled land not belonging to large landholders but to slightly better-off neighbors and relatives, who themselves had only a small plot and let part of that to the share-cropper, more to help him than from a desire for systematic exploitation. To organize such share-croppers in their own exclusive interest would be extremely difficult; many peasants who leased a part of their plot would be opposed. Whenever the differences between tenants and the lesser landlords were minor, both could be united into one organization that benefited the small owners in such a way as to enable them to give more favorable share-cropping or tenancy conditions to the tenants.

There are always problems, such as exploitation by money lenders and merchants, common to both tenants and small owners. The peasant organization can concentrate its struggle on these problems, trying to bargain for more favorable credit or marketing terms. Particularly where there was a tendency for money lenders, through loans and mortgages on the land of small owners, to try and gain possession of larger tracts of land (a situation that occurred in Indonesia and several other countries), organization of peasants appeared highly feasible.

In some areas of Java, new types of landlords have emerged, who by clever manipulation of indebtednesses, have acquired much land formerly held by small landholders. The *hadjis* in Indonesia can probably be considered such a group of new landlords, often much less considerate of the peasants' interests than the traditional landowners.

The degree to which certain tenure patterns, or changes in such patterns, occur in a particular area or village (even more than in a clear-cut, landlord-tenant division) should be investigated carefully. It appears that the BTI in Indonesia was successful in preceding organization and action by such research into the "class contradictions" in the villages. Such research has been nonexistent or rare in most other cases. Particularly in countries where a complicated land-tenure structure exists, it seems to be crucial that any organizing effort evaluate those contradictions so that the conflict-model can be applied effectively.

THE STRATEGY OF PEASANT ORGANIZATION: ESCALATION AS A REACTION TO ELITE RESISTANCE

Once a peasant organization has come into existence, a process of consolidation and of gaining strength will generally follow. It has been recognized by many leaders and organizers that to obtain concrete benefits through struggle is the best way to consolidate and strengthen an organization. Cases of abuse are presented to the courts, and mass demonstrations and public meetings are held to support petitions for justice or land. Initially, the only steps undertaken are those to obtain justice, as indicated by the existing laws. This has happened in all the cases described above. Meetings were held and a petition, with or without direct support from a sympathetic or paid lawyer, was presented to competent authorities. Often, however, the authorities stood aloof, or openly chose the side of the large landholders, despite the fact that the peasants had the law on their side. Continuous frustration, leading nowhere, encountered in following the slow course of legal procedure, prepared the ground for more radical peasant action to the limit of the legal possibilities.

It was not only the existence of an organization with a large membership, as such, that was the crucial factor in getting things changed, but also the way in which such an organization presented its demands and demonstrated the bargaining power to back them up. Generally some form of direct action from the peasants made it clear to the authorities, as well as to the vested interests and landholding groups, that the demands were serious. Among these forms of direct action, the peaceful or symbolic occupation or invasion of the lands considered to be exprobable was probably the most effective, and the most generally practiced.

Land reforms generally occurred only after such direct, usually nonviolent, action by peasant organizations had taken place. The "unilateral actions" in Java, or the occupations of estates by the Bolivian peasants in 1953, are two examples. Some such actions were merely symbolic, designed to draw public attention or exercise pressure. In other cases, they effected immediate changes in the cultivation system or property relations. In most cases, such activities have been purposely nonviolent, a form of civil-disobedience strategy. In several cases, the peasants even had the law on their side, and it was the authorities who failed to maintain or implement it. Effective or symbolic occupation of land, bringing it into cultivation or just organizing a "sit-in"on it, could not possibly be seen as violence, if violence is understood to be intentional damage to lives or goods.[7]

[7]   For a discussion of some examples of land invasions, see Huizer 1972b.

Similar nonviolent forms of direct action are the strike and the demonstration. An instance of a strike was the refusal of the peasants, organized by Hugo Blanco in La Convención, to observe the obligatory period of unpaid work days for the landowner; or as happened at times in Japan, to give the landlord the part of the yield he claimed. One of the many forms demonstrations can take is the sit-in or mass rally in front of courts, government offices, or landlords' houses, as has happened in northeastern Brazil, Peru, and Japan.

Peasant organizations and their leaders gain experience by organizing a strike, by symbolically occupying land, or by a mass demonstration. Such undertakings are risky in the sense that they may fail and lead to disillusionment. The many cases where errors were made without much damage being done, and needed experience for an effective movement gained, appear to justify the risks involved.

It seems that a tolerant and benevolent attitude on the part of the authorities regarding the peasants' efforts to gain strength is helpful and important. This happened in the Bolivian revolution of 1952, when political groups at the national level needed the support of the peasant movement in order to overthrow the old regime and establish and consolidate a more liberal one. Also, the Sukarno government in Indonesia depended on peasant support as a counterbalance to the increasing influence of the army.

Frequently, however, nonviolent or civil-disobedience actions by peasants are not tolerated by the authorities. They may give the rural elite complete freedom to react violently, or even give them active support by using the army to repress the peasant movement. Despite the fact that peasant activities are generally not violent, the local and national press, the authorities, or the landlords themselves have interpreted such actions as violent and have retaliated with violence. It cannot be emphasized enough that in almost all cases where real violence occurred, it was introduced either by the authorities or by the landlords as a reaction to increased pressure from the peasants. It is this escalation of repression that then gives the peasants a clearer consciousness of the need for overthrowing the system under which they live. The cases of Zapata in Mexico, Hugo Blanco in Peru, and Luis Taruc in the Philippines demonstrate that the ruthless repression of moderate peasant action makes the peasants potential revolutionaries, willing to use violent means to defend themselves and change the social system radically. A great deal depends, at this stage, on the kind of guidance the peasants get from their leaders or allies.

One factor contributing to the escalation of the actions of peasants against the overall system was the increased knowledge peasants gained of their rights. Particularly in the stage where the landed elite began to repress, combat, or corrupt efforts by the peasants to exercise pressure, the latter learned to see clearly the illegal, not to say criminal, nature of the landlords', or of the government's, approach. Traditionally, the peasants' high respect for law and order is a guarantee of security. As can be seen from the cases in Peru, northeastern Brazil, and Mexico, whenever landlords used illegal means to terrorize peasants, the latter initially tried to find a solution by appealing to the appropriate authorities. Only after insistent demands to qualified authorities that they enforce the laws failed to produce results, did the peasants start to see the landlords as a class, as their main "enemy."

It has frequently been documented that legal authorities in the rural areas of most countries interpret the laws generally in favor of the landlords, even if this means circumvention or violation of the law. Peasants will sometimes resign and give up, in a resentful or embittered way, efforts to improve their lot. But whenever the legitimacy and acceptance of the prevailing system is seriously undermined by the way this system attempts to maintain itself, it requires only a relatively small effort to transform the new awareness of repression among the peasants into a stronger revolutionary consciousness.

At this stage, the need usually arises among the peasants to gain weapons to defend themselves against injustice and repression. In cases where peasants did acquire weapons, such as in Bolivia in 1953, they could prevent the elite from further escalation of their violent actions. The land reform process in Bolivia was carried out without any violence because the peasants could check the power of the landlords. When, in the Convención valley, the first steps were made by the peasantry to acquire weapons, the government decided that lands would be distributed to appease them, thus, essentially preventing the movement from becoming a threat to the national political system.

When peasants, as a result of the repression by landlords and army, gain a clearer understanding of the need for overall radical change, and the weapons to struggle for it, they can become outright revolutionaries, as was shown by Zapata's movement and by that of the Huks in the Philippines. One important question in this context is how consciously revolutionary the peasants become. If by this term it is understood that peasants accepted a Marxist interpretation of society or Communist Party doctrines, it would seem that most of them were not consciously revolutionary. Research undertaken among peasants imprisoned for political reasons after the Arbenz government in Guatemela was overthrown (with support of the anti-land-reform forces, including the United

Fruit Company) in 1954, showed that the peasants were on the whole not ideologically indoctrinated by communism, but, rather, were awakened to ideas of democracy and social justice (Newbold 1957: 338–361). Also, the peasants who had participated in an uprising stimulated by the Indonesian Communist Party in 1926, and who were imprisoned in the penal colony in the swamp lands of Boven-Digul, could hardly be considered sophisticated communists, as was noted by one strongly anticommunist author (Brackman 1963: 19, 34). However, imprisonment of peasants in the Boven-Digul swamps or in jungle, such as Ichilo in Bolivia (where between 1946 and 1953, 250 peasant leaders were kept), does not make peasants less radical or less politically conscious, but just the opposite.

In the Philippines, Indonesia, and Japan, guidance was given to the peasantry by socialist and communist political groups who took up the land-reform issue and organized the peasantry around it. In other cases, a leftist political group took up the peasants' cause once the latter had shown itself to be a strongly organized body. They tried to become allies of the peasants. This happened in Mexico and Bolivia, in particular.

There was, in such cases, considerable variation in the control exercised by the political parties over peasant organizations. Some, such as the movement created by Zapata, were almost completely independent and followed rather closely their own purposes. The movements in La Convención and in the Cochabamba area, although supported by political groups, had a dynamic of their own, the membership at times pushing the leadership beyond the goals set. The organizations created after 1952 in areas other than Cochabamba in Bolivia, mainly through the MNR party, were relatively more controlled. The *Ligas Camponesas* had their own representatives in the National Parliament of Brazil and appeared to be controlled by no specific party, although strife among groups to gain influence within the movement was noted.

A dilemma faced by most growing peasant movements has been whether or not to relate the conflict-model strategy clearly to a positive ideological purpose. Although all were socialist-oriented, Rojas in Bolivia and Juliao in Brazil were less clearly defined than Abad Santos, Aidit, or Hugo Blanco. Ideological obscurity may sometimes have the tactical advantage of being slower to arouse the repressive forces of the elite. On the other hand, not having a clear ideology behind its activities may leave a movement in the air, once it has gained enough strength to bargain effectively with the "enemy" or even to eliminate his influence. Then the organization may be without a clear purpose and might easily lose its strength or deteriorate.

In order to utilize to the full the potential for organized efforts, it seems crucial to orient the initial struggle not only against the "enemy" but also in favor of objectives having a wider scope, that the organization may be kept on the move after it has gained strength in overcoming the main obstacles. Examples of places where this did not happen were Japan, Bolivia, and Mexico. The peasant organizations in Japan had as their main purpose the struggle with the landlords, first, to get better tenancy conditions and, later, to get an effective redistribution of land. Once this purpose was achieved, the peasant organizations, which could possibly have played a role in mobilizing the peasants for further efforts related to the solution of basic problems or the building of a socialist society, deteriorated. The possibility, which came to the surface later, of coopera- tive farming to overcome the disadvantages of small holdings, had to be tackled completely anew. In Bolivia the "feudal" class structure was broken in 1954, but after that the peasant movement became a willing instrument of the government to maintain a new status quo and check the struggle of miners and other workers.

It seems particularly important to anticipate the difficulties and prob- lems that may arise once the main demands, around which the peasants had rallied, are being fulfilled. It is important to orient the struggle in favor of the demand for land in such a way that the implications of the reform process itself, and any that may arise after its implementation, are already within focus before they actually come up. In this way the peasant organization will not immediately collapse after its main goal has been achieved, but will remain active and mobilized. Also the fact that post-re- form measures and needs are being discussed before the reform has actually taken place, gives perspective to the struggle, and may boost the morale of the organization. Also, the peasants understand exactly what they are heading for, thus lending realism to the activities in favor of reform. Destructive elements in the old structure become clear in the light of the new aims, giving a greater justification to the struggle. Although at times motivated by a great deal of resentment against the traditional and re- pressive system, peasants are, on the whole, very respectful of law and order, and radical measures will be more easily endorsed if seen as leading toward a new and just order.

CONCLUSION

The Philippine, Indonesian, Bolivian, and Peruvian movements have demonstrated clearly how peasant movements reacted to intolerance or resistance from the elite by becoming a class-conscious, revolutionary force at the national level. This happened not because the peasantry was by nature revolutionary, but rather in spite of their prudent, traditional, and evolutionary approach. All these movements gained considerable success because they were not violent explosions of peasant discontent, repressed as quickly as they came up (as has happened with many move- ments in the past). Rather, they all started with a careful grass-roots or- ganization that took up the most strongly felt grievances of the peasants — the counterpoints within the dominant traditional system — and tried to build up slowly around those grievances. Only by going carefully, and remaining well within the rules of the game, could the first steps be made toward creating representative interest groups against the heavy weight of traditional patronage and economic repression. Only after the rural elite reacted to minor peasant demands and organizational success in ways clearly counter to the prevailing laws, and often including violence, did the peasant organizations become more radical. It is quite probable that at any stage toward greater radicalization and escalation of demands, the peasant organizations would have accepted a compromise if the rural elite had been willing to give them a fair chance. The elite generally did not do this. The intransigence of the elite, more than anything else, was the reason that peasant organizations finally took a revolutionary stand, demanding the radical overthrow of the system as a whole, and acting accordingly. It is surprising that in view of so much historical evidence, the elite has continued to follow the same fatal course.

REFERENCES

ALAVI, HAMZA
    1965   Peasants and revolution. *The Socialist Register:* 241–277.
AOKI, K.
    1947   *Nihon nomin undo shi* [History of the Japanese agrarian movement], six volumes. Tokyo.
BANDSBERGER, HENRY A., *editor*
    1969   *Latin American peasant movements.* Ithaca: Cornell University Press.
    1972a *The revolutionary potential of peasants in Latin America.* Lexington: Heath Lexington.
    1972b Land invasions as a non-violent strategy of peasant rebellion. *Journal of Peace Research 2.*
BRACKMAN, ARNOLD C.
    1963   *Indonesian communism: a history.* New York: Praeger.
COSER, LEWIS
    1956   *The functions of social conflict.* Glencoe: Free Press.

DORE, R. P.
  1959   *Land reform in Japan.* Oxford: Oxford University Press.
GEERTZ, CLIFFORD
  1963   *Agricultural involution.* Berkeley and Los Angeles: University of California Press.
HINDLEY, DONALD
  1951–1963   *The Communist Party of Indonesia.* Berkeley and Los Angeles: University of California Press.
HUIZER, GERRIT
  1971   "Betting on the weak: from counterpoint toward revolution," in *Buiten de grenzen.* Edited by W. F. Wertheim, 104 ff. Meppel: Boom Boeken.
  1972a   The utilization of conflict in community development and peasant organization: a case from Chile. *International Review of Community Development* 16.
  1972b   Land invasions as a non-violent strategy of peasant rebellion. *Journal of Peace Research* 2.
  1972c   *The revolutionary potential of peasants in Latin America.* Lexington: Heath Lexington Books.
MARX, KARL
  1963   *The eighteenth Brumaire of Louis Bonaparte.* New York: International Publishers.
NEWBOLD, STOKES
  1957   Receptivity of communist fomented agitation in rural Guatemala. *Economic Development and Cultural Change* 5:338–361.
STAVENHAGEN, RODOLFO, *editor*
  1970   *Agrarian problems and peasant movements in Latin America.* New York: Anchor Doubleday.
TARUC, LOUIS
  1953   *Born of the people: an autobiography.* New York: International Publishers.
TOTTEN, G. O.
  1960   Labor and agrarian disputes in Japan following World War I. *Economic Development and Cultural Change* 9: 194–204.
UNITED NATIONS
  1971   *Popular participation in development: emerging trends in community development.* New York: United Nations.
WERTHEIM, W. F.
  1966   Indonesia before and after the Untung Coup. *Pacific Affairs* 39:7.
WOLF, ERIC R.
  1969   *Peasant wars of the twentieth century.* New York: Harper and Row.

The Anthropologist as Societal Ombudsman

RICHARD F. SALISBURY

Since April 1971 my colleagues and I, of the McGill Programme in the Anthropology of Development, have been involved in two projects of what may be called applied anthropology, one in New Guinea and one in northern Canada. Both, it is felt, imply a somewhat new conception of the role of the anthropologist as an intermediary in trouble situations between central agencies and local groups. A report on the two projects and an analysis of the conditions under which this role emerges is timely.

THE PROJECTS

The substantive findings of both projects have already been published as *Problems of the Gazelle Peninsula of New Britain* (Salisbury 1971) and *Development and James Bay* (Salisbury, et al. 1972) so that the nature of each can be summarized here very briefly. In New Guinea a dispute between two factions in the most politically sophisticated and wealthiest language group, the Tolai, had escalated over the previous four years into violence. The issue, as then phrased, was between a "nationalist" faction favoring the development of local government within the framework of ordinances set up for the whole of Papua New Guinea and a "separatist" faction demanding idiosyncratic institutions for the Tolai. Attempts by the central government of Papua New Guinea and by educated Tolai residents elsewhere had failed to obtain agreement between the factions. The attempts of the government to enforce ordinances and maintain services (e.g. keeping roads open) had involved tacit support of the "nationalists" and had exacerbated the polarization.

In July 1971, presumably feeling that most avenues had been tried and that trying an anthropologist might help and could not make things worse, the administrator of Papua New Guinea asked if I would act as a consultant to investigate the situation and, if so, under what conditions. Although the role of consultant for governments is an established one, this role in its usual form was impossible for an anthropologist aware of the strong feelings among the Tolai and knowing that any solution imposed from outside would be no solution. At the same time it would have been an abdication of responsibility to Tolai friends NOT to try to assist them in solving their difficulties, and it would have been a confession of intellectual bankruptcy NOT to stick by the diagnosis of Tolai problems in political development given in my earlier study (Salisbury 1969) which anticipated all the issues of 1971.

The problem was to specify conditions that would make a new role possible. Briefly, the conditions then asked for were the publication of any findings, and agreement by all parties to my conducting an investigation. As far as was practically feasible, given the formal requirement that my report be first submitted to His Honour the Administrator, and given the condition that "the parties" could be approached only informally, the conditions were agreed to. Research was conducted from August 1 to August 31, 1971, at which time a final report was submitted.

In the northern Canadian project the announcement was made in April, 1971, by the premier of Quebec that a 6,000,000,000 dollar hydroelectric scheme would be inaugurated involving damming the major rivers flowing into James Bay and inundating about a third of the hunting territories of various Cree Indian bands, with whom members of our program had been working for six years. We protested that such a decision had been taken without adequate investigation of the social and ecological impacts of the project on the area and without any consultation with the local people. We were asked, in reply, what social research should have been done, and whether we would do it. We indicated the research needed but said we would do it only if the Indians agreed to our doing so and had full access to our findings.

An understanding was soon reached with the Indians of Quebec Association, including provisions that workers from the program would undertake FIELD projects only after these had been specifically approved by the Association and only if no Indian group wished to conduct them itself. It took longer before the statutorily-established James Bay Development Corporation accepted the desirability of public access of findings, but once convinced, they actively (and financially) supported our reporting back of the findings to the Indians of Quebec Association and to the Cree Indians.

The study was begun in January, 1972; a report based almost exclusively on published materials and on going unpublished research by members of the program (and here I must acknowledge the work of Harvey Feit, Jacqueline Hyman, Ignatius LaRusic, and Peter Sindell) was completed in June; feedback of results to Indian groups (and some fieldwork commissioned by the Indians of Quebec Association) lasted into August; and a final report was submitted in September.

Lest it be thought that I am claiming that anthropologists can SOLVE problems, I would hasten to add that the issues in both areas are still, in late 1972, involved in intense controversy. But what has happened in both areas has been that a central planning agency (the central government and the Development Corporation) has become much more sensitive to the issues as they appear to the local people and has changed its policies following the reports. On the other side, and here I speak with much less confidence and optimism, many local people have realized the complexity of issues and the possibility of obtaining what they wish through a variety of courses of action of which they had not previously been aware. What is occurring, in short, is that local people are bargaining and negotiating on their own behalf, and on terms closer to equality, with central agencies which had previously appeared distant and all-powerful.

In such a situation the potential contributions of an anthropologist are twofold. The first is to translate and make intelligible to people with a particular perspective the viewpoint of a different group — to phrase locally significant issues in terms understandable to policy makers and to explain to local people the ways in which planners and administrative bureaucracies go about their work. The second is to use the accumulated knowledge of the discipline to suggest possible courses of action TO BOTH SIDES — be it how to overcome organizational problems in small businesses or how to avoid the problems of hinterland denudation by large northern settlements. I stress TO BOTH SIDES, for I am convinced that when an anthropologist commits himself to one side only, he nullifies many of the benefits that his professional training could give to that side. He is not able to retain any confidence from the other side and so is unlikely to make an accurate analysis of that side's point of view, while any analysis he makes of his own side's point of view is unlikely to carry weight with the other side.

More generally, a major finding of anthropology over the last twenty years has been that to understand and to change any social situation requires a knowledge not only of the internal dynamics of the situation but also of the nature of the macrosystem which provides parameters for the situation. An anthropologist who confines himself to attempting to change only one aspect — the macrosystem OR the microsystem — is ignoring this finding, at his peril.

FIELD RESEARCH METHODS

In both studies traditional procedures for nonapplied anthropological research were adopted and found suitable. First, basic sources of data were reviewed to suggest problems requiring detailed investigation and analysis. Second, introductions were made with officials concerned with the area. Third, relationships were established with significant individuals at the local level. Fourth, open activity as a participant-observer, data collector, and analyst established an awareness of the anthropologist and his distinctive role. Finally, the data were analyzed and immediate feedback provided to informants at all levels. Reviewing these stages and the modifications required may serve to clarify the problems involved with the societal ombudsman role.

If we consider the stage of specifying the problems requiring detailed investigation, three observations can be made. First, speed was essential if either of the studies was to have an impact on a situation that was in rapid flux. Meeting this demand was possible only because the investigators had previous experience in the areas and had remained in touch, and so could cut the time needed for the first stage down to a minimum. The availability of investigators at short notice was fortunate but could not always be relied upon to be the case, even though training of workers has been more systematic and concise studies of limited periods have been stressed in our training program.

Second, in neither case did basic descriptive materials need to be collected since previous studies had been done. And third, theoretical work on similar problems in other areas provided a series of possible interpretations of the situations which were neither those assumed by central planners nor those believed in by local people. Caribbean studies of the role of "separatist" groupings in wider region politics provided insights into the New Guinea situation; studies of Eskimo population growth and migration to cities provided a different point of view on the impact of northern industrial development from that held by individuals believing that the major impact of dams was an ecological one.

The three observations hang together. If anthropology is to find applied value in this way, there is a need to maintain a continuing flow of descriptive anthropological studies of communities everywhere. Only a few will be of significance for advancing theory, though basic theory is vital. A majority would serve to provide information needed WITHIN the communities to help them operate and to provide the base for specialist studies, should these be needed in crises. A constant supply of researchers would then be available to communities to call upon in times of crisis. While these could be specialists, located in universities or institutes but keeping up links with regions in which they have worked, it seems simpler and ultimately more desirable for local people with training to find employment conducting research in their own communities. The foreign anthropologist studying an exotic community may well become a thing of the past when the techniques and findings of anthropology are learned and applied by researchers to their own societies.

The second stage of establishing relationships at the central official level involved for the ombudsman dramatically different procedures from those of the traditional anthropological study. Since he had been invited by senior officials, neither "permission" nor access to information was a problem. The problem, from an anthropological viewpoint, was how to treat senior officials as informants, in order to build up a realistic picture of the structure of officialdom and its policies that could be communicated to local people. The realistic picture in both the cases considered is not that of a monolithic, intransigent, and insensitive hierarchy, but rather that of a set of well-meaning individuals pursuing many conflicting ends, believing in a number of objectively inaccurate stereotypes, but trying to be consistent within a framework of "the law" and "the regular channels." Describing such a picture would make comprehensible to local people the seeming stupidities of planners, while also permitting local people to see the means by which their own wishes can be obtained from planners. But to do so without giving the impression that one agrees with what the planners have said, and without betraying the confidence of any individual informant within officialdom is difficult. If one does not practice the same tact and confidentiality in discussions with officials that one exercises in interviews with other informants, one cannot expect to play a useful role.

The other danger of being officially briefed and sponsored is, of course, that one's impartiality is suspect to nonofficials. I know of no way of overcoming suspicion, which I take to be an entirely justified reaction, other than behaving completely openly. The openness must start from the very first, when the possibility of such work is first broached, and must not be left exclusively to official press releases. Press reports before I arrived in New Guinea emphasized my status as a "government expert" and seriously jeopardized my work; direct contacts with all parties and an avoidance of the press avoided many difficulties in Canada. Publication of final results, however, is a vital part of openness, though not the whole story. The ombudsman must be consistent in maintaining openness on all sides. A government official must know that you are going to talk to an opposition politician from the local area and that you will not necessarily actively uphold the government position; a village radical must know that you have an appointment with the district commissioner tomorrow morning. Both must know that not only will you respect what they tell you in confidence and not identify them in any way that would bring them harm but also that the content of what they say will be treated as public information.

Confidentiality of private information is one thing, but the OPEN TRANSMITTAL of information when informants want it transmitted, and in a form that is understandable to the recipient, is crucial to the ombudsman role. Traditional analyses of this role have emphasized that the ombudsman communicates complaints from individuals to officials while having authority over some officials; the obverse is also true: the ombudsman must convey information about official policies and structures to the individual citizen.

Even though openness is necessary to overcome suspicion, it does not by itself create confidence. Anthropologists have a long way to go to engender confidence among officials, as Cochrane (1971), an administrative official in the Solomon Islands, has forcefully argued. This confidence can only come if anthropologists use as much care in their analysis of officialdom and in their relationships with individual officials as they do in the analysis of any other culture. It is less widely admitted that anthropologists often do not have the confidence of local people. But, with individual exceptions, in New Guinea and among American Indians anthropologists are viewed as useless seekers after exotica, unable to help local people over issues that they feel are significant, or offering help but then leaving the community when the going becomes difficult.

The articulation of local concerns in a language understandable by officialdom is thus one major way of gaining trust; a second way is the accurate and informed analysis of official policy and procedures. It requires, I maintain, a professional ethic of scientific impartiality and openness, which this paper attempts to spell out. Even so, one must recognize that suspicion exists and is normal; to try to overcome it by deceit is both unethical and self-defeating. If openness does not overcome it, then there is no answer but to discontinue the work and to publicly state the reasons why.

The third phase — introduction to locally important people — and the fourth phase — data collection — have been discussed to some extent in the previous section. In brief, the anthropological ombudsman must behave no differently in relation to officialdom from the way he behaves in relation to community members. Local opinion, voiced by local leaders, has as much significance for him but is also liable to exactly the same degree of distortion and selective perception as the views of officials. Not only the same degree of interest and attention but also the same degree of considered scepticism must be paid to local views. The stance of neither agreeing with nor opposing an informant, but of wishing to understand exactly what his opinions or policies are, is, in my experience, the ideal field approach to obtaining a precise statement of those views. It is not merely an interviewing technique but a consistent practice of what one can state explicitly, namely that the anthropologist will express publicly but anonymously the view of the informant even if the anthropologist does not himself agree with them.

The first corollary of this approach is that those sections of any report spelling out local views must be made available to local people for comment and correction before the report appears in final form. In New Guinea I was fortunate that, with the permission of the administrator and thanks to the ability of a skilled Tolai radio interviewer, I was able to present such a preview in Tolai over the local radio station to an audience of an estimated 60 percent of the population. Feedback was rapid and positive.

A second corollary is that one must clearly indicate that the anthropologist ombudsman is in no sense a replacement for "regular channels" of local expression of opinion. Local politicians are, by definition, the spokesmen for their communities and the individuals most concerned to explain to local people (in positive or negative terms) the impact of central policies on local communities. The anthropological ombudsman can only stress that he may have certain abilities enabling him to make those local views intelligible to central officials, and certain knowledge of channels, not available to local politicians, that can supplement direct action by them. Any final settlement of problems must eventually be made through negotiation by local politicians, and the anthropological ombudsman must diligently work to avoid preempting their role. Preempting it would weaken the local community in the long run and result in conflict with those politicians, at a time when providing them with information about their constituencies and about officialdom would make them more effective.

But what one can provide for local people is more than simply information about channels of communication in centralized bureaucracies. A range of generalized findings exists about development — processes of urbanization, business organizational structures, political mobilization and decentralization, manpower training and brain drains, cultural identity and education, industrialism and dependency and many more topics — about which people at large (and here I would generalize even to developed countries) know little. What is generally current "knowledge" is often stereotyped and inaccurate and leads at the local level to the adoption of courses of action typified by the well-known *kago* cults in New Guinea. Though these may seem exceptional and bizarre to outsiders, twenty years of experience of *kago*-thinking has brought home to me the point most dramatically made by Peter Lawrence (1964), that they are a self-consistent and logical reaction, given certain premises about the role of ancestral spirits, to what New Guineans have observed of "development" over the past fifty years. The reactions of people to social change in other areas, based on equally unprovable assumptions, would seem equally bizarre to those who do not share their particular assumptions. More accurate comparative knowledge of the development process is vitally needed.

The anthropologist, as a professional specializing in knowledge about these findings, has an obligation to make them available to people at large and not merely to officials in central bureaucracies. In discussions with local people about their own opinions, this obligation can be easily fulfilled and knowledge communicated by phrasing one's considered scepticism of their opinions in terms such as, "But have you considered what happened in Area X, where they did Y?" In such an indirect way one can introduce ideas to people without advocating them oneself. One encourages an informant to clarify his own position to the listener and to himself by showing that a number of alternative positions exist beside his own and that of his antagonist. If, in so doing, the informant sees advantages in the third position, it is a matter of his own choice if he takes it up. He has not been forced into it by the anthropologists. The anthropologist is only an information source, not an advocate of a particular policy. As an ombudsman he is a catalyst in a situation where the actors are the local people themselves in interaction with central officials and planners.

CONCLUSIONS

It is clear that the ombudsman role for the anthropologist can exist only under certain circumstances. I take it as axiomatic in the world of today that in all areas the need exists for increased communication between central bureaucracies and smaller, relatively powerless local or grass-roots groupings, and that the relative powerlessness of those groupings depends in large part on their lack of access to information. The need for ombudsmen is universal, but the emergence of ombudsmen implies more. In the first place, there must be relatively enlightened central bureaucracy. It must accept that local views may differ from its own, may be justified, and should be listened to, but that it is not omniscient and can only profit by obtaining clearer expressions of local problems to which it must then respond. It must also be ready to explain its own policies and procedures to the general public and must be willing to trust information intermediaries with discretionary powers to reveal information. Such an ideology of "participatory democracy" is not universal, and the projects reported here may have been possible only because of the enlightened nature of officialdom in the two countries.

In the second place, the emergence of an ombudsman role implies that ordinary people of a particular locality place confidence in an outsider appointed and paid by an official organization and trusted by that organization. The experience of national officialdom in many villages of the world makes this condition a rarity on the world scene. Priests, doctors, and lawyers fill some of the specifications, but rarely all of them, since local trust in them often varies inversely with their involvement in national organizations while official trust varies inversely with their community involvement. In any case, their technical preparation does not equip them for the dual role. By contrast, the anthropologist is specifically trained to shift perspectives and to evoke personal trust in small communities while retaining professional status in the wider society. They are often the first nongovernmental professionals that villagers get to know well.

The third necessary condition for the emergence of the ombudsman role is that it be possible to diagnose the nature of the disjuncture between central official planning and local practice and TO DO SOMETHING ABOUT IT other than forcing local practice to change. Many disciplines can provide experts who can diagnose how official plans could be improved from a central viewpoint, or how local practice should be changed. Something is very commonly done following official reports of such "experts," but often without remedying the disjuncture. Anthropologists by their training have been habituated to diagnosing what is wrong from the viewpoint of villagers, but then getting nothing done about it because they are unable to communicate their diagnosis to national planners.

Anthropology as a discipline needs to develop its theory of how local level changes can produce national level consequences, and must develop in its practitioners the ability to talk to national planners in their own language. If they succeed, more of their recommendations will be acted upon by planners (at least, if one assumes the same level of good-will among planners in different societies). Whether or not the information and general theory communicated by anthropologists is seen as useful by local people is even more crucial. For that to happen it has to be good advice, and it has to be acted upon. As I have indicated, our own efforts are still being weighed in the balance of experience.

In short, anthropologists with some additional training seem excellently situated to fill the role of societal ombudsman, should such a role emerge. The societal ombudsman is needed when apparently insoluble problems emerge in local societies as a result of central policies and plans. It involves an investigative role, accepted by the central bureaucracy to the extent that the investigator has status and is given cooperation by all officials, but outside the "regular channels" of the bureaucracy. The role must be accepted by all parties to the situation. It must be primarily a role of open communicator of information, in a form that respects individual privacy and confidentiality, and this flow of information must be both upwards and downwards. As an interpreter of foreign cultures the anthropologist should be able to communicate to officials about small societies by speaking an "official" language. In practice he often cannot, as he speaks a language special to anthropologists. But if the anthropologist is prepared to approach official bureaucracies with the same aims of understanding a "foreign" language and culture, he will do a better job. If, at the same time, he has technical knowledge of the processes of developmental change, he could phrase the aims of planners in terms comprehensible to local people, while also suggesting to the local people ways of achieving their wishes which they did not previously realize.

By this means he can remain the professional anthropologist, dispassionately evaluating information, conducting research, and communicating the findings of his own research and of the discipline TO BOTH SIDES. By acting as an information broker he can be a catalyst for solving problems whose solution is achieved by negotiations between local groups and officialdom. Although his contribution of knowledge aids both sides, his major usefulness is to the relatively less knowledgeable local groups, who can then use his knowledge to bargain with officialdom on a relatively equal basis. Anthropologists can, sometimes, be useful to their subjects.

REFERENCES

COCHRANE, G.
    1971   The case for fieldwork by officials. *Man* 6:279–284.
LAWRENCE, P.
    1964   *Road belong cargo*. Manchester: Manchester University Press.
SALISBURY, R. F.
    1969   *Vunamami*. Berkeley: University of California Press.
    1971   *Problems of the Gazelle Peninsula of New Britain, August 1971*. Port Moresby: Government Printer.
SALISBURY, R. F., F. G. FILION, F. RAWJI, D. STEWART
    1972   *Development and James Bay*. Montreal: McGill Programme in the Anthropology of Development.

Biographical Notes

RAYMOND APTHORPE is Professor of Development Studies at the University of East Anglia, Norwich, England. He previously worked for the UNRISD in Geneva and for the UNDP in Asia. From 1957 to 1968, he worked in Africa where he was Professor of Sociology and Dean of the Faculty of Social Studies at Makerere University College, Kampala. He has published widely on development and social change, including *People, Planning and development studies* (1971) and *Rural cooperatives and planned change* (1972).

BENGT-ERIK BORGSTRÖM (1944–) received his B. A. from Stockholm University in 1968 and his M. Phil. degree in anthropology from the School of Oriental and African Studies, University of London, in 1971. He did his fieldwork in Nepal from October 1971 to April 1973 and is currently working on his Ph. D. Thesis in anthropology at the University of Stockholm.

ANNIKA BORNSTEIN-JOHANSSON (1940–) was born in Stockholm. She received her B. A. from the University of Stockholm in 1963. From 1963–1966 she taught sociology at the same university and worked for the Swedish Department of Social Affairs and the Swedish International Development Authority. In 1968 she received a post-graduate diploma in social medicine and anthropology from the University of Edinburgh. From 1969 to 1974 she was employed by the FAO, first at the Nutrition Division in Rome and later as a sociologist at a Nutrition Programme in the Yemen Arab Republic, where she was carrying out research on social aspects of nutrition.

GLYNN COCHRANE (1940–   ) was born in Northern Ireland. He studied modern history and political science at Dublin University where he received his B.A. and his M.A. degrees. He received his Ph.D. in anthropology from Oxford in 1967. He served in the British Overseas and Diplomatic Services 1961–1967. He has lived in the United States since 1968 where he is Professor of anthropology and public administration in the Maxwell School of Citizenship and Public Affairs at Syracuse University.

J. H. DE GOEDE (1939–   ) is Associate Professor of Social Development Planning at the Asian Institute of Technology in Bangkok, Thailand. He received most of his education at the Free University of Amsterdam, the Netherlands. After receiving his B.A. he specialized in Urban Sociology and Anthropology in which areas he completed his doctoral examination. He carried out applied social research in low income residential areas of Karachi, Pakistan. Before coming to the Asian Institute of Technology he taught urban sociology and anthropology at the Free University of Amsterdam.

ADEL P. DEN HARTOG (1937–   ) is a nutrition officer in the Food Policy and Nutrition Division of the Food and Agriculture Organization of the United Nations, Rome. He studied Human Geography and Sociology at the State University of Utrecht. After a field assignment in tropical Africa, he received post-graduate training in food and nutrition. He has also carried out several studies in the field of food habits.

BOGUSLAW GALESKI (1921–   ) was born in Warsaw, Poland. He studied philosophy at the University of Warsaw where he received his M.A. in 1951. He received his Ph.D. in 1959 in economics of agriculture with a dissertation on rural social structure. In 1962 he took his habilitation in rural sociology with a study on rural social change. Since 1970 he has been Professor of Sociology in the Institute of Philosophy and Sociology, Polish Academy of Sciences. His numerous publications include works on social structure, industrialization, collective farming, social and cultural change, consumption patterns, and diffusion of innovations. Among his recent publications are *Basic concepts of rural sociology* (1972, Manchester University Press) and *Studia nad Społeczną Strukturą Wsi* [Studies on rural social structure] (1973, Ossolineum).

TARIQ HUSAIN (1940–   ) received his B.Sc in Mathematics and Physics in 1958 and his M.Sc. in Physics and Nuclear Physics in 1960 from Karachi University, Pakistan. In 1965, he received an M.B.A. in Operations Research from McGill University and in 1966 did subsequent graduate work in Econometrics at the same institution. He is an economist in the Projects Department of the Europe, Middle East, and North Africa Region of the World Bank and has been engaged in research in the Economics Department of the World Bank. He has worked in the general area of investment decisions under conditions of uncertainly with extensive use of modelling and computer simulation. His research has been reported in the World Bank Working Papers, and he occasionally teaches at the Economic Development Institute of the World Bank.

H. M. MATHUR (1937–) is Director of the HCM State Institute of Public Administration, Jaipur, Rajasthan, India. He received his M.A. in anthropology from Lucknow University in 1958. He also taught there for a brief period before his appointment to the Indian Administrative Service in 1959. An administrator with long and varied experience in the field of development policy and administration, he is interested in development studies from a social science, particularly anthropological, perspective. He has contributed to several journals, and is currently writing a book on anthropology and the development process in Third World nations.

DAVID PITT (1938–) is Professor of Sociology at the University of Auckland, New Zealand. After an undergraduate degree in history he did a B.Litt. and Ph.D. in social anthropology at Balliol College, Oxford. He has carried out research on social and economic change in the South Pacific, Southeast Asia, and Central Europe. He has also worked for a number of United Nations Agencies, including UNESCO (Paris), ILO (Geneva), UN Center for Development Planning (New York) on development problems. His recent books have included *Tradition and economic progress* (1970, Oxford University Press), *Social Dynamics of Development* (1975, Pergamon, Oxford), and *Emerging pluralism* (1974, Longmans).

CLAUDE ROBINEAU (1930–) is Director of Researches of ORSTOM in Paris. He has specialized in Economic Anthropology. Doctor ès-Sciences économiques and Doctor in Sociology (Sorbonne), he successively worked in Comorro Islands (East Africa), Souanké (North Congo) and Tahiti. Among his chief publications are *Société et économie d'Anjouan* (1967, Paris, ORSTOM), *Evolution économique et sociale en Afrique centrale: Souanké* (1971, Paris, ORSTOM), and *Tahiti et Moorea* (1970, Paris, ORSTOM). He is working now on tradition and modernity in the Society Islands (Eastern Polynesia).

HENRY J. RURZ (1943–) is Assistant Professor of Anthropology at the University of California, Davis. He received his B.A. from Lawrence University in 1966, an M.A. from the University of Hawaii in 1967, and a Ph.D. from McGill University in 1973. His special interests include the political economies of Oceanic societies, where he has undertaken field research in the Marshall Islands in 1967 and in Fiji in 1969–1970 and in 1974.

RICHARD F. SALISBURY (1926–) was born in London, and studied anthropology at Cambridge, Harvard, and the Australian National University. His first fieldwork was in the New Guinea highlands in 1952–1953, concerning social and economic change. Since then he has returned frequently to New Guinea, and done other field studies in the Caribbean and the Canadian North. He is currently Director of the Programme in the Anthropology of Development at McGill University, in Montreal and involved in applied research on the impact of development projects on small-scale societies in the Canadian North and elsewhere.

PAUL STREETEN (1917–) is Warden of Queen Elizabeth House, Director of the Institute of Commonwealth Studies and a Fellow of Balliol College, Oxford. He was Professor of Economics at the University of Sussex and a Fellow of the Institute of Development Studies. Before that, he was Deputy Director-General of the Economic Planning Staff of the Ministry of Overseas Development. He was a member of the Board of the Commonwealth Development Corporation and is now a member of the Royal Commission on Environmental Pollution. Recently, his main interest has been focused on the international aspects of development. Among his recent publications is *The frontiers of development studies.*

CARL WIDSTRAND (1928–) has been the Director of the Scandinavian Institute of African Studies at Uppsala, Sweden, since 1962 and is Associate Professor of Anthropology in the University of Uppsala. He has written extensively on African problems.

Index of Names

Index of Subjects